"The words in this book have th[...] change for anyone who reads them.[...]

—Dr Mukesh Jain, Australia

"This book will help you achieve your dreams if you follow the methods and take the right action with the right advice"

—Dr Rajesh Parmar, minister of religion, spiritual leader, India and United Kingdom

"I am really excited about Rachanaa's book. I mean the topic is so good: procrastination. So often in this day and age people want to achieve more in life, but something stops them.... Procrastination is that thing, and her book is so exciting.... Rachanaa is a dynamo … and this book is going to just explode as soon as it hits the market."

—Gerry Robert, best-selling author, Canada

"This book is the best book I have ever read. Rachanaa is an exceptional communicator and sideways thinker. She tackled the subject of procrastination with bravery. This book hits the nail on the head, as it addresses a shortcoming in most people's lives. I now understand more about procrastination and taking action, and I am now applying the teaching in my life. I recommend this book to whoever wishes to change their lives. What this book will uncover will surprise you."

—James Hwindingwi, BA theology, ambassador of heaven, United Kingdom

"Awake your Dreams is a phenomenal book. I am on my way from being a lazy chap to an efficient person in whatever I do, be it at work or on a personal front. Thank you, Rachanaa, for helping me reach my desire via the DREAMS system ideology."

—Jimish Shah, senior consultant, Jersey

"This is a superb guide and a page-turner written by Rachanaa Jain to achieve and live your dreams."

—Juginder Pall Jain MSc, Professor, Singapore

"This book will enable you to stop procrastinating and start moving in life and will really help you to achieve your dreams."

—Milan Daftary, entreprenuer, India

"Speed of implementation is everything in business. Otherwise ideas and growth will die a slow death! This book will enable you to stop procrastinating and help you implement your ideas at a fast speed."

—Philip Chan, author, United Kingdom

"An easy-to-follow book written for today's ever-changing world."

—Rachita Jain, teacher, Australia

"Nowadays people don't have time to read big books. This book is only 130 pages, and the reading time is 45 minutes. So you can read and take action immediately."

—Sachin Jain, director at Younique Recruitment, United Kingdom

"All leaders, entrepreneurs, and success-oriented people need this potent solution to transform their results. If you are serious about success and need to take more effective action, then this book is perfect for you. Rachanaa Jain has created a powerful solution for the biggest problem that 99 per cent of entrepreneurs face today"

—Tony Dovale, Formula WON Results-Beyond-Reasons creator, president of LifeMasters.co.za, South Africa.

"Everyone dreams of success but very few people achieve it. Most people dream, procrastinate, but do not have an action plan to realize their dream. Most people are not focused. They lose direction, or get confused ending up in doldrums. Rachanaa's book "Awake your dreams subtitled Stop Procrastinating Start Achieving" is a simple solution to helping people achieving their dreams. I strongly endorse it and recommend everyone who has a dream to read it and realize their dreams.

– Vinod Jain, director at Win Five, Malaysia & Australia

"This is a quick self-help book which will offer immediate methods for taking action. I read the whole book in two hours, and I was so impressed that it actually motivated me to take action to achieve my dreams."

—Zakir Hussain, director of Strivez Ltd, United Kingdom.

AwakeYour Dreams

Stop Procrastinating!

Start Achieving!

Rachanaa Jain

Foreword

This book is dedicated to the loving memory of my late grandparents, Himmatlal Daftary and Jayshri Daftary, and my late uncle, Viren Daftary.

I would like to thank God, the angels, the ascended masters, the universe, and all my family and friends in this life and in past lives. This book is also dedicated to you, the readers.

Acknowledgements

I would like to express my gratitude to the many people who helped me see this book through: to all those who provided support; talked things over; read; wrote; offered comments; allowed me to quote their remarks; and assisted in the editing, proofreading, and design.

I would like to thank all the staff at AuthorHouse who made my dream a reality by publishing this book. I would also like to thank Gerry Robert for inspiring me to write and publish this book. Above all, I want to thank my husband, Sachin Jain, and the rest of my family, who supported and encouraged me in spite of all the time it took me away from them. It was a long and difficult journey for them. I would also like to thank Milan Daftary, Pragna Daftary, Kuldeep Daftary, Krupali Daftary, Jimish Shah,

Seema Jain, and Subash Jain for helping me in the process of selection and editing.

Thanks to all my teachers and friends, without you, this book would never have found its way to the Web. Last but not least, I beg forgiveness of all those who have been with me over the years and whose names I have failed to mention.

All Rights Reserved

Notes to the Readers

While the author of this book have made reasonable efforts to ensure the accuracy and timescales of the information contained herein, the author and publisher assume no liability with respect to loss or damage caused, or alleged to be caused, by any reliance on any information contained herein and disclaim any and all warranties, expressed or implied, as to the accuracy or reliability of said information. The authors make no representations or warranties with respect to the accuracy or completeness of the contents of this work and specifically disclaim all warranties. The advice and system contained herein may not be suitable for every situation. It is the complete responsibility of the reader to ensure they are adhering to all local, regional, and national laws. This publication is designed to provide accurate and authoritative information in regard to the subject matter covered.

CONTENTS PAGE

Introduction

1. PROCRASTINATION AND WHY WE DO IT 15

2. PROCRASTINATION TYPES AND COST 34

3. HOW TO TAKE ACTION WITH THE DREAMS SYSTEM 49

4. DESIRES 57

5. REASONS 67

6. ENEMIES 71

7. ADVICE 76

8. METHODS 81

9. SETTING TIMESCALES 111

After Word

Bibliography

About The Author

Introduction

Your life is meant to be full of abundance, and you are meant to have a life of your dreams. You are meant to have everything that you desire and love. Your life is meant to be full of happiness, peace, and fortune. If you want to learn to dance, you are meant to dance. If you want to write a book, you are meant to write a book. If you want to be a millionaire, you are meant to be a millionaire. Whatever your desire is, you have the power to make it real. I strongly believe that dreams are within reach. All you have to do is visualise and believe in what you want to be. Create an action plan, and the universe will guide you through the next step to make it a reality. It's important that you believe in what you desire and take action. Procrastination will not take you any where and is costing you more than you think. The chapters in this book will help you understand procrastination, how procrastinators think, the cost of procrastination, and how to take action with the six-step DREAMS system, helping you to create a plan of action with proper vision. With this system, the universe will guide you, and you'll turn your dream into reality.

Procrastination and Why we do it

According to the Oxford English Dictionary, "Procrastination is the action of delaying or postponing something." Some call it a thief of time. It's obvious that when we delay our responsibilities, they will pile up and it will take longer to do them later on. Today, distractions like social media are a form of procrastination and are major time-wasters. It's crucial to understand the importance of time and avoiding procrastination, as it will cost us dearly in the long run. We often put off important tasks. This happens for numerous reasons, but also because we are sometimes just lazy or disorganised.

Sitting in a chair, looking at your phone, or watching TV will lead you nowhere in life, and it's time to analyse this and start taking action. This chapter will explain more about procrastination and explore some of the research on its effects and why people choose to procrastinate.

Procrastination develops first in our minds and thoughts before any delaying actions take place. We all have innumerable thoughts in a day, and more of these are negative than positive. So we need to train our brains to think positively. Otherwise our negative mind-sets can lead to putting things off, depression, anxiety, and much more.

Many procrastinators give the greatest importance to the least prominent tasks, such as chatting with friends on our mobiles, perusing social media sites, and watching TV, rather than focusing on truly important responsibilities, such as sending a report, studying, or meeting deadlines.

Procrastination can give us immediate relief; it allows us to follow our egos. However, in the long run this can prove detrimental, as it will take longer to complete a task. A lot of people are scared of taking action, because doing so involves pain and suffering. They don't realise that the suffering will be much greater if they don't act immediately.

Procrastination can badly damage us. It affects our emotions, self-esteem, morale, and health to a great extent.

Procrastination promotes lethargy. If you are never out of your comfort zone, then this avoidance can potentially become a habit. It takes a long time to change a habit. Since everything starts with thoughts in our conscious as well as subconscious minds, it's imperative that we understand the thought processes of procrastinators and non-procrastinators. So let's see how the brains of non-procrastinators and procrastinators work.

BRAIN OF PROCRASTINATOR and NON PROCRASTINATOR

A non-procrastinator is an action-taker and gets on with a new project immediately; whereas a procrastinator wants to watch TV, clean his or her desk, have a nap, chat with a mate, and post on Facebook, having no concept of time at all and then postponing important tasks until tomorrow. Procrastination becomes a habit due to delaying tasks on a daily basis. Perhaps delaying day-to-day creates even more anxiety about the amount of work to do and thus creates more desire to procrastinate.

Research on Procrastination

Numerous research studies have been conducted on the behavioural patterns of procrastinators and why they procrastinate. For details on some of this research, see Image 3. According to research conducted by Brandon Gaille, "20% of the population of the world are chronic procrastinators. They are making their lives very difficult and potentially reducing their life span due to constant procrastination and task avoidance!"

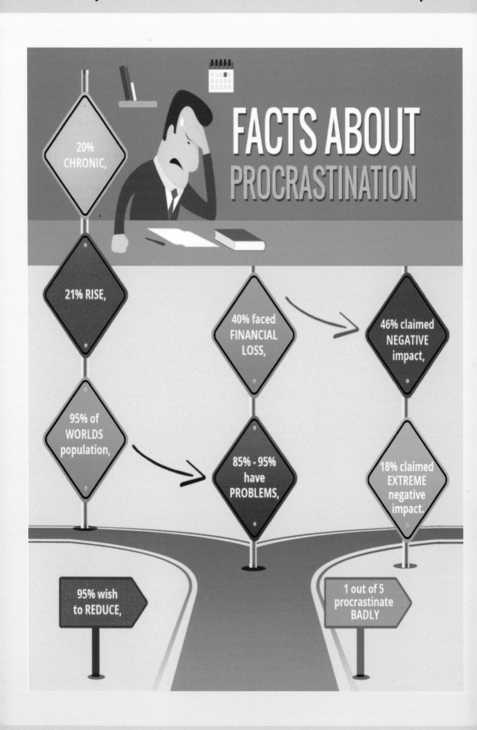

Procrastination is on the rise. In fact, Gaille found that procrastination has more than quadrupled in the last thirty years. There has been a 21 per cent increase, up from 5 per cent (1978) to 26 per cent (2002) among people in the United States, making them poorer, fatter, and unhappy. Gaille (2013) further states that 95 per cent of people have procrastinated at some point in their lives. In addition, 85–95 per cent of students have problems associated with procrastination; this is because of the latest technology, which is more fun than studying. Forty per cent of people have experienced financial loss due to procrastination. In studies conducted by Ferrari and Tice (2000), 60 per cent of male participants procrastinated when men and women performed an identical task twice. In an online survey, 46 percent of the 2,700 respondents claimed that procrastination had "quite a bit" or "very much" of a negative impact on their happiness, and 18 per cent claimed procrastination had an "extremely negative effect". Further, 95 percent of procrastinators wish to reduce this behaviour, and one out of five people procrastinate so badly that it potentially jeopardises their health, relationships, job, and credits. Procrastination is clearly getting worse in our society, and scientists are trying to figure out how and why this is happening.

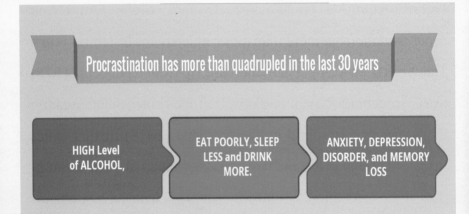

Procrastination has more than quadrupled in the last 30 years

HIGH Level of ALCOHOL,

EAT POORLY, SLEEP LESS and DRINK MORE.

ANXIETY, DEPRESSION, DISORDER, and MEMORY LOSS

Laziness is Procrastination OUT OF CONTROL.

PROCRASTINATION AND DISORGANIZATION are integrally linked.

BEYOND SELF-DISCIPLINE, STRESS.

STUDYING is pushed back.

SELF-DEVELOPMENT and PERSONAL MAINTENANCE

Time spent UNSTRUCTURED.

FOUR CAUSES OF PROCRASTINATION ARE ANXIETY, HIGH FRUSTRATION LEVELS, TOLERANCE AND REBELLION

Procrastination's rapid growth is a huge problem, but not just because of responsibility avoidance. Procrastination predicts higher levels of consumption of alcohol among those who drink. Also, one study by a procrastination research group looked at 374 undergraduates and found that students who put things off were more likely to eat unhealthily, have insomnia, and be alcoholics. Procrastination can lead to anxiety, depression, and other disorders and illnesses related to memory. Laziness is procrastination out of control and is sometimes a symptom of disorganisation. In fact, procrastination and disorganisation are integrally linked. The problem with procrastination often goes beyond self-discipline and comes when one whips oneself from stasis to stress. The effect, according to (Bill Knaus, 1993), is that people who procrastinate experience delays in two key personal areas: self-development and personal maintenance.

But why does this happen? Sometimes it's a matter of distraction. In the university environment, particularly in student accommodations, there is usually something more enjoyable than studying that students prefer to do instead. For most students, only a few hours each day are spent in classes and labs. The majority of their days are unstructured, and they are responsible for deciding what to do and when to do it.

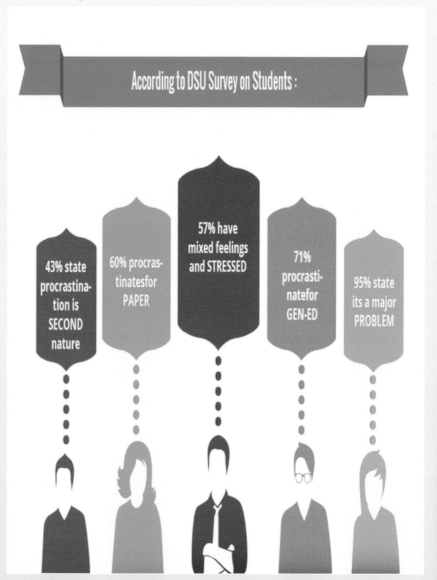

According to a De Sales University student survey Figure 3, 57 percent of students feel a mix of liking procrastination, because it gives them a rush, and disliking it, because it makes them feel stressed. 43 percent admitted that they procrastinate because they have done it for so long that it's become second nature to them. 60 percent procrastinate more on papers than other assignments. 71 percent said they procrastinate more for gen-ed classes than other classes. Finally, 95 percent said that procrastination is a problem for the majority of college students.

We all know the experience of staring at the cursor blinking away on a blank document and thinking of something else. Although physically we are present, mentally we aren't really there and don't want to complete the task. Procrastination is eating away students' productivity, especially before exams. Indeed, 85–95 per cent of students have problems associated with procrastination. These students are clearly and communally motivated to put off until tomorrow what they should do today. Research conducted on Facebook and its effect on procrastination found that there is a big link between social media sites, such as Facebook and Twitter, and procrastination. At work, emails, the Internet, and games are just one click away, which makes procrastination very easy to adopt.

Why Do People Procrastinate?

There are many reasons people procrastinate. Some of these include lack of skills, poor mind-sets, pain avoidance, lack of drive, bad attitudes, self-limiting beliefs, fear of failure and fear of success, poor decision-making, and perceptions.

Lack of skills is one reason people procrastinate. If you don't have certain skills to complete a project, it's pretty normal to avoid it. This can be any form of deficit, such as being a slow writer or bad at painting. Every person is different, and we all lack some skills. Some of us are embarrassed for others to see our lack of skills, and that is another reason why we avoid certain tasks. However, if we lack something, then we should not just avoid it. In fact, we should embrace it, take the task as a challenge to turn things around, and make it happen.

I believe we can easily turn our weaknesses into our strengths, and our lack of skills can easily be rectified by stretching ourselves and taking guided action.

Poor mind-sets have an important impact on our lives. From the time we are born, we are feeling and thinking; so it's very important that we feed our brains with correct and positive thinking. Otherwise negativity can lead to a bad destination in life. It's very easy to let negative thoughts into our brains, which then create more negativity. This cycle of negativity feeds our subconscious minds and can potentially lead to fear, stress, and anxiety.

Pain avoidance causes procrastination when we don't want to get out of our comfort zones and want to get everything without taking any actions. Research has shown that a lot of people avoid doing certain tasks or activities such as working on a science project or studying theory because they are associated with pain. Naturally, people don't want to bear any form of pain, so they keep on putting these unpleasant tasks off.

Lack of drive is a typical cause of procrastination. When we don't like a task, we don't consider it a high priority. We just don't feel enthusiastic to take any further action. We sometimes avoid certain tasks for a period of time because they are not pleasant, such as cleaning the toilet, sorting out the laundry, and other chores we don't find interesting. But these are necessities that we have to do at some point. So taking the first step in not putting these chores off is great start for procrastinators. Bad attitudes cause procrastination when our perceptions and attitudes towards certain tasks are bad. Some people think negatively of a task which has been assigned to them. This negativity often stems from our attitudes of superiority. We may think: I am a manager, and she is telling me to do this task which is nowhere near my position or standards. I am way above her to be asked to do this small task. While a task may be beneath your station, instead of complaining about and avoiding it, you should accept it as a learning experience or a chance to help others out and show that you are a team player.

Self-limiting beliefs occur when our minds and hearts play games with us. When we listen to these beliefs, it can lead to procrastination. Some people say to themselves: I am not good enough.　I don't deserve this. I want it all. These are all self-limiting beliefs which prevent us from acting and lead us nowhere in life.

Fear of failure and fear of success are two of the most common reasons people put off important tasks and decisions. Again, negative thinking causes fear in procrastinators because they potentially see a negative outcome if they complete a task. For example, we might think: I will buy that property on a buy-to-let scheme and take a loan which will need to be paid off within six months. But what if I lose my job and am not able to pay off the loan? Then I'll get into trouble. Here, fear of failure is stopping us from acting.

Sometimes fear of success also prevents us from acting. We might think: I don't want to be rich and famous, because I will be become very rude and arrogant and will have media following me around. If anything negative happens, then it will be exposed to the public. I am better off where I am; I don't want to reach the top.

Poor decision-making is another reason to procrastinate, as we sometimes are not able to judge whether a task is important or not. In this way, we can end up putting a high priority on a low-priority task, and vice versa, because we don't make the right decisions.

Sometimes procrastination occurs when we take a very long time to make decisions. Then, in the interim, we make no decisions, which can potentially cost us, as we might miss out on a good opportunity.

Perception causes procrastination when we perceive a task as negative even if it really isn't. There is a saying that "perception is reality", which means that what we perceive we conceive. So it's important that our perception towards given tasks are positive. If they're not, then we might delay action, which can potentially make us lose out on time, money, or opportunity.

Broadly, the real reason we procrastinate is because taking action will cause us a certain amount of pain. Let's do a simple exercise to understand this theory. Think of an action you have been avoiding. It can be any of the examples already listed or something specific happening in your life. Imagine yourself, rather than avoiding, taking action. How does that make you feel? Do you feel uncomfortable or hostile? When we stay in our comfort zones, we pay a huge price for staying there. Staying in our comfort zones, we can miss out on new opportunities, ideas, and relationships which come our way. Even worse, procrastinators waste the most valuable asset a human has time. We all are born on this earth with a life purpose, and our time is limited. Every moment is an opportunity we'll never have again. While procrastinators act as though they have infinite time, deep down they know they're just wasting time. However, procrastinators don't know how to free themselves and take responsibility for their valuable time.

We are not born as procrastinators; rather, we develop habits of procrastination. It's a behaviour we see in all around us in our day-to-day lives, such as in parents, work colleagues, teachers, and friends. We sometimes admire these people, and so we follow in their footsteps.

Procrastinators are not honest with themselves, which hurts

their egos, as they are not being their authentic selves. When we procrastinate, our inner selves cry a little. Procrastinators actively look for disruptions, particularly the easy ones, so that there is no pain in their lives. These are ways to avoid our fears, such as of failure. I strongly believe that we should live each day thinking that there is no tomorrow, like it's our last chance, and make the most of our present by grabbing those opportunities and taking action.

Now it's time to test yourself to find out if you are a procrastinator. If you tick any of the boxes in the checklist below, then you are a procrastinator.

PROCRASTINATOR TEST

Tick the Box Applicable

	Yes
I don't like to prioritise a task.	
I tend to start on low-priority tasks first and fill my day with them.	
I read and check emails all day but avoid responding or taking action.	
When I sit down to perform a high-priority task, I often immediately get up to make a drink.	
I leave high-priority tasks for a long time before acting, even though I know they are important.	
I like to delegate my tasks to other people.	

I prefer to complete my tasks perfectly, without any mistakes.

I like to clean my work environment (such as desk, chair, bins, etc.) before starting a task.

I let myself watch TV before starting an important task.

I convince myself I can do something tomorrow.

I get scared even thinking about an important task.

I let myself take a quick nap before I start an important task.

I prefer to thoroughly research a task before taking action.

I prefer to share my pictures and thoughts on social media sites rather than working.

I sometimes start a task but then get an idea for another task which is less important and focus on that task instead.

Please Note: Delaying an insignificant task is not necessarily procrastination; it can just be good prioritisation. Delaying an important task because you are feeling particularly tired isn't necessarily procrastination either, so long as you don't delay it for several days. If you have an honest reason for rescheduling something important, then you are not necessarily procrastinating; but if you are simply finding an excuse because you really just don't want to do it, then you are.

Procrastination Types and Costs

We've all procrastinated at some point in our lives. We get caught up in other activities and put some of our more important tasks on the back burner, only to feel bad later that we didn't act on them earlier. Usually it costs us a lot more to complete an important task after we've put it off.

While we've all done it, there are actually many different types of procrastinators. For example, perfectionist procrastinators chronically postpone completing tasks because they fear their work is not good enough. Deep down, they believe that making a mistake means they are failures.

I have identified sixteen different types of procrastinators. We are all at least one type out of the sixteen featured, and some of us may be a mixture of a few. Read the following list and find out which type(s) you are. If you can identify the type of procrastinator you are, you can then take the steps necessary to minimise your procrastination.

Types of Procrastinators

Abstract thoughts are more pleasant to think about than the real-life actions that need to be taken. I find it difficult to plan details and follow through with a task

The Dreamer

I am alright under pressure so I can leave until the last minute.

The Disaster Maker

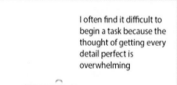

I often find it difficult to begin a task because the thought of getting every detail perfect is overwhelming

The Perfectionist

Too many tasks are risky, I am better off in my comfort zone and avoid change

The Fidget

1) The Dreamer – This type thinks abstract thoughts are more pleasant than the real-life actions that need to be taken. They find it difficult to plan details and follow through with a task. They usually like to daydream about what they want but don't take action to achieve these dreams. They find it challenging to plan and complete a task. They've formed a habit in their minds and their auras which has led them to find happiness by only dreaming of their desires.

2) The Perfectionist – This type often finds it difficult to begin a task because the thought of getting every detail perfect is overwhelming. They usually want everything to be perfect. Sometimes they think a task is just not good enough, and then they feel overwhelmed and don't even start the task.

3) The Disaster-Maker – This type believes they are good under pressure and so can leave tasks until the last minute. They are usually overly confident that they will be able to achieve their objectives, even if they put it off. The end result is typically disastrous, and they are embarrassed of the out come.

4) The Fidget – This type thinks that too many tasks are risky and that they are better off in their comfort zone and avoiding change. They usually are extremely fearful of taking risks, want to play it safe, and don't like change; so they are happy staying where they are in their lives.

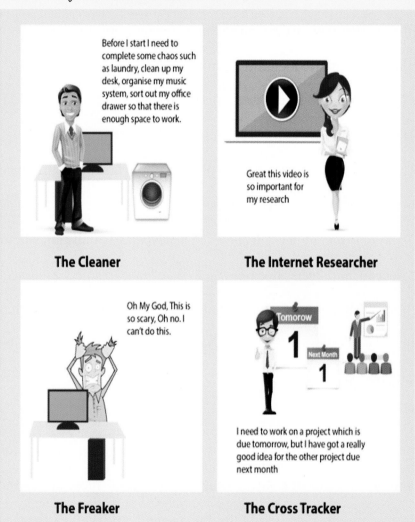

The Cleaner

The Internet Researcher

The Freaker

The Cross Tracker

5) **The Cleaner** – This type has thoughts like, Before I start, I should really do the laundry, clean up my desk, organise my

music system, and sort out my office drawer so I have enough space to work. They usually have cleaning as their priority and like a clean environment, which leads them to delay very important tasks to focus on cleaning instead.

6) The Freaker - This type scares themselves out of taking action. They may think, Oh my God. This is so scary. Oh no. I can't do this. They are often worried, fearful of failure, and lacking confidence in their ability to achieve certain tasks.

7) The Internet Researcher – This type is usually all about research and feels at ease when they have studied a subject thoroughly before they decide to take action. Sometimes what they deem "research" is only loosely related and the delay can be very expensive.

8) The Cross-Tracker – This type tends to put off work for a project which is due soon in favour of pursuing a good idea for another project due later. They usually think most about the future rather than living in the present and get easily side tracked thinking about tasks which are needed later than that at hand.

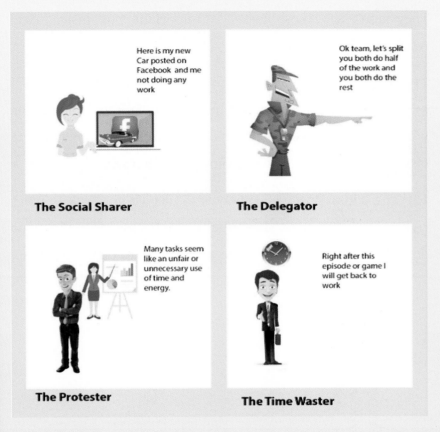

9) **The Social Sharer** – This type would rather post pictures to Facebook than do any work. They usually are social extroverts who love to go out with family and friends. Working or achieving goals are often the lowest priorities for them.

10) **The Protester** – This type tends to think of certain responsibilities as unfair or unnecessary uses of time and energy. They consider their procrastination a form of protest, as they feel it would not be fair to them to complete important tasks.

They don't see these tasks as important but instead feel rebellious about them.

11) The Delegator – This type divides the work and delegates it to other people. Delegators usually do not want to do any of the work, and because of their position, they can actually delegate tasks to their staff. Then they do no nothing but relax.

12) The Time-Waster –This type thinks, I'll get back to work right after this episode. They usually avoid a task by wasting time doing unnecessary activities like watching TV or playing games.

13) The Over-Doer – This type finds it difficult to prioritise or say no to other demands. They usually want to achieve everything and can't prioritise their tasks, as they get involved in personal affairs which take up their time.

14) The Perpetuator – This type thinks, I was going to start thirty minutes ago; but it's too late now, so I'll start tomorrow. They usually delay the work process by getting up to do other things, like make a cup of tea, and then convince themselves that it's then too late to accomplish their task that day.

15) The Napper – This type believes they will feel more energised to work after a quick nap. They usually feel self-pity and want to look after themselves. They like to take breaks by sleeping or taking a quick nap before starting an important task.

16) The Snacker – This type usually loves to eat and munch food before they would start any task.

Costs of Procrastination

Life is not difficult, but living is difficult. Life is nothing but energy. There are many forms of energy: love, food, money, work, respect, creativity, technology, freedom, assets, physical strength, mental strength, and so on. Most of us have difficulty understanding how to acquire energy and how to find healthy energy. How does our inability to understand how to acquire energy cost us. What does it cost us? It can cost our health due to us stressing about completing a delayed action. And this can also lead to procrastination and may cost us more than we realise. If we are trying to pinch pennies, cut corners, and stretch a dollar as far as it will go, we can't actually afford to let procrastination become a threat to the budget. As we saw earlier in Image 3 Facts about Procrastination, it's clear that 40 per cent of people have had financial losses due to procrastination.

When asked about the cost of procrastination, multi-millionaire business tycoon Michelle Mone says:

If you are going to do something, you should get it done. I am all or nothing. I think once I am committing to doing something, I just finish it off and don't really start something else until that project is finished. I do multitasking as well in between that, but

I will not move on to another serious project until it's done, because there are so many people who only do 70–80 percent, I don't believe in that. I think you have to finish things at 100 percent. If you don't take action, it can really affect your business, and it can really affect your relationships.... I think you've just got to go for it and do your best and do with sheer determination.

Due to modern technology, such as email and the Internet, procrastination is just a click away, as indicated by Professor Piers Steel. He further states, "That stupid game Minesweeper – that probably has cost billions of dollars for the whole society", adding that "the U. S. gross national product would probably rise by \$50 billion if the icon and sound that notifies people of new e-mail suddenly disappeared".

Procrastination is costing us big time. For example, delaying filing taxes on average costs a person 400\$ a year in the U. S., and last-minute Christmas shopping with credit cards was five times higher in 1999 than in 1991, according to Steel. In a review of more than 500 economic and psychological studies about putting off unpleasant chores, Steel found that in the past quarter century, the average self-score for procrastination (using a 1-to-5 scale, with 1 being no delaying) has increased by 39 percent. Procrastination can affect all areas of our lives, including our relationships, health, careers, finances, credits, emotional health, energy fields, and much more.

As you can see in the following image 10, the person who procrastinates is surrounded by grey, unhealthy, negative energy due to negative thoughts, worry, fear, laziness, stress, ill health, disasters, bad debts, drained energy, demotivation, lack of decision-making, perfectionism, and a bad attitude. In contrast, the person who does not procrastinate is surrounded by colourful healthy, positive energy has positive thoughts, strong beliefs, prompt actions, and an attitude of gratitude. If we become aware of our energy fields, we are able to switch quickly from negative energy fields to positive and to start taking actions promptly. The examples that follow highlight different ways procrastination can cost you.

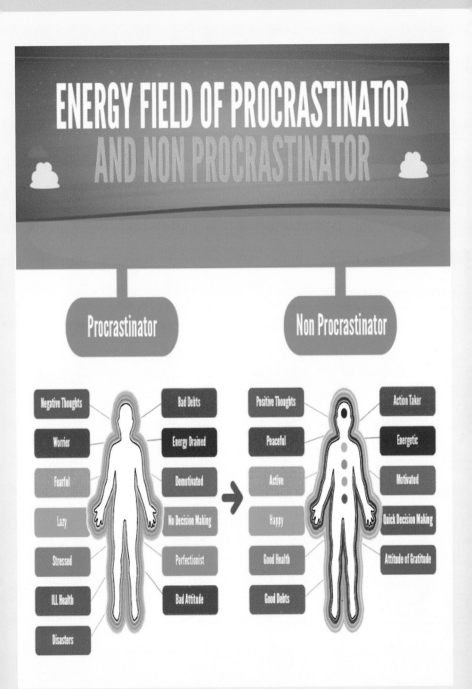

Home Repair Projects

Procrastination can put a dent in your pocket if you don't act on home repairs. Small tasks, like using loft insulation or wall insulation, can help you save money in the long run and avoid potential future concerns. Likewise, use of LED lights or sunroof windows can potentially save you money and hassle. Home improvement is small but a great start to stopping procrastination.

Clutter

Clutter around the house does not create good energy, and it encourages laziness and bad debts, as per Fengshui. So it's highly recommended to not clutter your house. If clutter and procrastination join forces, then your living situation will be very bad. Eventually your entire house will be full of clutter and mess, and you will end up spending a lot of money on a home-cleaning service or a lot of your own time clearing the mess. Collecting and keeping unnecessary items is a bad start. You should regularly declutter your house and be proactive, rather than reactive.

Expenses

Payment procrastination can lead to expenses that multiply due to late fees and unnecessary interest. On top of this, you can develop bad credit and a bad reputation. Bad credit, as you probably know, can lead to all sorts of problems, especially when you are planning to buy a house. With poor credit history, no lenders will lend you money for a mortgage or other loans.

Sometimes we put off buying certain necessities. If you have procrastinated buying a new mop to clean your floors and then slip in liquid, you could be seriously hurt. Not having the tools you need, can cause health concerns and is painful mentally as well as physically.

Budget Issues

Procrastinators often delay taking timely actions and can miss out on temporary special offers. In this case, you may end up paying double the price you would have earlier. Another example might be if you try to get the best deal on car insurance and in doing so don't insure your car for few days. If you then have an accident which leads to huge repairs, it will cost a fortune since you don't have insurance.

Almost everyone has been guilty of procrastination at one time or another. It's easy to put certain activities, such as home repairs and budget-planning, aside in favour of doing things you find more enjoyable. But when you consider how much your procrastination is costing, you might quickly decide that home repair, budgeting, clearing clutter, and establishing a system of organisation are matters that deserve your immediate attention.

Procrastination costs us dearly, especially affecting health. As we saw, college students who put things off were more likely to eat poorly, sleep less, and drink more, compared to others who acted promptly. Evidence also suggests that the stress of procrastination can compromise our immune systems. Students who procrastinated were more likely to suffer from colds and flu, gastrointestinal problems, and insomnia. Procrastinators can change their behaviours, but this can potentially consume a lot of cognitive energy. And while it doesn't guarantee transformation, behavioural changes can be achieved through highly structured alternative therapy.

How to take action with the Dreams system

As we've learned, the costs of procrastinating can be enormous; as Quek (2014) states, "When we procrastinate on our goals, we are basically putting off our lives." Since procrastination is an emotional reaction to and poor mind-set about what we have to do, activating the rational part of our brains to identify the costs of procrastinating is a great strategy for getting unstuck. As explained by Abraham Hicks, 2007 if we know how we are emotionally connected, then it's very easy to switch frequencies from low to high and from bad feelings and low vibrations to good feelings and high vibrations.

Procrastination is a low-frequency emotion. As you can see in the Image 11, it's actually nearly the lowest frequency, alongside insecurity, guilt, and unworthiness. The only emotions with lower frequencies are fear, grief, depression, powerlessness, and despair. If we know that procrastination is near the bottom frequency level, then to achieve our desires, we need to be at the top, engaging emotions with high frequencies and good   feelings. We just need to know how to get there.

There are numerous levels of emotion, and as you can see level 1 starts with joy, appreciation, empowerment, freedom, and love. Procrastination is at level 21. The difference is twenty levels upwards, which is a big jump and likely not going to happen overnight. This kind of level-jumping will involve immense pain, persistence, acceptance of change, and continuous improvement.

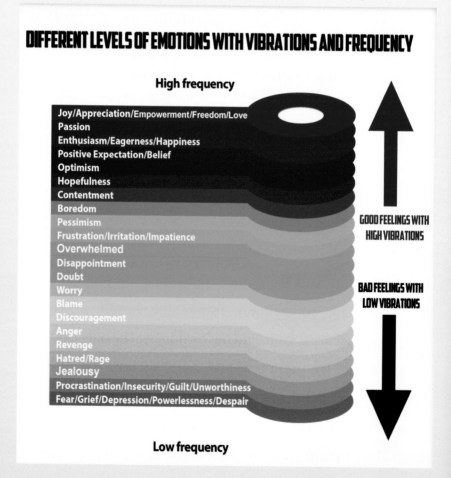

Mind-sets play a vital role in our success. We need to have good mind-sets to achieve our dreams, whatever they are, small or big. However, a lot of people, while aware of what mind-set they need to achieve success, don't take the necessary steps to achieve that mind-set. Procrastinators especially love to be in their comfort zones and get tied up in cycles of negativity. As Researched by Dave Rogers 98 per cent of the world's population has a poor mind-set, and those are the people who are procrastinating. That leaves only 2 per cent of the world's population with a rich mind-set; they are people who are action-takers, the millionaires and billionaires of the world. This 2 per cent of people utilises their brains wisely, achieving anything they want with positive thoughts and actions. As shown in the Image 12, those with bad mind-sets who stay in their comfort zones experience depression, fear, lifelessness, boredom, security, stability, ease, and comfort; while those with rich mind-sets are far away in the achievement zone, experiencing confidence, financial freedom, security, peace, lifestyle, prosperity, fearlessness, blue-sky thinking, wealth, abundance, health, and fulfilment.

THE MINDSET

Achievement only comes when you get out of your comfort zone and into the stretch zone, where you can achieve small dreams and desires. However, if you want to find a truly rich mindset, then you have to leave the stretch zone and bear the pain of the panic zone. Then you can go even further; by reversing your negative traits, you will reach the achievement zone, where your big dreams turn into realities.

In order to take back your time, you need to embrace change and be ready to accept the pain. When we move away from pain, it only increases and, like a ghost, haunts you. However, if you face it, it will run away. I learned this lesson when I was studying at School. I didn't like history, and it was painful for me to study for that class. I used to procrastinate and wound up barely passing the exam. However, I realised this was the only subject negatively affecting my overall performance. I knew if I could just study the subject, I would easily pass and better my academic record. To help motivate me, I decided to approach the subject with creativity and started drawing images of everything I had to memorise. This made history much more interesting to me, and I was able to remember everything about it. Soon I started enjoying and then even loving history and I did eventually ace the class.

Life is the same: if we can embrace the pain, we will gain and pain will turn into power. Now that we know more about procrastination, the reasons behind it, the different types, and how much it can costs us, we can begin to look at how to combat it. This philosophy on pain can help anyone who procrastinates. The challenge is that desiring pain is not natural for most of us. That's why we need a system; to turn that pain into gain. If there was a magical cure to stop procrastinating, then scientists would have found it by now. While there isn't a magical cure, there are numerous steps which we can use to quit procrastinating.

To this end, I created the DREAMS system, a six-step process for turning your dreams into realities. This system (seen in the image 13 that follows is a step-by-step manual for taking action and eliminating procrastination.

The DREAMS System

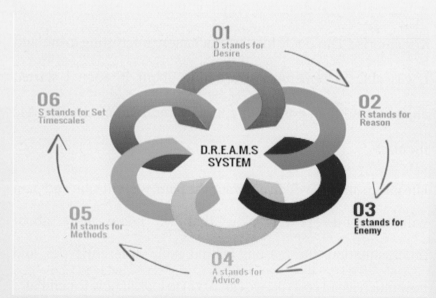

Desires – discovering that which your heart really desires by analysing yourself as a person.

Reasons –understanding why that desire is so important to you and the underlying reasons behind it.

Enemies– identifying that which might stop you from taking the necessary steps to achieve your dreams.

Advice– finding the guidance you need to turn your dreams into reality; taking the right actions with the right advice.

Methods– figuring out which methods and techniques will allow you to turn your dreams into realities.

Setting Timescales– identifying when you are going to reach your goals and what the potential consequences might be if you don't.

No matter what your next step is in life, consider the DREAMS system as inspiration and motivation. The steps are quite simple and easy to remember. Begin applying them when you can and emotionally absorb them in pursuit of your aspirations. By following this system, you can achieve any type of dream you have – personal, business, familial, and universal. However, this system will only work when you stop procrastinating and start achieving. Reaching your passions won't necessarily come easily. It's going to take real dedication and commitment, and you must be willing to put in the necessary hard work and effort.

When things get tough and it seem like nothing is going right, you must remember deep down that things will turn out okay. You must believe and have faith that you will achieve your dreams despite any obstacles that appear.

It may not happen as planned or at the exact time you expect, but ultimately, with precision, desire, and effort, you can achieve anything.

If you're a pessimist or lack confidence in your ideas, you will get exactly what you expect. Change your attitude and outlook before it drains your spirit of growth and expansion; keep faith that your time for flourishing and thriving will come.

Now it's time to take action! The chapters that follow highlight each step of the DREAMS system in detail.

Desires

According to the Oxford English Dictionary, "Desire is a strong feeling of wanting to have something or wishing for something to happen." When we desire something or someone, we feel excited by the thought of that item, event, or person. We want to obtain that desire in reality and are motivated to take action. To this end, there are numerous motivation theories on human desire and how it can help us to take action.

As human beings, we receive 20,000 thoughts a day, and those thoughts are a mixture of positive and negative. Through the power of these thoughts, we consciously or unconsciously create our own destinies. If we focus on positive thoughts, then we attract the energy of the universe and can achieve goals faster. Emotions play a very important role in our lives; they determine who we become.

We all have desires related to work, sports, hobbies, and other passions. Desire is the fuel which keeps the human engine moving, because, as humans, we have a tendency to keep chasing what we want until we reach it. Of course, our level of accomplishment depends and how badly we want our desires to manifest. Without desires our lives would be meaningless, with no purpose or drive to achieve; so it's very important that we know what our life purposes are. There are numerous aspects that influence our abilities to achieve our desires. These include personality characteristics, personal experiences, and circumstantial factors.

When asked what makes her a success, Michelle Mone answered

> My recipe for success is I wake up in the morning [with] this real fear of failure in my tummy, and that's what keeps me going. I always say if you go to bed satisfied and have done just as much as you possibly can do, you wake up determined for another day. I just love business. Yes, there are lots of issues and lots of challenges; but as long as you have got a solution to that challenge, then I think you will keep on and you will survive.

In other words, Mone is saying that we need to truly love and have sheer determination for our desires to achieve success. In this chapter, we will look at realistic desires as well as imaginary desires, those desires that are potentially unseen.

Research done by Sean that our desires are real when they are tangible – that is, when we can see and feel them. We are more emotionally connected to these real desires vs. the imaginary, intangible desires which don't have much of an emotional impact on us as we can't see, touch or feel in reality.

When desires are big, they stimulate us to go get of our comfort zones and take action. When we want something badly, despite the difficulty in getting it, we find motivation to do so. In this way, having bigger desires is good. However, it can sometimes take a lot longer to achieve a big desire than a small one. Smaller desires that are easier to fill can thus boost our confidence and makes us want to achieve more. So it's important that we have a mixture of desires – some small and some big – to keep a balance and avoid demotivation.

Think of a time when you've had a bad dream whilst deep asleep and then awoke in the morning to find that it was only a dream. Remember how you straight away felt at ease and how the fear which you had earlier vanished because it was only imaginary and not in real life. Its human nature to fear the consequences involved in real-life scenarios, when the potential for fear is not just in our dreams. We want to avoid reaching that point. In addition to keeping a mix of big and small desires, we should also have a mixture of real and imaginary desires. This, too, helps balance our lives, as we sometimes take realistic desires for granted. Procrastinators especially do this, as they know that these realistic goals are practical and can be achieved, while imaginary ones are less tangible and have an unknown end result.

I believe that whatever you desire, whether realistic or imaginary, already exists in the universe; it's simply a matter of taking action and making your dream a reality. However, different people have different viewpoints, and those are their realities based on their perceptions.

According to Bill Cosby, "In order to succeed, your desire for success should be greater than your fear of failure." This means that your desire should be your main point of focus, rather than worrying about what could happen and fearing failure.

This also means that you need to know what it is that you genuinely want so badly that it your will make it. This might not happen the way you plan it, but it will happen. And you should have full faith that you will get what you desire eventually.

In order to get what you desire, you must know exactly what you want and be specific about it, rather than just saying, "I want to be rich." Being rich can mean numerous things, so you need to be clear with yourself and the universe as to what you desire.

There is saying that "energy flows where the intention goes", so it's important that your desires are strong enough for the energy to flow in that direction for you. It's also important to know how badly you want to achieve something. I would suggest you take a pen and paper, write down all your desires, and then score them on a scale of 1 to 10, with 1 being the least desirable and 10 being the most desirable. Then see which items are 10s. Because if you only score a desire at 1 or 2, you stand very little chance of achieving it as it's not important. However, if your desire scores a 10, then you stand a very high chance of achieving it. It's your intentions which flow the energy and turn it your dreams into reality.

Many of us think we know our life purposes, and in most cases we do. However, some of us think and act differently; we're a bit confused – especially the procrastinators. To that end, here is an example from my life which helped me identify my life purpose and my desire.

When I was a child my father used to have me read newspapers, journals, reports, and magazines every week to highlight everything I liked in the articles with a smile and everything I disliked with a grumpy face. He compiled a file for me over the years. Many years later my father showed me those articles and explained that, since childhood, I've liked helping people and reading about appreciation, rewards, recognition, holidays. I hated anyone being discriminated against, abused, or bullied, especially women. Eventually after reading so many articles, I saw a pattern in what I liked and disliked and what I really desired and didn't.

That's why I am writing this book: to serve my life purpose of helping people take action.

In the same way, by doing a similar exercise over a period of three months, you will easily be able to identify your true, authentic self: who you are and what you truly desire.

Types of Desires

There are four main types of desires: personal, familial, business and universal. These desires can fulfil different aspects of your life.

Personal Desires

A personal desire is a wish to achieve something on a personal level. These are very special desires, considered personal only in the concept of dreaming, rather than according to our general perceptions or opinions. These are unique to each individual and need to be interpreted using one's own life experiences and circumstances. Everyone has desires for personal achievements. These can be a promotion, buying a car, going to the gym, getting married, or trying a new service. Link aspects of your night-time dreams to your waking life, and ensure you take into account any developing instincts resulting from those dreams, including the way they make you feel. A good way to know whether you truly desire something is to imagine yourself achieving it, and then ask yourself how you feel about it. If it makes you feel happy and cheerful (level 1 emotions), you should pen that down. Never rush into anything on the account of a dream. Always remain rational.

Familial Desires

A familial desire is a wish to achieve something together with your family. Mostly, family members desire to have or maintain good relationships with each other. So they want shared happiness, joy, kindness, and nurturing, as well as a place to live. Families wish for their kids to attend good and reputable schools, colleges, and universities, and later to have stable incomes. These desires are normally related to family life and general family well-being.

Business Desires

Business desires are visions of achievement in business or our careers.

Successful businesses start with desires. These desires begin in the mind, and then the inventors or entrepreneurs implements them to make them real.

Business desires can be to grow from A to C, to acquire and expand to different territories, to improve productivity or performance, to make a difference or help others, or to create something unique. This desire is a special venture which starts with a great idea. Many people desire to have their own businesses because they are fed up with the rat race and working for someone else. Having your own business gives you a sense of achievement and allows you to live your dreams.

Starting your own business is a lot of hard work and requires commitment, passion, patience, consistent input, and potential risks. As stated by Michelle Mone, "If you have a dream, you've got to believe it in your heart. You should never, ever give in, never give in. Be around positive people; no one wants to work with negative people. And just never stop. … Go for it. You will have your highs and lows, but the secret is [to] get up again with a smile."

It's important to put a lot of thought, care, and planning into whatever idea you decide to use; and thorough research is required. After all, 80 per cent of new business start-ups fail in their first two years. Doing your research and taking the right advice is imperative. Otherwise you may be out not just your dreams but also your life savings. Success will happen when you take good advice from a coach (which we will look at more closely in chapter 7).

Universal Desires

Universal desires are very big dreams. These are often desires of spiritual people who want peace on earth, for people to take action to achieve their dreams, help for the poor, or good health for everyone. These desires are your life's purpose and potentially come from not only present lives but also past lives.

Reasons

According to Wikipedia "Reason refers to our capacity for consciously making sense of things; applying logic; establishing and verifying facts; and changing or justifying practises, institutions, and beliefs based on new or existing information."

With desire comes a reason for it and what it brings to you. Without reasoning, there really would be no logically structured plans or explanations. Goals can't be reached through desire alone; you must understand the reasons for that desire. According to Friedrich Nietzsche, "Given a big enough why, people can bear almost any how."

If you don't have a reason to get out of bed in the morning, it won't matter how healthy you are, will it? If you don't have pleasures, positive goals, love, or meaning in your life, why bother with self-management? We all need reasons to live, but sometimes we don't or forget what they are.

Every day we dream about our desires, and we are constantly moving ahead towards them. Sometimes we are so focused on our objectives that we don't have time to wonder why we desire what we desire. We never ask which part of my mind is this coming from?

Let's do a simple visualisation to identify your why. Relax and focus your thoughts on the latest desire you achieved. It can be anything, small or big. Imagine that achievement as a journey which has easy roads and tough roads, short roads and long ones. Think about why you took that journey and what helped you to complete it. Go deep into your memories. Identify how it all began, why you decided to go after that desire, what obstacles you faced, how you overcame them, and finally how it felt to achieve that desire.

Types of Reasons

To enable you to understand the reasons behind your desires, I have identified the following eight basic reasons people want to achieve their dreams.

1) To Identify Your Life's Purpose

Achieving your desires is related to your life's purpose. We are all destined to fulfil our life purposes. And by achieving different desires, we are able to identify what it is that we truly desire. When our different desires bring positive feelings, it's a sign that we are making progress towards our life purposes.

2) To Find a Sense of Achievement

Achieving your life purpose gives you a sense of achievement and boosts your ego. It's a positive feeling of joy and happiness.

3) To Solve Your Problems

Everyone has problems, and one reason we desire a certain dream is to solve a problem affecting us.

4) To Keep Yourself Motivated

As your body needs food, and so you feed yourself; your mind, in the same way, needs motivation to achieve desires and move forward in life.

5) To Overcome Past Failures

Everyone has failed at some point in an attempt to reach a goal. Sometimes we want to prove ourselves wrong by creating that desire again and achieving it. This will also provide a sense of accomplishment.

6) To Feel Good and Happy

We all deserve to be happy and feel good about life. Sometimes we desire to achieve emotional happiness, which boosts our confidence.

7) To Achieve Prestige and Status

In some cases we want to take advantage of the benefits that certain desires allow us to achieve. We want a unique identity and status in society, as these makes us feel happy.

8) To Spend Time with Family and Help Others

We all want to be loved and respected by our families and friends. It gives people pleasure when they can do something for others, such as charity work or helping a family member.

Enemies

In researching why people do not achieve their dreams for this book, I did a survey. The many responses I got included answers such as "I am not worthy"; "I am not decent enough"; and "There is an inner voice that is preventing me". Based on the answers I received, I discovered that our minds are always battling when making a choice. The battle is between our egos and our hearts. Our hearts generate true feelings of a situation, whereas our egos are more about anxiety and biases. So when we make a decision based on our minds, beliefs, and egos, our inner selves cry a little; this is because we are not being our true selves.

I realised that our real enemies are our egos and our biases, which get in the way of our victories. We all are good at some things and bad at some things; but that should not stop us from craving an achievement that we are not good at, because we can turn around and make our flaws our greatest powers. We are unique and have different opinions. Some of us believe we don't have the ability to achieve something due to lack of trust in ourselves; others are nervous that something might go wrong and panic. These are called self-limiting beliefs. I believe we, or our egos, are our own worst enemies, as we often believe we can't achieve our goals. Our egos keep on telling us that we can't do this or that. I have identified seven different types of enemies within us that keep us from taking those next steps toward success.

TYPES OF ENEMIES

Pride:
I am the best

Exasperated :
Don't get in my way

Appetite :
I need to have it all

Obstinate :
I refuse

Self Devastation:
I need to end it all

Misery:
Don't blame me

Self Criticism :
I am the worst

1)   Obstinacy

This happens when you are stalwart and refuse to accept responsibility or take charge. It is tempting to put off responsibilities or shift the duty to someone else. In fact, the longer you wait, the less likely you are to get something done. Taking responsibility is an important component in the application of the DREAMS system.

2)   Pride

This self-limiting belief acts as an enemy when you think you are too good for a task or overly confident in your abilities. This type of egotism can be hazardous and cause you to avoid a task or be too liberal in your approach. Some of us have the mistaken belief that we must be flawless at all times and that losing is a bad thing. However, I believe that losing can teach us some important life lessons.

3)   Exasperation

When we are exasperated we are irritated with ourselves and then tell other people not to get in our ways. This can limit us. Sometimes this exasperation comes from lack of desire. From the time we are born, we are compared to other people. It becomes really difficult then to distinguish between what we truly want and what has been forced on us. Sometimes when we are working on an assignment and realise how much we have to accomplish in a short timescale, we feel scared and start procrastinating. This can also affect our level of enthusiasm, and we feel irritated and flabbergasted. But we must remember that we are in charge of ourselves

4)   Self-Devastation

This fourth self-limiting belief acts as an enemy when it affects your self-regard. You say to yourself, I need to end this; otherwise things will get most vile for me. With this enemy, we are in the panic zone. We freak out when it comes time to take action to achieve a desire, and we end up giving up instead.

5)   Self-Criticism

Self-criticism acts as an enemy when you start to think, I am bad and can't do anything myself, or, I am the foulest. There are many other hindering thoughts that could be added to this list, especially when you dwell on your own understanding of skills and comprehension while completing some tasks.

6)   Misery

When we are in despair we limit ourselves, because we don't like to be answerable for our activities or wrong decisions. When in despair, we often try to put the burden on someone else.

7)   Appetite

This final self-limiting belief acts as an enemy when you are keen and want everything all at once and to be a jack of all trades. However, in reality this is not typically feasible.

Advice

The Oxford English Dictionary defines advice as "guidance or recommendations offered with regard to prudent action".

In our day-to-day lives we consciously and subconsciously take advice from people. Whether it's for a recipe or a movie or a night club, we are always checking and asking before we take action. The same principle applies when we want to achieve a desire. Taking action is important, but taking the right action at the right time and place and in front of right people is more important. This proper action can only come from advice taken from people who have previously experienced what you are.

Since childhood, I've been inspired by successful people and always loved studying them and their habits to understand what worked for them. Over time I realised one thing all successful people had in common: they had a coach or a mentor giving them good advice and guidance to support their decisions, showing them the right paths. Many successful entrepreneurs, whilst sharing their wisdom during an event or conference, have addressed their gurus, teachers, and coaches. Successful entrepreneurs often insist these coaches are the reasons for their success, and they always thanking them.

It's always good to take advice, especially if you want a new desire. Good advice can help you gain confidence about whether you are taking the correct actions to achieve your desires. That's why it's imperative to take advice from the right people and follow it through.

There are different forms of advice that you can take, from different types of advice-givers. I have identified three different types of advice-givers from whom we should take advice in order to turn our dreams into realities and to make the right decisions

Types of Advice-Givers

1. ACCOUNTABILITY PARTNER

An accountability partner can be your friend, spouse, or relative, someone who is at professionally at the same level as you and willing to help you for free. It should be someone you fully trust, since you'll have to share your desire with him or her. You will also have to familiarise your partner with the action steps you'll need to take to achieve your desires. You will then both work together, agree to certain action steps, and discuss your progress on a weekly basis: what went well, what you achieved, and where are you going next. You can return this help by helping that person achieve his or her desires as well.

2. MENTOR

A mentor should be a person who is at a higher position and more experience than you, someone who has achieved what you want to achieve and is willing to help you for free. This can be a teacher, parent, relative, or other accomplished well-wisher. Similar to the accountability partner, you both must agree to certain action steps to be taken and time scales and should meet on a fortnightly basis to review your progress.

3. COACH

This should be someone who is a professional coach, with numerous stories of successfully turning people's dreams into realities. This is some one who you pay fees to. You should meet your coach on a monthly basis, or more if necessary, to track your progress and ask any questions. This is the person whose advice is most important, and you should discuss any future decisions or actions before implementing your plans and listening to his or her advice. Coaching can help you with all your desires, whether personal, business, or universal. A coach can help you stay motivated in times of distress, move forward confidently, and take the right steps at the right time in right place. So it's important, whether you have a big dream or a small dream, that you have a coach who will assist you in achieving your dreams. Taking the right advice is extremely helpful in reaching success.

Choosing the right person to coach you is equally important. If you choose someone who's not a good fit with you, it can potentially hinder your progress. To that end, here are some helpful questions to ask yourself when choosing a coach. These questions should help you find what you are looking for and decide whether someone is a fit. Meet around three or four different coaches, and then sit down and ask yourself the following about each :

Did we get along well during our meeting?

Did I understand everything he/she explained?

Was I inspired by him/her?

Will he/she help me with my emotional as well as physical desires?

How approachable was he/she?

What areas of expertise did he/she have?

How many success stories did he/she have within my industry sector?

How successful was he/she?

If you answer all the questions positively, then it's a fit and that person is the perfect match for you to work with. If you answer some of the questions negatively, then continue your search until you find the right coach.

Methods

Procrastination is a habit stemming from a deeply rooted pattern of behaviour. That means that you won't break it overnight. You can change your habit only after persistently not practicing it, so use as many methods as possible to maximise your chances of beating procrastination. Whether we are aware or not, whether we like it or not, we continuously manifest all aspects of our lives into our thoughts and feelings. The universe creates whatever we focus on, what we give great emotional feeling to, to support our purposeful or unconscious desires it manifests into reality.

It takes thirty days to change a habit, and I have come up with many different methods in this chapter which you can use to break your habit of procrastination and to start taking action. Some methods will work better for some people than for others. Sometimes you just need a new approach to beat procrastination, and these methods will help motivate you to take action.

There are several methods you can use to take action. I have identified eleven. You can use all the methods, some of them, or only one; it's your choice. Try experimenting with all the methods in order to better understand yourself and which method(s) will work best for you. The choice is entirely yours.

Reversal of Desire

As we've seen, procrastination can lead to not taking action. So if we find a method which will stop you from procrastinating, then you are left with no choice but to take action. This method is called reversal of desire. Here's how it works: First begin the process by visualizing the pain that you are avoiding as a dark cloud in front of you. Notice how you are fed up with the ways it has stopped you from achieving desire, and tell yourself that you are determined to conquer it. Imagine the cloud changing its colour from dark to light and then a clear blue sky in front of you. Imagine yourself being extremely happy.

If you practise this method every time you want to put off a task, you will form a habit of moving towards gain all the time.

When you experience joy in previous instances, you automatically switch to joy again, turning pain into action. This is called "living the dream", and it has amazing effects on people's lives. This is no mystery but rather a result of agreements with the universe. As you may know, the planets are always moving forward, and change is the only constant. So by embracing change and putting ourselves in forward motion, we are in harmony with the universe. This leads to opportunities, people, and places unknown to us before.

Manifestation of Dreams

According to Merriam - Webster, manifestation is "a public demonstration of power and purpose". This is to say that you have the power within yourself to do whatever you desire. Imagine this power as ordering from the cosmic kitchen of the universe. For example, if you went to a restaurant and simply told the waiter that you wanted food, he would be confused, as there are many different varieties of food available at restaurants. We normally explain which food we want, how we want it, and when we want it (such as starters first and then the mains, whether you want all the toppings or alternates, and whether you want drinks or just water).

Normally we know what we want to eat and order exactly what we want at a restaurant. The same principle applies with the universe. If we request specific desires and use the powers within us, we can manifest any dream into reality. We all have power to achieve our dreams, no matter how many challenges we face. All we need to do is place our orders – very specifically describing what we want, knowing that our order has been placed, and having faith that the universe will deliver it. However, if we are not consciously aware then the universe will get confused and might deliver a reality different from our desire.

We may think we know how to manifest our desires, but if they don't turn into realities quickly enough, we tend to lose faith and give up. The power of manifestation only converts dreams into reality when we keep the faith going and wait patiently for the universe to deliver.

If we disrupt the order of the universe by allowing our egos to play games, then we focus on what we don't want. So it's important to continuously manifest our desires; and if we give full power and energy to them, they will manifest faster than we expected. Ask yourself whether you are manifesting what you desire or sending confusing messages to the universe.

In 2008 I was cleaning my house and came across my dream sheet, which was dated two years prior. In it I had affirmed a desire; and at that time, I realised I had achieved that desire within six months of manifesting it. In this way, I discovered how powerful manifestation is. Because of this incident, I am sharing my dream sheets with you to adopt for your desires.

You should write out these dream sheets on a blank piece of paper with a circle drawn in blue ink and affirmations inside the circle. The content should be positive, as if you have already achieved your desires and are feeling very happy with your success. Remember that this needs to be done with full faith, and then it will work wonders for you, as it did for me. Start by creating four circles for different types of dreams:

1) **Personal Dreams** –Inside the circle, write:"Yes, yes, yes! I am so grateful that my dream of being _____has come true, and so it is_____. Thank you, God. Thank you, universe."

2) **Family Dreams**–Inside the circle, write. "Yes, yes, yes! I am so grateful that my family life is going _____, and so it is _____.Thank you, God. Thank you, universe."

3) **Business Dreams** – Inside the circle, write: "Yes, yes, yes! I am so grateful that I have professionally achieved _____,and so it is_____. Thank you, God. Thank you, universe."

4) **Universal Dreams**– Inside the circle, write: "Yes, yes, yes! I am so grateful that this world is _____ and so it is_____. Thank you, God. Thank you, Universe."

Next, fold each dream sheet eight times and keep them in a God box near the temple or prayer area of your house or office.

Manifest these dreams every morning until they turn into realities and in full faith.

MANIFESTATION OF DREAMS

Personal Dreams

Yes, Yes, Yes I am so grateful that my dream of being the best seling author has come true and so it is.... Thank you God, Thank you Universe.

Family Dreams

Yes, Yes, Yes I am so grateful that my family life is going so blissful and we are all so happy together with great understanding and so it is.... Thank you God, Thank you Universe.

Business Dreams

Yes, Yes, Yes I am so grateful that my business at Devine Messages Ltd is growing day by day and I am financially free and I choose to work because I want to and not because I have to and so it is......Thank you God, Thank you Universe

Universal Dreams

Yes, Yes, Yes I am so grateful that this world is getting better and people are helping each other and are in peace and harmony with everyone and so it is.... Thank you God, Thank you Universe.

Meditation and Visualisation

The Oxford English Dictionary defines meditation as the "focus [of] one's mind for a period of time, in silence or with the aid of chanting, for religious or spiritual purposes or as a method of relaxation". In simple words, meditation involves focusing on a desire for a certain period of time.

Start your day by spending ninety minutes before 9 a.m. on meditation and visualisation. The first thirty minutes should be meditation for mental improvement, such as prayer and visualisation of what you desire. The next thirty minutes should focus on physical improvement activities, such as yoga, exercise, gym, and relaxation. Then spend the final thirty minutes on actions to improve your financial status.

Before starting a meditation you need to create the right atmosphere for success. You have to be ready to transmit the energy of what you desire to the universe so that it can respond to your order. You need to turn off all distractions (such as your phone, laptop, and iPad) and be in a quiet space where no one will disturb you for some time. Now sit on a mat on the floor, folding your legs if possible; get comfortable; close your eyes; and take some deep breaths to relax your mind, body, and soul and to calm your emotions. Breathe in peace and breathe out negative energy.

You should start the meditation by inviting the spiritual force you have faith in to call the universal energy you choose to surround you. This spiritual force can be God, Jesus, Mother Mary, angels, fairies, Dr Usui, Master Choakok Sui, spirits, ascended masters, Buddha, life forces, Mahavir, Mother Kwan Yin, all the great ones, all the spiritual teachers, or the helpers. The main purpose of this meditation is to connect to the universal life-force energy of love and light so it surrounds you. This energy is the true source which will fulfil all your desires.

There are many ways to meditate. I use twin-heart meditation, which uses universal healing by calling the golden light to flow through all the chakras in your body. Now choose what you desire, open the dream sheets you created earlier, and visualise that you have already achieved them in full faith and are very happy with the out come. Now ask the universe to fulfil your desire. Say, "I accept the fulfilment of this desire now." Now you have placed the order with the universe to grant your wish, and you know that your order is in progress and that the finished product will be with you soon. When you visualise achieving a desire, including the smallest details, you send a clear message to the universe. Keeping a clear vision helps keep you from succumbing to any negative thinking that comes your way.

The Dream Book

A dream book is a method which will allow you to put your fantasies in a book. Achieving personal dreams is something that everyone should strive for. There have been numerous studies that show that setting goals and writing them down is a great tool for obtaining these dreams. Setting and achieving dreams provides fulfilment. Make dreams for yourself and set out to do them. Become the person you want to be. Do not listen to people who belittle you.

To achieve your desires, create a dream book and place pictures in it of everything you desire. This dream book should be like a photo album of pictures of everything that you desire. The image that follows is an example of my dream book. As you can see, I have attached pictures of everything that I desire, from personal dreams to universal dreams.

The best way to manifest your dreams is to visualise your dream book ten minutes before you go to sleep, focusing on every dream individually and the love and joy you'll feel when achieving. This technique really worked for me. When I was focusing on my dreams before going to sleep, I started having dreams of what I wanted and then, in my dreams, turning it into a reality. When I awoke in the morning I would feel very positive that my desires had turned into reality in the night. The only thing left then was for my desires to turn into reality during the day. The psychology behind this involves focus and the unconscious mind. When we focus on something before we sleep, it goes into our unconscious mind and then turns into reality whilst we sleep.

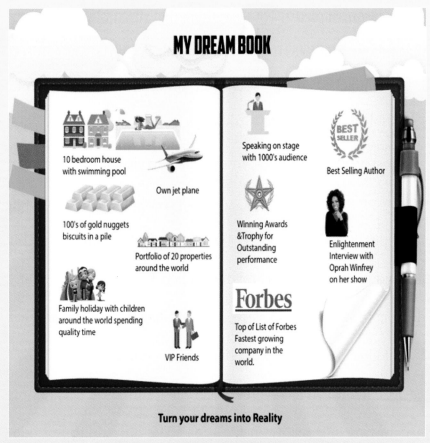

The Gratitude Book

We spend most of our lives not being physically present. Without being conscious of this, we are often more engaged in thoughts about situations, people, and events somewhere else than what we are doing at present. Success lies in being grateful for what you have at present and finding happiness in the small things in life. Once we appreciate what we already have, we then use these assets to our advantages, attracting more abundance into our lives. Writing down everything that you are grateful for on a daily basis in your gratitude book creates a habit which leads to positive thinking and an infinite flow of abundance. It helps you to be thankful to the universe for everything that you already have, which in turn blesses you with more desires turned real. I have created a sample gratitude book which you can use to create your own and to start experiencing abundance in your life.

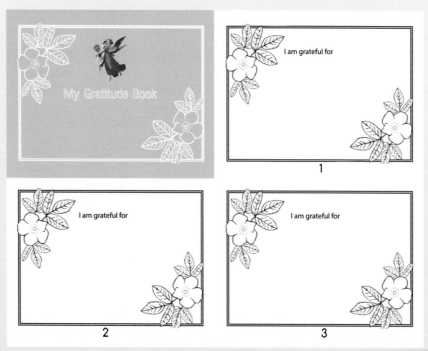

Affirmations

Affirmations are a method of achieving desires by declaring what you want. I learned about affirmations whilst learning reiki and realised how powerful they are. I also realised that when you affirm something and when you share your desires with someone, you increase your chances of achieving them in reality. Affirmations also shorten the timescale of achieving desires.

You should read all your affirmations loudly or in your mind, with your hand on your heart, and whilst taking some deep breaths. The following are examples of affirmations, but you can create your own as well. Practise affirmations on a daily basis

- ☞ I am divinely perfect. All of my needs will always be met along my way.

- ☞ I have plenty of money to share with charities or people in need.

- ☞ My life is full of abundance, joy, and blessings.

- ☞ Opportunities knock on my door, and I open the door with both arms open.

- ☞ I am grateful to have all the abundances in my life.

- ☞ I am getting richer by the day.

- ☞ My life is beautiful and full of happiness, peace, and love.

- ☞ I am blessed with fantastic health, wealth, and positive thoughts.

- ☞ I am rich doing what I love and am passionate about.

- ☞ I am completely financially secure.

- ☞ All of my needs are met now and will continue to be in the future.

- ☞ My loved ones are safe and secure.

The Little Black Book

Creating a little black book will allow you to understand yourself and your life's purpose. This book is your tool for analysing yourself and discovering your strengths, weakness, and what areas you need to improve on for the future. To create your little black book, begin by writing down what went well each day, every day. This can be anything, even the small things that went well, such as "reached work on time" or "completed all my to-do tasks". Then write down areas to improve on and learn from. This can also be something small, like "give my seat away to someone elderly or pregnant on the train" or "try to better achieve tasks on time".You should also specify the activities that influenced your mistake. Finally, write down your to–do list for the next day. This can simply be errands and chores, such as "order new PC", "go food shopping", or "pay bills". This list is a proactive approach to action steps for the next day. This way, all you have to do the following morning is open up your little black book, and you are ready to take action. This saves time.

MY LITTLE BLACK BOOK

1st January :
What Went Well ?
What areas to learn and improve from?
1st January
Things to do tomorrow

2nd January
What Went Well ?
What areas to learn and improve from ?
2nd January
Things to do tomorrow

3rd January
What Went Well ?
What areas to learn and improve from ?
3rd January
Things to do tomorrow

years into the future is another method for achieving your desires. This helps you to focus on what you want to achieve and how you are going to do it. Adding a clause of consequences for not achieving your tasks on time also helps you to be more accountable and responsible towards your goals. When you declare something, you attract the universe to help you achieve it. I have created a sample contract which follows. You can create something similar to mine, but with your own desires and action plans.

The Contract

Writing a contract of your success for five, ten, and fifteen years into the future is another method for achieving your desires. This helps you to focus on what you want to achieve and how you are going to do it. Adding a clause of consequences for not achieving your tasks on time also helps you to be more accountable and responsible towards your goals. When you declare something, you attract the universe to help you achieve it.

I have created a sample contract which follows. You can create something similar to mine, but with your own desires and action plans.

My Five-Year Contract for Success : 2015 to 2020

I, Rachanaa Jain, hereby agree and commit to create meaningful and lasting change in my life and to doing all of the work required as part of this process. I will take the following steps to achieve my dreams of _____.

1) I will stop procrastinating and implement my ideas at high speed.

2) I will commit to surrounding myself with the right people and limiting my exposure to the people, things, and ideas that pose as risks to my success.

3) I will write in my gratitude book and my little black book daily.

4) I will visualise the items in my dream book every night for ten minutes before I sleep.

5) Every night I will write a plan of action for the following day.

6) I will do everything required to take that next step to achieve my dreams and keep moving forward day by day.

7) I will start my days by spending ninety minutes on meditation: consisting of thirty minutes for spiritual improvement through prayer, thirty minutes for physical improvement through

exercise, and thirty minutes for implementing scheduled actions to improve my financial status.

8) I will choose to think and speak only positive words.

9) I will keep my thoughts positive at least 51 per cent of the time each day.

10) I will regularly take breaks and treat myself.

Failure to achieve my dreams will lead to consequences from the accountability partner.

Name: Rachanaa Jain   Accountability Partner : ABCDEF

Signature: RSJ   Date: 1st January 2015

The Obituary

Writing your own obituary will help you think differently and make the most of the present. This exercise will make you think about how you want others to remember you when you leave this world. What footprint do you want to leave behind? There is a saying that when you are born you cry, and the whole world smiles. Thus, when you die you should leave a legacy behind so that you smile but the whole world cries. With this in mind, why not plan our lives and our purposes by writing our own obituaries?

I did just this, and my obituary follows. This obituary allows me to create my own destiny by envisioning and writing about how long I want to live, what I want to achieve, and what legacy I want to leave behind. This exercise helps you think about your life purpose and your true desires. Please use this example as a template to create your own obituary.

My Obituary

At about 1a.m. on 31 December 2085, Rachanaa Jain was granted a long-held wish when, in the presence of loved ones, she died as she had lived: with great dignity, peacefully, and without causing any fuss. She was one of two daughters of Milan Daftary and Pragna Daftary.

As an author, healer, entrepreneur, and coach, Rachanaa was able to demonstrate her writing. A gifted psychic and healer, she gave freely of these talents. During her time she changed the lives of numerous people and turned their dreams into realities. She helped the needy by donating to charities regularly as well.

She was a self-sufficient lady with firm ideas on morality, politics, and world events and a good sense of humour. She could converse at great length with much interest. She used to say, "Live each day like it's your last, because today is a present." She often told stories of angels to her grandchildren, who are proud to have a grandmother like her.

Having achieved all of her ambitions and never being a shrinking violet, Rachanaa Jain enjoyed every minute of life. She was a star, and an alternative therapy centre is being built in her memory. What a wonderful life and death. Such people make this world a better place to live in.

The Mind Diet

Shakespeare said, "There is nothing either good or bad, but thinking makes it so." So it's important that we think and feed our minds well. We have all heard the phrase "five a day". That is, eating a combination of five fruits and vegetables a day has great health benefits and decreases our chances of cancer and heart diseases. The same principle applies with our minds.

The mind diet truly works if we feed our brains correctly so as to achieve our desires. If we feed our minds with positive thoughts, then we have positive results. We need to ensure that nothing harmful or toxic goes into our minds in the same way we do with our bodies, adding benefits to our minds as we do with our bodies. We need to be careful with our bodies and look after them in same way we need to be careful with our minds and what goes inside them.

We must also make sure that there are a higher proportion of positive thoughts in our minds than negative. Our minds, bodies, and souls are all interconnected; and if we get the ingredients right for all three of them, then we can have blissful lives full of love.

Sometimes we keep our homes and cars clean, tidy, and clutter free to create a healthy environment to live in; but we don't realise how important it is to value our minds. The same concept that applies to our outward environments applies to our minds. We should not clutter them with harmful thoughts.

As we have five fruits and veg a day, I have discovered five mental fruits a day that are essential for a successful mind. These are abundance, recreation, pleasure, spiritual exercise, and education.

Our minds are sources of infinite wisdom; and this wisdom is only created when we feed our minds with the correct mental fruits, which will bring us immense success and turn our dreams into realities.

We always think about what we are going to say or do before we take action. So if we plan for good in our minds, then our bodies and souls will automatically do well. All the inventions in the world, such as computers, telephones, and tablets, were created in someone's mind first. Then the inventor took action to achieve it.

There is a saying that the pen is mightier than the sword. This is true, as you can win wars in your mind first, and then you will in reality. In the same essence, thoughts have the power to create our destinies. So naturally, healthy, positive, successful thoughts mean our minds will be healthy and positive and will bring us success.

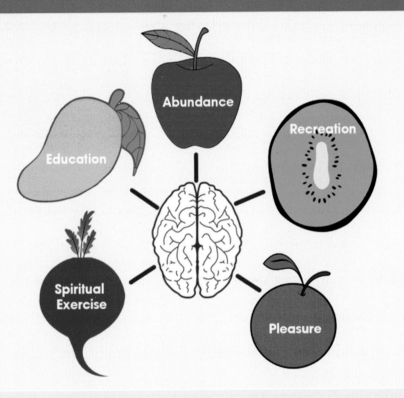

Five Mental Fruits

Abundance– Practicing this on a daily basis is a good mental fruit to feed your mind, as abundance practises will open doors for you. If you believe in your mind that you are able to achieve a task or desire and if you create an action plan, then, due to your intentions being positive, the universe will direct you and push you forward to achieve your dreams.

Recreation– This includes relaxing and taking regular breaks. Taking breaks doesn't mean you postpone a task until tomorrow; rather, it means taking short, relaxing breaks, which can help your mind to be at level 1 again and make you work more efficiently and faster than before.

Pleasure– This refers to having fun and enjoying what you do. If you enjoy what you do, then you are naturally happy. The results of your work will be satisfying, which also helps boost your confidence to achieve more desires. So having fun and taking action simultaneously helps build a healthy mind.

Spiritual exercise– Manifestations and affirmations, which were covered earlier in this chapter, are forms of spiritual exercise. Visualising yourself achieving a positive outcome also puts your mind at ease. It makes you happy and feeds your brain. Achieving something gives us a sense of accomplishment, makes us feel happy and fearless, and helps us to be more driven.

Education– We need to keep learning different subjects and topics. Continuous learning and education help us to gain results faster and more easily and makes us experts in our fields. Knowledge is power, as they say, so it's highly important that we implement our learning and share our wisdom.

Do It or MissIt

I often say, "Do it or miss it." We all have many choices to make every day, deciding to do it or lose it. Life opens so many opportunities in a day, and it's up to us to do it and take action. If we don't, we miss the chance, and somebody else gets the chance to make their dreams come true. The choice is totally yours, and you create your future. This is how we either "do it or miss it".

The Dreams Jar System

The dreams jar system will help you to accomplish your financial desires. As a child I created a system for achieving, a system I still use today. I learned if you appreciate yourself first by putting money into a dreams jar, then you are more likely to achieve your dreams; this is because you'll have money for your dreams set aside. I learned in a workshop once about managing my income in a systematic way. This involves the allocation of income to different jars for different aspects of your life, which will unconsciously create abundance, allowing you to achieve your dreams.

There are six different jars that you need to create, each with a percentage of your income:

dreams jar – 10 percent

savings jar – 10 percent

knowledge jar – 10 percent

needs jar – 55 percent

fun jar – 10 percent

charity jar – 5 percent

I also learned that you should always pay yourself before you

pay your bills. For example: You want to get a job because you do

not have money and are struggling financially. Then what you

need to do is take whatever money you have, say one pound,

and divide that into six accounts (jars), allocating as indicated previously. With 10 per cent in the dreams jar, you will have ten pence to be financially free in the future, and so on with the rest: ten pence in the savings jar to invest in future assets, ten pence in the knowledge jar for gaining knowledge and improving skills, fifty-five pence in the needs jar to pay bills, ten pence in the fun jar toward enjoyable activities and holidays, and, finally, five pence in the charity jar to donate to a charity as a way of giving back. When I started the jar system I realised that I had already been doing this informally anyway and my money was increasing day by day for years.

I also strongly believe that the key to living is giving. So give as much as you can in different forms, as you shall receive it back.

Setting Time Scales

According to the Collins English Dictionary, a time scale is "the span of time within which certain events occur or are scheduled to occur considered in relation to any broader period of time". After that span of time ends, everything that was set within it loses its value if not completed. Here is an example of its usage in a sentence: "It is very likely that these companies now will show excellent profits on a two-year timescale."

Every great achievement starts with a desire. Setting a reasonable timescale to meet a desire will assist you in reaching it. The process of creating a timescale will help you to stay motivated and on track. Additionally, this method can aid in blocking out distractions that would otherwise deter you from getting to the final result. Some of the world's top athletes and business executives use timescale techniques to gather momentum to pursue their desires.

Whilst planning for your desires, it is very important to do a realistic and careful time estimation and allocation. The delivery of the entire project depends on proper estimation of time, and you have to remember that timing is everything in life. The importance of setting a timescale is in efficiency and feasibility. The more efficient you are, the less effort you will have to put into time management. More time amounts to more money invested, which makes you able to go one step further on your path.

The potential consequences of not meeting the time scales you set can result in a huge amount of loss. You can lose value on many tasks you do if you are contracted for a project that you don't complete in the defined span of time. This might also result in loss of reputation for you and your business, leaving an impression on others that you are not professional or serious.

Whilst making a timescale for a project, it is important to do the allocation so that some margin is there incase of emergencies, unavoidable break downs, or interruptions. Time scaling and allocation require experience and the ability to handle unforeseen events.

To overcome and avoid potential mistakes which could ruin your whole journey, you should always make a backup plan that won't slow down your business, make it less effective, or affect your capital overall. The best way to overcome potential mistakes is by making a plan before starting on anything you plan to do.

Regularly monitor your desires and performance with the set time scales with your accountability partner, mentor, or coach to avoid any missed deadlines. This will also help you stay motivated and will allow you to self-evaluate as to how far you've gone and what the next step is. This will help you to keep your momentum going. Motivation is very important in achieving a desire.

Working on timescales limits your opportunity and creates restrictions. However, making the most of every opportunity to expand your skills will allow you to view these restrictions in a positive way. Flexibility also draws creativity and positivity, which will encourage you to be more practical and able to deal with potential future problems. Prioritizing your tasks enables you to achieve any time scales with more flexibility and transparency. It is a more proactive approach than the reactive approach, which causes missed deadlines.

Proper planning is the key to success for achieving any time scales, as is committing to realistic time scales. The following are some reasons we should have time scales.

Limited Time

We all have twenty-four hours in a day; it's limited. Therefore, it's important to make the most of your time if you want to do everything. It takes to achieve your dreams.

Achieve More with Fewer Efforts

When we balance our time wisely, we are able to stay focused and are efficient in achieving our desires. Visualise yourself running a marathon and stopping every few minutes. It will take you very long time to reach the finish line this way. So it's important that we utilise our time wisely.

Good Decisions

Life gives us so many options, and it's very important to choose the right ones. Managing your time wisely allows you to make the right decisions, make the right choices, and avoids future pitfalls. When you are pressured for time and are procrastinating, you are more likely to make hasty decisions which can potentially put you at risk.

Quick Success

Managing your time is critical to success; when you manage your time, you are able to control and are accountable for your own life, rather than being controlled by others. You are able to achieve more in shorter timescales, make better decisions, and work more competently. This leads to quick success without stress or worry.

More Knowledge

When we govern our lives and are responsible and are proactive in our approaches, then results are bound to be efficient and fast as well. We are able to learn more and at fast speeds. We have seen that in university or school some students are sharp and pass the exams faster than others are, because they know how to handle their time wisely and have a balance between work and play. Being proactive also helps you to stand out from your competitors. Imagine if you can do this for your career how far you will then reach in life.

Less Stress

Procrastination leads to stress. Then we panic and become frustrated that whatever we wanted to do is not happening on time. Time is so critical in making you successful, so it's important that you manage your time efficiently. When you plan ahead, set time scales, and follow them through, then you can accomplish more in less time and have more time for your family and friends.

You can also be stress free, as events are happening according to a plan and, in some instances, even early. This brings a sense of satisfaction and builds your confidence and happiness.

Quality Work

Everyone needs some time to relax and a work-life balance to live a healthy and blissful life. Regrettably, not everyone is able to do this. We sometimes find ourselves racing against time, caught up in doing our tasks and left with no extra time in hand. Often procrastinators face this challenge of having no time left because they keep on delaying their tasks; then it all piles up at the last minute. Instead, if we plan ahead and organise appropriately, it leads to efficient, quality work.

Self-Control

When you regularly organise and plan ahead, then you are less likely to put things off. Managing time leads to efficiency and creates a life of discipline .These are the reasons setting time scales and managing your time is so important.

Afterword

Now you should have a firm understanding of procrastination, the types and costs, and how to take action using the DREAMS system. You should now be able to take action by implementing some of the eleven methods highlighted. As stated in the Sacred Sukhmani by Harbans Singh Doabia (2011), "If anyone wants four boons (Dharm, Arth, Kam and Mokh) faith, wealth, fulfilment of desires and salvation; He should engage himself in the service of holy men." So engage yourself in charity and prayers, as this will lead you to the life of your dreams.

We are all given choices in life, and you now have several choices among the methods listed in chapter 8. Now it's decision time. Decide which method or combination of methods will fit your personality, and make a decision.

So, are you going to do it or miss it? The decision is yours, and I am sure you will make the right choice by taking the right advice. I recommend you try it all out, take action now, and make your dream a reality.

Bibliography

BOOKS

Hicks, Esther, and Jerry Hicks, Ask and It Is Given (Carlsbad, CA: Hay House, 2007)

Sacred Sukhmani by Harbans Singh Doabia (2011)

ONLINE

Knezevic, Milana, "Procrastination: A Student's Worst Enemy?" Guardian (9 May 2012)

<http://www.theguardian.com/education/mortarboard/2012/may/09/students-procrastinating-exams>

Saul Mcleod "Maslow's Hierarchy of Needs" (2007)

<http://www.simplypsychology.org/maslow.html>

"Viewpoint: Why Do We Procrastinate So Much?" BBC News Magazine(27 August 2012)

<http://www.bbc.co.uk/news/magazine-19389707>.

"If you procrastinate, don't put off reading this" Associated Press (11 January 2007)

<http://www.nbcnews.com/id/16580741/ns/health-mental_health/t/if-you-procrastinate-dont-put-reading/>.

Timothy A Pychyl "Perfectionism, Procrastination, and Distress" (28 October 2012)

<http://www.psychologytoday.com/blog/dont-delay>

Serendip Student "Procrastination Habit or Disorder?" (29 April 2013)

<http://serendip.brynmawr.edu/bb/neuro/neuro02/web1/jmary asis.html>

Timothy A Pychyl "I'll look my Health Later: The Costs of Procrastination" (16 April 2008)

<https://www.psychologytoday.com/blog/dont-delay/200804/ill-look-after-my-health-later-the-costs-procrastination>

Piers Steel, University of Calgary "The Nature of Procrastination: A Meta-Analytic and Theoretical Review of Quintessential Self-Regulatory Failure" (24 April 2007)

<http://studiemetro.au.dk/fileadmin/www.studiemetro.au.dk/Procrastination_2.pdf>.

Dave Rogers "2% versus 98% - who has the world's wealth" (28 November 2010) <http://www.examiner.com/article/2-versus-98-who-has-the-world-s-wealth>

Brandon Gaille "17 Lazy Procrastination Statistics" (13 December 2013) <http://brandongaille.com/17-lazy-procrastination-statistics/>

"Bill Cosby" BrainyQuote.com.XploreInc, 2015.

(1 February 2015)

http://www.brainyquote.com/quotes/quotes/b/billcosby132430.html

Dr Timothy Quek "The Problem of Procrastination"(2002) <http://webhome.idirect.com/~readon/procrast.html>

About the Author

Rachanaa Jain is a successful entrepreneur, business woman, coach, and healer. As the founder of Devine Messages Ltd, she has transformed many people's lives. A reiki master, neuro - linguistic programming (NLP) practitioner, pranic healer, magnified healer, numerologist, vaastu and fengshui expert, and oracle card reader, Jain has helped numerous people take guided actions to identify their true potential and to turn their dreams into realities. What makes her unique is her ability to tap into others' problems, read their past and present, and recommend solutions which will create bright future for them. She conducts workshops worldwide for her signature program to heal minds, bodies, and souls. She strongly believes in karma and that "the key to living is giving". She is involved in voluntary charity work and loves helping people with disabilities. She regularly donates to charities in India to help poor people, women, disabled people, and orphans. 5 percent of the proceeds of this book will be donated to the charity Give India. For more information on Rachanaa Jain, visit her

websites: <www.rachanaajain.com>;

<www.authorrachanaajain.com>;

<www.devine-messages.co.uk>.

About the Book

Awake Your Dreams focuses on a common problem faced by many people: procrastination. We often find ourselves procrastinating, even though it causes us much anxiety later. A question people frequently ask their therapists and coaches is, "Why do I keep on procrastinating?" Author Rachanaa Jain deals with just that in this book. Even though most of us know exactly what we need to do, we often put those tasks off until the very last minute. And this is not just a one-time thing. Often this behaviour becomes a pattern that keeps repeating itself, and we find ourselves trapped, swirling down the familiar whirlpool of stress and anxiety because of our own procrastination.

Procrastination has many negative effects. Putting off work for later and finishing up at the last minute only depreciates the quality of our work. This can give us a bad reputation with colleagues, family, and friends, and may even get us into serious trouble. In short, it can cost us big time.

This book will enable readers to change those perceptions that inhibit and limit their efforts to change dreams into realities. With the DREAMS system, Jain puts forward an effective six-step system to help prevent people from falling into trenches of procrastination that only hinder true success. These guiding steps will allow readers to find the motivation to get out of their comfort zones and try out new things.

This book touches over important points, such as why we often find ourselves procrastinating, even when we have important tasks at hand. Awake Your Dreams is aimed at helping readers bring out the power they have within themselves to turn their dreams into realities. In addition, readers can hope to achieve an effective and healthy "mind diet", which will help them heal their spirits, bodies, and minds.

www.lifepath101.org/yourchoice

Congratulation on joining the 2% with a rich mind-set.
Would it now be okay to introduce you to the lifestyle you deserve?

See why I chose this particular business opportunity.
I look forward to hearing from you, teaming up with you and
helping you on your journey."

I HAD A CHOICE AND SO DO YOU
CLICK ABOVE TO SIGN UP A FREE ONE TO ONE SESSION

Yarlini Sivanesan is a health and wellness network marketing enterpreneur and
owner of lifepathnon. She is focucsed on empowering lives every day to
give them better health and financial freedom.

HOW TO TURN YOUR BUSINESS INTO THE NEXT GLOBAL BRAND

If you want to know how . . .

Book-keeping & Accounting for the Small Business
*How to keep the books and maintain
financial control over your business*

The Small Business Start-up Workbook
*A step-by-step guide to starting the
business you've dreamed of*

How to Make a Fortune on the Internet
*A guide for anyone who wants to create
a massive – and passive – income for life*

How to Grow Your Small Business Rapidly On-line
*Cost effective ways of making the internet
really work for your business*

howtobooks

Send for a free copy of the latest catalogue to:

How To Books
Spring Hill House, Spring Hill Road,
Begbroke, Oxford OX5 1RX, United Kingdom
Tel: (01865) 375794. Fax: (01865) 379162.
info@howtobooks.co.uk
www.howtobooks.co.uk

HOW TO TURN YOUR BUSINESS INTO THE NEXT GLOBAL BRAND

Creating and
managing a
franchised
network

Brian Duckett
and Paul Monaghan

howtobooks

Published by How To Books Ltd,
Spring Hill House, Spring Hill Road,
Begbroke, Oxford OX5 1RX, United Kingdom
Tel: (01865) 375794. Fax: (01865) 379162.
info@howtobooks.co.uk
www.howtobooks.co.uk

ISBN 978 1 84528 208 0

British Library Cataloguing in Publication Data
A catalogue record for this book is available from the British Library

Cover design by Baseline Arts Ltd, Oxford
Produced for How To Books by Deer Park Productions, Tavistock, Devon
Typeset by PDQ Typesetting, Newcastle-under-Lyme, Staffs.
Printed and bound by Bell & Bain Ltd, Glasgow

NOTE: The material contained in this book is set out in good faith for general guidance
and no liability can be accepted for loss or expense incurred as a result of relying in
particular circumstances on statements made in this book and the book is bought and
sold on that basis. The laws and regulations are complex and liable to change, and
readers should check the current position with the relevant authorities before making
personal arrangements.

Contents

Acknowledgements   ix

Preface   xi

SECTION 1 – THE BASICS

1. **Introduction**   **3**
   Who is this book for?   3
   What is franchising?   5
   What can be franchised?   7

2. **Business format franchising – a growth option for your business?**   **9**
   What makes a good franchise?   9

3. **The franchised network development plan**   **15**
   The franchisee   15
   The franchisor   18

4. **The franchisor/franchisee relationship**   **22**
   Becoming a different business   22
   What are franchisees?   23
   The importance of listening   24
   The rules   25
   The roles   26
   Maintaining contact   27

5. **Pilot operations**   **29**
   Testing the business concept   29
   Testing transferability   29
   Testing franchising   30
   Testing the effect on the business   31
   Testing new ideas   32

6. **Building the franchisor management team**   **33**
   The team roles   34
   Recruiting and training the management team   37

7. **The franchise operations manual**   **38**
   Why is the manual important?   38

How to get franchisees to use your manual 42
The importance of using experienced manual writers 44

8. The franchise agreement **46**
How, and when, to choose your lawyer 46
Items to consider 47
Negotiation 51

9. International franchising **53**
The franchisor 57
The master franchisee 57
The area developer 58
The unit franchisee 59

SECTION 2 – PRACTICAL FRANCHISE MANAGEMENT

10. How to market a franchise **63**
The marketplace 63
The economic cycle 64
How many franchisees do you want to recruit? 65
Why a franchise? 66
Why this franchise? 67
Franchisees' former employment status 67
Marketing for franchisees 68

11. How to recruit franchisees **83**
The background to franchise recruitment 85
Developing the recruitment process 86
Recruitment records 94
Preparing to start trading 96

12. How to get the best results from franchise exhibitions **98**
The decision to exhibit 98
Preparing to exhibit 102
The run-up to the exhibition 105
On the day 106
After the exhibition 106

13. How to help franchisees prepare and review their business plans **108**
Why have a business plan? 108
Annual business planning 110
Who writes the business plan? 111
What should be in the initial business plan? 112
What should be in subsequent business plans? 115
Monitoring performance against the business plan 116
Finally . . . 117

14. **How to write the franchise operations manual**   **118**
    Developing a good manual   118
    How to protect your manual   126

15. **How to develop and deliver a franchisee training programme**   **128**
    Developing the training programme   129
    Training topics   131
    Delivering the training   134
    Documenting the training process   136

16. **How to monitor franchisees' performance**   **138**
    Why monitor performance?   138
    Protecting your brand   140
    Protecting your income   142
    Protecting your customers   142
    Protecting other franchisees   143
    Protecting franchisees from themselves   144
    Monitoring performance against standards   144
    How is performance monitored and by whom?   151

17. **How to motivate franchisees**   **155**
    What motivates franchisees?   155
    A theoretical approach to motivation   156
    The franchisee life cycle   157
    Know your franchisees   158
    Developing motivational strategies   159
    Some practical motivational ideas   160

18. **How to get the best from field visits**   **165**
    The franchise support team   166
    The role of the franchise support manager   167
    The role of the field visit in the franchise relationship   170
    Planning the field visit   172

19. **How to manage franchise unit resales**   **178**
    A new way of thinking   178
    The resale process   180
    Recruiting for resales   190
    Marketing the resale opportunity   190
    The mature network   191

20. **How to monitor your performance as a franchisor**   **193**
    The franchised network healthcheck   193
    Franchisee satisfaction surveys   195
    Staff satisfaction surveys   196
    Customer satisfaction surveys   197

21. **How to avoid legal problems for you and your franchisees** **199**
    What could be the consequences of prosecution or litigation
    for you or your franchisees?   199
    What are the potential problem areas?   200
    Additional subjects relating to the franchisor's specific risks 203
    How to avoid the risks   205

Section 3 – advanced franchising

22. **Becoming an international franchisor**   **209**
    Taking the decision to go international   209
    Preparing the international development plan   211
    Developing the franchise offer package   212
    Setting the fee structures   213

23. **Becoming a master franchisee**   **216**
    Advantages   216
    Points to consider   217

24. **Meeting your international match**   **219**
    The process   220

25. **Negotiating the international arrangements**   **225**
    Master franchise agreements   225

26. **Buying or selling an existing franchised network**   **231**
    Items for consideration   231
    Preparing the business for sale   234
    The franchised network healthcheck   235
    Types of buyer   237
    The sales process   238

Appendices
A. A typical franchise development work programme   240
B. Franchised Network Development Plan – typical contents   244
C. Franchised Network Development Plan – Financial Factfind
    Questionnaire   245
D. Franchise agreement – example contents   260
E. The Diploma in Franchise Management programme   262
F. The Franchise Training Centre Workshops   264
G. Further reading   272
H. National Franchise Association and other useful websites   273

Index   **275**

Acknowledgements

This book would not have been possible without the experiences of the many hundreds of clients around the world with whom we have worked, and from whom we have learned, over a combined period of nearly 50 years. Franchisors tend to be very open about their businesses and will share both the good and bad times that they go through, mostly in the hope of sparing others some of the pain that inevitably goes with creating and managing a franchised network. We haven't singled any of them out, but they know who they are and we thank them.

Thanks too to our colleagues in Howarth Franchising who these days continue the work we started and who similarly share with us the experiences of all their clients. We are particularly grateful to Farrah Rose for her contribution to the international chapters, Iain Martin for his work on buying and selling franchised networks, and Stafford Cant for his almost unique interest in, and talent for, producing operations manuals.

Finally, nobody who has built themselves a career in franchising can fail to acknowledge the guidance and wisdom of Martin Mendelsohn, an eminent franchising lawyer for over 40 years, and himself a prolific author of books on the theory and legalities of franchising. Martin has been a true friend and mentor to Howarth Franchising and we hope this book will be seen as a practical complement to his contributions to franchising literature.

Preface

Franchising, in the context of this book, started in the USA in the early 20th century, largely because people saw successful businesses being developed and wanted to be a part of their growth by opening their own businesses using a proven formula and established name.

The most recent estimates available from the World Franchise Council and the International Franchise Association indicate that there are now some 16,000 franchised systems operating in 140 countries around the world, with a wide range of products and services being delivered by more than 1.6 million franchised outlets, with total sales of US$1 trillion.

The 2007 NatWest/British Franchise Association annual survey of franchising shows that there are 781 franchised systems operating here, with 31,600 franchised outlets employing 371,600 people with total sales of £10.8 billion.

Different countries collect their statistics in different ways but, however you look at it, franchising is big business, domestically and internationally.

Franchising cuts across all sectors whose businesses operate through branch networks – hotels and restaurants; car hire and servicing; real estate and letting agents; sandwich and coffee shops; domestic and commercial cleaning and maintenance; mobile product distribution of all sorts; care services for the elderly; and business-to-business services such as printing and sign-making.

Some franchisors are big global brands, some are simply regional networks, most are somewhere on the journey between the two. What they have in common is a proven business system which others can easily be taught to operate profitably. If that sounds like your business then the world is your oyster – limited only by your vision, your desire and your willingness to learn.

Whichever country you are operating in, the best place to find a list of franchisors operating there, and a list of experienced advisers who can help you, is the website of the relevant National Franchise Association. A list will be found in Appendix H on page 273.

Section 1
The basics

1
Introduction

This book came about for a number of reasons, but mostly because various people asked us for it! Those people fell into various categories, and each had a valid reason for their request. As a reader of this book you will likely fall into one of those categories, listed below, yourself.

Our potential readers were all looking for practical franchising advice from those with years of experience of how franchising works in practice, rather than a book containing only the theory and the dry legal stuff. Franchising is a people business, not a legal business, and understanding how the people work is what makes it a success.

WHO IS THIS BOOK FOR?

Potential franchisors

These are owners of businesses who want to expand their business by opening more branches, and for whom franchising is one of the options. They could of course just grow organically by opening more outlets and employing more managers themselves, but franchising may offer the opportunity to do so more quickly by using other people's money and enthusiasm to open individual offices, shops, restaurants, salons, surgeries, units, van rounds, service centres, or whatever they call their outlets. Those who have no experience of franchising should start with Section 1 of this book, the Basics, in order to get an overview of what's involved. They can move on to Section 2, the detail of Practical Franchise Management, later.

Existing branch network operators

Owners of existing branch networks may also be looking to add more branches by franchising, to run alongside their existing company-owned outlets, so they could fall into the classification above. They could also be looking to convert all or some of their existing outlets to franchised outlets, possibly even by converting existing managers to franchisees, in order to harness the power of franchising to transform their performance. They too should start with the Basics chapters and move on to Practical Franchise Management later.

Practising franchisors and their management and support teams

Many people working in franchised organisations have evolved into their current positions, as indeed have their companies, without necessarily understanding how things happened as they did, or why they happen as they do. Other than out of interest, it's probably too late for them to read the Basics chapters, but in Practical Franchise Management they will find plenty of advice to help them in their current roles – and they may be particularly interested in finding out what their franchisees are thinking via a franchisee satisfaction survey. (See Chapter 20, page 193.) They should simply dip into the book and pick the chapters most relevant at the time.

Diploma in Franchise Management candidates

Most of these will be franchisors in the early stages of development, or their managers in established networks, but they are going through a programme at the Franchise Training Centre (see Appendices E and F) which exposes them to all aspects of franchise management including those disciplines with which they are not (yet) involved. Franchise sales managers need to learn about monitoring franchisee performance; franchisee administration support personnel need to learn about motivating franchisees; field support staff need to know how to assess a franchisee's financial performance, and so on. Everyone needs to understand the franchisor–franchisee relationship. These candidates can also dip in as and where they feel the need.

Mature franchisors

As a franchised network approaches maturity or capacity in its domestic market it needs to consider whether to grow the business or to get out. It can only be one or the other because simply doing nothing will be the start of a downward spiral. Readers in this category can go straight to Section 3, Advanced Franchising, where they can consider the options of taking their business overseas, starting a new network by importing a system from overseas, buying an existing franchised network or simply selling up.

Potential international franchisors

Some businesses just know they want to go international, whether or not they franchise at home. International development using the right franchising model may be the way to do it. If they have no previous experience of franchising, the Basics chapters will be useful first, then cut to the chase and go to Advanced Franchising.

Franchisees and potential franchisees

OK, we're fibbing. No franchisees or potential franchisees have ever asked us for a book, but they would all benefit from reading this one to find out how good franchisors do things properly. They can then compare these methods with those of the franchise they are thinking of joining, or the one with which they may already be involved. If we can stop one potential franchisee from joining an ill-prepared system; or help one franchisee to get his franchisor to improve what he does, then all the effort that has gone into this project will have been worth it.

WHAT IS FRANCHISING?

Before going any further, and to make sure we're all on the same page (which we must be if you're reading this) let's define what we mean by franchising in the context of this book.

Business format franchising

We are talking about '**business format franchising**' which, put simply, is 'a business relationship where one party **allows** another to operate clones of a **proven** business system in return for initial and ongoing fees'. We are not talking about rail franchises or film franchises, or any other variations on the theme.

Why have two words been highlighted in that definition? Because they underpin the whole franchisor–franchisee relationship, of which you will read much more later.

The franchisee is **allowed** by the franchisor to operate a branch of the franchisor's business, using the latter's name and business systems. If the franchisee stops using the name and system properly they will no longer be allowed to use it and they will lose their business and whatever they have invested in it.

The franchisor should only be offering a system, and any addition to the system, which has been tested, and **proven** to be capable of duplication, over a period of time, at a number of outlets, with a number of people having been trained how to do it. They should not be offering to franchise something they think is just a good idea.

Get everyone understanding those simple points and you have the basis for a long and happy career in franchising.

Growth franchising

The majority of businesses considering franchising do so because they want to grow, so these can be called **growth franchises**. Franchisees provide the financial and human resources to open new branches so the total network ought to grow more quickly than it could organically. Within this category there are two types of business:

- established businesses which have been going for at least a couple of years, sometimes decades, which are looking to add new branches, either domestically or internationally;

- brand new businesses, sometimes little more than a good idea, which want eventually to grow by franchising once they are established. As will become apparent from later chapters, these businesses need to go through a slightly longer development process to become franchisors.

Conversion franchising

There are also two types of **conversion franchises**:

- a business which already has a number of outlets (it could be ten, it could be a thousand or more) may see advantages in converting some or all of them to franchised, rather than company-managed, units. The costs and hassle of day-to-day operation are transferred to the franchisee, who may or may not be the previous manager. The latter is more motivated to operate profitably because it is their own business;

- a business adds further outlets to its network by converting existing, competing, businesses to operate under its brand. Many small business owners are good unit operators, but they lack the skills to develop their marketing, research and development, and so on. For them, joining a franchise brings those added benefits. For the franchisor, it means acquiring a franchisee and a site, and taking out a competitor in that local market, all in one go.

Neither type of conversion is as easy to achieve as it may sound and it is essential to get experienced advice from those who have been involved in such projects before.

WHAT CAN BE FRANCHISED?

Just about any business which can operate as a branch network and which meets the criteria outlined in the next chapter can be franchised, and both franchisors and franchisees come in all shapes and sizes.

Job franchises

These are sometimes known as *man-and-a-van* franchises because they often involve someone going round providing a service or products to either businesses or consumers, but they also include *white-collar* franchises where an individual provides some sort of professional service, often working from their own home, particularly if customers do not need to visit them. The franchisee may be the only person involved in his business, many of the customers may be provided by the franchisor, and sometimes the franchisor will handle most of the invoicing and other administration.

Management franchises

The end product or service could be the same as that provided under job franchises, or it could involve the need to operate from specific retail or other business premises, but here the franchisee is managing a team of people rather than doing everything themselves. Many job franchises evolve into management franchises as they become established and early franchisees take on multiple territories, or simply grow their businesses so that they need to employ others. Different skills are required of the franchisee and it is important that franchisors realise what these are when recruiting their franchisees.

Investment franchises

Some projects which require large capital investment, such as hotels or larger restaurants, may attract franchisees who simply put up the money and engage either a manager, or indeed the franchisor, to operate the business and produce a return on their investment and capital gain on resale.

Whichever category you fit into, we hope you will find the book useful. If you have any comments, or would like to know more about something specific, please send an e-mail to
info@howarthfranchising.com

2

Business format franchising – a growth option for your business?

Any business that can operate as a branch network, and that wants to grow, should at least consider franchising as one of the options. However big you want it to become – biggest in your region, biggest in the country, or biggest in the world – franchising may be able to get you there. It depends largely on your vision, and only you can create that. Remember – everyone started with only one outlet.

Much of the project work undertaken in our business starts with someone contacting our office saying, 'I've got this business. Is it franchiseable and, if so, how do I go about it?' Sometimes the question is, 'I've got this great idea for a business, can I franchise it?' The easier question to answer is the second one because the simple answer is 'No'. You can only franchise a successful business format, not an idea. Turn your idea into a successful business, at your own expense and risk, then we can see about franchising it with you. That's not to say that you can't develop your idea into a business with the long-term view of growing it as a franchise, and it's never too early to start considering franchising as an option for eventually growing your business.

WHAT MAKES A GOOD FRANCHISE?

Let's assume the business in question has now been going for a few years. There are five things we look for to help us decide whether it may make a good franchise. We call this Five-Star Franchising. It doesn't matter if not all five attributes are yet in place – that can be remedied – but they will need to be in place before the franchise opportunity is launched. Listed below are the five things we initially look for.

Proven format

This means that the business must have a track record of operating profitably – and operating profitably in the format in which it is intended to be franchised. If the business currently operates from retail stores of about 100 square metres in a secondary location you cannot plan to franchise 500-square-metre stores in shopping malls. Similarly, if you only have one shop and it is bang in the middle of London's Oxford Street, don't imagine you can open hundreds of smaller stores on the High Street, either in Oxford or anywhere else.

If you want to franchise a different format, test it yourself to prove it works, then franchise it. The same applies when you are established as a franchisor and you want to introduce significant changes to your system.

Profitability is important, not least because you cannot franchise a business in order to get it out of trouble – franchising will not save a failing business. You cannot clear your overdraft by recruiting ten franchisees, each of whom stumps up a franchise fee equal to one-tenth of your current debt, and you cannot get rid of loss-making stores by handing them over to franchisees. Underperforming stores can sometimes be transformed by turning the managers into franchisees but the underlying business format must be proven to be successful elsewhere.

The format will need to be documented in detail, in an operations manual, and as many as possible of the Intellectual Property (IP) constituents of the system must be protected by legal means, for example trademarks, store designs, bespoke software, unique colours, and the manual itself. The franchisor needs to own the rights to these items as otherwise he cannot license the franchisee to use them, and cannot stop anyone copying them to compete with his franchisees. A good consultant will take you through an IP audit, and introduce you to a specialist lawyer.

Easily duplicated

The easier it is to find sites for additional outlets, the easier it will be to develop a franchised network. Most small businesses are relatively easy to duplicate – all the franchisee has to find is an appropriate office, industrial unit, retail store, or whatever the business currently works from. In many cases this can even be the franchisee's home, which certainly keeps the overheads down and means they can start trading very quickly. Many franchisees start by working from home, then move into business premises once they get established.

Difficulties arise where the optimum premises are either hard to find or hard to acquire. Prime retail locations are notoriously difficult to come across, as they are in great demand and agents tend to have waiting lists of big-name prospects. They are equally difficult to acquire as landlords naturally prefer to go with an existing big business as a tenant rather than a start-up franchisee. Sometimes this can be solved by the franchisor taking the head lease and subletting to the franchisee, but the pros and cons of this need serious consideration.

The more outlets a business has when it starts to consider franchising the better, because it has already proved that the concept can be duplicated. Having said that, of course, every business started out with only one outlet.

Easily learned

The easier it is for someone to learn how to operate, or manage, the business, the easier it will be to find appropriate franchisees – and the quicker they will get into action, the quicker they will start recouping their investment, and the quicker they will start paying franchise fees. Most small businesses, and just about all successful franchises, are fairly easily learned – that's the beauty of them. Indeed a franchisor will continue to spend years making it easier because that's how both parties increase efficiency and profitability.

Easy doesn't mean anybody can do it, however; it means the appropriate person can. There is a lot about the franchisee profile in Chapter 11, 'How to Recruit Franchisees'. Sometimes the work that is actually done in the franchisee's business is very skilled, and may even require formal professional qualifications, such as being a vet, an optician, a dentist or some other professional activity. Obviously the franchisor cannot take just anyone and teach them these skills in a short enough time-frame – but he or she could find a franchisee who has the marketing and management skills to run a multi-disciplinary health practice, leaving everyone to do the bits they are best at.

People may say, 'If the business is easily duplicated and easily learned, why does anyone need a franchisor? They could just set up for themselves.' They are missing the point. What a franchisor is offering is a system that is easily duplicated and easily learned. The system will have taken many years, many mistakes, and a lot of resources to refine. That experience is what the franchisee is buying into, and getting benefits from, from day one. If restaurants were so easy to set up by inexperienced people, it wouldn't be the case that 50 per cent of them go out of business in their first year of trading.

Profitable for both parties

The franchising business model has to work for both parties – the franchisee has to be happy and making money; the franchisor has to be happy and making money.

When we have the initial discussion with someone thinking about franchising their business, there is no way either of us can know whether this particular criterion can be met. That's why the first stage of any project is the Franchise Development Plan, but it is essential to embed into everyone's mind at an early stage the principle that franchising has to work for both parties.

The trick is to get the balance of what 'happy' and 'making money' means for everyone concerned. Many franchisees are happier than when they were employed, because they are perceived as being independent and they consider themselves to have a better lifestyle.

They may be earning less money, and working longer hours, but they are happy. Others get into franchising to build their fortune and then go on to bigger and better things. The franchisor must know, and be honest about, which of these types of franchisee he is likely to be able to satisfy, and indeed which of them he wants in his network.

Similarly one franchisor may be happy with the ego trip of having 100 or more branches operating under his name, even if he makes no more money than he did before. Another may only be happy if he is earning £1 million or more a year.

However good the potential franchisee, or the franchisor, and however well they get on with each other, sometimes it is not possible to match their income requirements and investment capabilities. In such cases they must be honest with each other, and move on to find a better match.

Franchising culture

Franchised networks need to develop a culture of mutual trust and support, where everyone is working together towards a common goal. That is why understanding the franchisor–franchisee relationship is so important from an early stage.

The best way to explain the franchising culture is to consider what happens when an area manager of a large corporate organisation visits one of his branches. The perceived wisdom is that if he tells the manager to jump, the manager will ask, 'How high?'

Compare that to a franchisor's field support executive visiting one of his franchised outlets. All he can do is *ask* the franchisee to jump, whereupon the franchisee will demand, 'Why?'

It's a fact of life that large corporate organisations find it very difficult to franchise all, or even parts of, their businesses successfully. This is partly because they cannot adapt to the above scenario, and partly because they will not accept that franchising is a long-term investment and commitment. Typically the franchise project is headed by someone who doesn't really 'own' it, they are just doing this as one of many projects on the way to their next promotion, and they don't have the time to learn the nuances of franchising. Existing big businesses typically need more professional franchising advice than do owner-managed businesses because the latter already have to know how to 'get' people to do things rather than 'tell' them.

3
The Franchised Network Development Plan

This is the numbers bit.

Like it or not, you need to read it.

Franchising will only work if both the franchisee and the franchisor are operating sustainable businesses, so that's why any franchising plan starts with the numbers.

THE FRANCHISEE

Firstly we need to calculate, how will it work for the franchisee? How much will they need to invest initially, not just in the upfront franchise and training fees but in the acquisition of equipment, premises, vehicles, staff and so on. Once they are set up and opened, how quickly will sales start to come in and what will be the associated expenses? What ongoing fees will be payable to the franchisor? When will the franchisee start making a profit, and when will their cash flow eventually be positive? Will the business provide enough to repay loans, pay the franchisee an acceptable salary, generate a sufficient return on their investment, and still leave money over to invest in the development of their business?

Most of the data for the above calculations will come from actual results achieved in the existing business. The more sophisticated that business, and the more there is available in the way of branch management accounts, the better.

What will not be available from the existing business are figures for franchise fees, simply because none are currently being paid. This is where the need for experienced advice first comes in, and it is a good point at which to explain what these fees may be, and how the franchisor may generate his or her income.

The upfront fee

This is the amount a franchisee pays to the franchisor to get into the game, and it may or may not cover training, rights to use the name and systems, an amount which enables the franchisor to amortise his development and recruitment costs, an amount which reflects the perceived value of the opportunity or territory, and a small element of profit for the franchisor. It may also be calculated with reference to what other similar systems are charging, and the general market price for franchises, but it needs to be accurately assessed for each system. Just because a competitor is charging, say, £30,000 upfront fee doesn't mean that's the right figure for your business – it may not even be right for their business if they didn't research it properly!

Many franchisors claim to make nothing from the upfront fee once they have deducted all their costs. Indeed some claim not to be breaking even with an individual franchisee until the latter has been trading, and paying ongoing fees, for at least a year.

Note that the upfront fee is not the same as the franchisee's total set-up cost, the latter of which includes all the other necessary purchases and expenses of getting an outlet opened. These may include acquisition of premises, equipment and vehicles; building works; shop fitting; initial stock purchases; staff recruitment and training; and various other items, the fees for which may go to third parties.

Some franchisors use the upfront fee in their franchise advertising, some use the total set-up costs. If you've seen figures in excess of about £40,000, they ought to be for total set-up costs not the upfront franchise fee.

Note also that a franchisor's business is not about selling franchises and bringing in upfront franchise fees, although these will inevitably be important in the short- to medium-term. The long-term goal is to generate continuing income from successful franchisees.

Management services fees

Sometimes incorrectly referred to as royalties, these fees cover the ongoing services provided to the franchisees by the franchisor. The range and quality of services, and the level of management services fees, varies greatly from system to system – even for businesses in the same sector – and they need to be assessed and set by an experienced practitioner. They must be affordable, and good value, for the franchisee; they must be sufficient eventually to pay for the franchisor's support infrastructure and to provide them with a reasonable profit, good return on their investment, and adequate funding to develop further the network and the business.

The majority of management services fees are charged as a percentage (anything between 4 per cent and 40 per cent, depending on the network) of the franchisee's sales (not profit, not cash received) and they are most often payable monthly in arrears. Sometimes they are simply a fixed regular amount regardless of the franchisee's performance, but the fairness and appropriateness of such an arrangement needs to be discussed with your consultant when initially creating the franchise structure.

Marketing fees

Many franchisors charge an ongoing fee, either a percentage or fixed amount, which goes into an identifiable pot to help pay for national marketing and branding activity. The application of such funds is usually accounted for to franchisees on an annual basis, and surpluses or shortages are carried forward as the pot is not intended to provide profit, or loss, for the franchisor. Local marketing activity on the franchisee's area is usually a separate expense, paid for by the franchisee.

Product mark-up

For some franchisors it makes more sense, or it is more appropriate, to charge franchisees a mark-up on products supplied rather than a percentage, or fixed, management services fee. Sometimes franchisors charge both, but the temptation to take too much from franchisees in too many ways must be resisted if it affects the viability of their businesses. One of the advantages of being a franchisee is to benefit, not suffer, from being tied to, or part of, a bigger buying group.

Supplier rebates

Some franchisors receive retrospective discounts from suppliers based on the total sales to their network, others prefer to pass these on in the form of lower prices, or added-value services, to their franchisees. Either approach is acceptable, but it is better for the relationships if the arrangements are transparent.

To complete the financial forecasts for a franchised outlet, the preliminary decisions on all of the above are fed into the model, and the outcome is assessed. Based on all current, accurate information and best-informed guesswork, does it look like an attractive option for a potential franchisee who fits the desired profile? If it doesn't, can any of the assumptions be (reasonably and credibly) adjusted to make it look better?

If so, do it.

If not, forget it.

All bets are off if the proposed structure cannot be made to work for the franchisee because, if that is the case, it will never work for the franchisor.

THE FRANCHISOR

If the forecast does work for the franchisee, we then move on to make sure it works for the franchisor.

Will there ever be enough franchisees, paying whatever they are going to be paying, to cover the costs of setting up the franchising business in the first place, and the ongoing costs of the support infrastructure that will be needed to support it? Unless you have done it before you will really need help here because there are many hidden, or naively overlooked, costs that go with establishing a franchised network. To name but a few:

- the Franchised Network Development Plan;
- territory analysis and demographic profiling;
- running pilot operations;
- preparation of the legal agreement;
- production of the operations manual;
- franchise marketing materials;
- launch marketing and promotion;
- employment of experienced staff;
- training of existing staff;
- membership of your National Franchise Association;
- associated professional advice of all sorts.

The total of such costs will vary from franchisor to franchisor, and from country to country, but in the UK you will typically have spent between £30,000–£50,000 on the above, in one way or another, before you sign your first franchisee.

You may think, 'That's OK, I'll get most of it back from the first franchisee in upfront fees.' However, even if that is the case, it does not mean that this is all the funding you need.

Consider how a franchised network develops. In the first year there will be few franchisees, probably five at best, and they will all be start-up businesses. Their sales will not be as high as they will be when they are mature, so your total income from percentage management fees will not be very high. However, you will need to provide all the recruitment and support services outlined throughout this book to those early franchisees because if you do not, those early franchisees will not succeed.

If your early franchisees are not supported, and do not succeed, you will find it hard to recruit others. If you fall behind with your recruitment schedule you will run out of money, your business will fail and so will those of your early franchisees.

So you will be spending much more on support than you are receiving for providing it, and you will need to fund that from somewhere.

On top of that, if you want to recruit more franchisees next year, you will need to be spending more on marketing and recruitment activity this year. That means even more money going out than there is coming in. All the amounts vary from business to business, which is why you need an experienced practitioner to help with your plans, but it is not unusual for a franchising project to have a total funding requirement of £150,000 before it starts to make money.

After that, profit growth can be considerable but you need to do the cash flow projections to know where the challenges lie. The calculations are more complex than you think, which is why we developed our own *FranchisedNetworkBuilder* software, but if you want to try it yourself there is a data collection template in Appendix C on page 245.

It doesn't matter what the overall funding requirement is provided you know its extent and can put funding in place to cover it. What does matter is not knowing what the requirement is, then running out of money and leaving early franchisees exposed. The major clearing banks, certainly in the UK, are very supportive of franchising projects and they have their own specialist franchise sections to advise their business managers on lending to both franchisors and franchisees. Details are available on the British Franchise Association website, listed in Appendix H on page 273.

The beauty of the Franchised Network Development Plan is that its preparation involves discussion of all the relevant issues that are likely to come up as the business evolves, and it provides a comprehensive action plan of what has to be done, who is going to do it, when it has to be done by, and what it will cost.

Financial projections, both for profit and cash, are established and can then be compared to actual performance on a regular basis. Assuming the levels of investment and return are considered acceptable all that has to be done is to press the button and get on with it.

A typical franchise development work programme is given in Appendix A on page 240. Examples of a contents list for a Franchised Network Development Plan, and of the financial forecasts, are presented in Appendix B and Appendix C respectively, on pages 244 and 245.

4
The franchisor–franchisee relationship

BECOMING A DIFFERENT BUSINESS

Many of the skills needed to develop and run a franchised network are the same as those required to run any other business. After all, the prospective franchisor must have established a successful business in order to be able to establish it as a franchise. Marketing, operations, finance, administration and people skills are required whatever the business, and whatever its chosen method of getting its products or services to the end user.

Franchising requires the franchisor to add franchising skills to those which he possesses in running the individual franchised unit, and this is a good time to point out that when a business decides to become a franchised network, it becomes a different business.

Whatever it is that the business does now – running restaurants, selling houses, cleaning offices, styling hair or hiring cars – becomes irrelevant when operating as a franchisor. Sure, there will need to be people providing technical advice on the activities mentioned, but the job of the franchisor is to recruit, train, monitor and motivate people who want to run their own business. Franchising skills are the same whatever the end product or service, and they all revolve around understanding the franchisor–franchisee relationship.

Many people do not appreciate that the quality of the relationship developed between the franchisor and the franchisee is fundamental to the success and longevity of the network. If all the services which the franchisor provides are franchisee-friendly, and appropriate, then that is likely to be a good start.

Taking the time and trouble to understand, and implement, the principles of the franchisor–franchisee relationship is what makes the difference between a successful franchisor and a failing, or at least underperforming, network. Knowing what motivates franchisees, realising what is unique about the relationship between them and their franchisor, and speaking the language 'franchise-ese', are critical elements in the process of practical franchise management, the promotion of which is largely the theme of this book.

So, what is different, indeed unique, about that relationship, and who is responsible for making sure both parties are aware of their roles and responsibilities within it? The answer to the second part of the question is easy. The franchisor. But to explain it, they first have to understand it themselves.

WHAT ARE FRANCHISEES?

Firstly let's consider, what are franchisees? It's easier to begin by exploring what they are not. For a start, they are not employees – even though they work to instructions and will hopefully be selected with as much, or more, care as would be an employee. They are not customers – even though the formal relationship will start by them buying something from the franchisor, and they will continue to be provided with goods and services in return for some sort of payment. They are not partners – whatever the franchisor's promotional material may say about working together towards a common aim, they are certainly not partners within any legal definition. So, they are none of these things, but they are all of these things and they will be expected to behave in many of the ways people in these categories would be expected to behave.

Above all, franchisees are people who trusted the franchisor to provide what they said they would provide during the marketing and recruitment process. Indeed they trusted him or her to such an extent that they were prepared to invest, often, their entire resources, and the future prosperity of themselves and their family, in a business venture which they were convinced was likely to be suitable for them. They were probably also told that they would receive initial training, and ongoing support, in order to facilitate their success.

THE IMPORTANCE OF LISTENING

Just rereading the previous paragraph starts to highlight where it can all go wrong. Replace the words 'likely' and 'facilitate' with 'guaranteed' and 'guarantee', 'convinced' with 'assured' and it may just be possible to understand what the potential franchisee heard, as opposed to what the franchisor said.

Prospective franchisees sometimes hear what they want to hear and not necessarily what they are actually told. Some convince themselves that the business is the most desirable opportunity available and do not hear what is said to them, not only by the franchisor but also by their own advisers.

Of course, franchisors may also hear things wrongly during the recruitment process and it is important for them to understand that that process lays the foundations for the relationship. Both parties must appreciate that there is no point in fudging issues. If they have difficulties in communicating at that stage, or do not want to hear what is being said to them, they are likely to be entering into a relationship which will hit problems.

Franchising, as a business sector, is notoriously short of empirical research, but various figures are regularly quoted which include the relative success and longevity of franchised outlets *vis à vis* independent start-ups, and what motivates franchisees. Interestingly, the former may affect the latter.

Franchised outlets are claimed to be anything between two and ten times less likely to fail, over a given period of time, than non-franchised businesses. A definition of failure is hard to come by because franchising can also help an unsuccessful franchisee to recover his investment by engineering a resale, so many franchisors would not count that as a failure. All this assumes of course that the original research, if indeed there ever was any, was based on franchised opportunities which had been properly developed and piloted.

Franchising attracts people for whom safety and security are among their prime motivators. The 'what motivates franchisees' research is said to include various surveys of franchisees who were asked, 'Why did you buy a franchise rather than set-up your own business?' and the quoted results from survey to survey seem to have been fairly consistent. Top of the list come things like marketing support, training, use of an existing brand, always wanted to run a business but was scared to go it alone, feeling part of something, and so on. Always well down the list is anything to do with a desire to earn loads of money. Indeed franchisees will often earn less in their new role than they did in employment, but they are happier with the lifestyle.

So when a franchisor hears a franchisee candidate saying they will work hard to make their outlet or area successful, he had better be sure they share an understanding of what 'hard work' and 'success' mean. If the franchisor hears 'I'll get up early and work 14 hours a day, seven days a week to make my business market leader in my territory' when the candidate is saying 'Once I've dropped the kids off at school, I'll be able to make at least three sales calls before I hit the golf course', then trouble is brewing.

THE RULES

1. The first rule of understanding and operating the relationship is that the franchisor must explain, unambiguously and in writing, right from the first contact with a franchisee candidate, that what is being offered is the right to operate a proven business system, and to optimise the potential of that system, at an agreed outlet or within an agreed territory, for a defined period, for the mutual benefit of both parties. During that process of explanation the franchisor should define 'optimise' and start to agree a plan, objectives and personal responsibilities for the progress of that business in order to deliver that mutual benefit. He should also explain what will happen if things don't go according to plan. Help will be provided if the franchisee *cannot* make it work; they will lose their business if they *will not* make it work.

2. The second rule is that a franchisor must make it clear to his own staff, and accept for himself, that if a franchisee has joined a system, and made a considerable personal investment and commitment, based on a promise of guidance, support and

established systems, then that guidance and support had better be there and those systems had better work. For recruitment staff, that also means not over-promising or offering services to a standard that will simply not be available – all discussions should be confirmed in writing.

3. The third rule is therefore that the standards required of each party must be written down somewhere, there must be processes for monitoring everyone against those standards, and for rectifying situations of poor performance. Franchisors should be equally determined, when necessary, to rid their system of poor performers whether they be employees or franchisees.

4. The fourth rule is that it is essential for support staff to treat each franchisee as an individual, and to make an effort to find out what their 'hot buttons' are at any particular time. Personal support and motivation can then be tailored for each franchisee in order to get the best out of them, and for them. For example, there's no point offering a franchisee schemes to generate more sales if he can't, or won't, employ enough staff to service the customers he already has.

THE ROLES

The franchisor must also understand, and make clear, what the respective roles include.

Broadly speaking, the franchisor's role is to:

*   develop the business and the operating system;

*   market the opportunity;

*   recruit and train good franchisees;

*   create and maintain standards;

*   monitor and motivate the franchisees to operate the system properly;

and the role of the franchisee is to:

*   operate the system to the required standards.

The franchisor is not there to do the job for the franchisee, and the franchisee is not there to reinvent the wheel. Conversely, the franchisees are not there to provide the finance and take the risk of testing the systems for the franchisor. The franchisor provides the right tools, the franchisee uses the tools right.

While it is normal to generalise about what motivates franchisees, it is important for franchisors to remember two things. Firstly, franchisees are individuals and the details of their prime motivators will differ, even if the themes are similar among all of them. Secondly, those motivators will change over time as the franchisee reaches different stages of development in the franchisee life cycle (see Chapter 17).

MAINTAINING CONTACT

Another important aspect of managing the relationship is to be careful not to ignore franchisees who are doing well. It is easy to forget about those who are happy and successful. They pay their fees correctly, and on time, and are relatively undemanding compared to those who are struggling. If they are ignored, sooner or later they will start to question what they are gaining for all the fees they are paying, compared to the lower fees being paid by the people who are being given all the attention, and dissatisfaction may creep in. It may only need a mention in a newsletter, or an award at conference, to keep them onside, but nobody will know that if they never talk to them.

They will also never know whether that franchisee is 'happy and content' or 'happy but wants to do better'. The former may well accept a field visit which involves a long lunch and a chat about the latest football scores. The latter will be offended and frustrated by such a visit and will prefer a business meeting devoted to analysing the performance of his or her business and proposing ways of growing it.

Hopefully it is becoming apparent that franchise support staff need to have finely honed influencing and assertiveness skills, rather than relying on authority and aggression. A field support manager who is used to telling employed branch managers to jump, and expecting them to ask, 'How high?' is going to find life very difficult when he learns that, even if he only asks a franchisee to jump, the reply will be 'Why?'

That does not mean however that someone from a culture where the customer is always right will find the job easy either. The franchisee is not always right, and they will often try to flex their muscles on the basis that, since they're doing the job every day, they know more about it than someone from the support office. They may well be right in that assertion, but if the person from the support office can factually point out where the franchisee is underperforming against agreed standards then they are entitled to insist that things get back on track and will again need those influencing and assertiveness skills. The franchising field is not a place for shrinking violets or people who prefer to avoid conflict.

It's all a matter of balance and of finding ways of using mutually acceptable methods to reach the shared goal of building a business network using a common brand and system. Being clear about the respective roles and responsibilities of the parties involved, laying down the ground rules right from the start, then continually monitoring to ensure compliance and improve performance, is the very essence and nature of the franchisor–franchisee relationship.

Its importance is clear:

- get it wrong and neither party will have as successful a business as they could;

- get it very wrong and neither party will have a business at all.

5
Pilot operations

Hopefully by now you are convinced that for franchising to work properly it must be based on a proven business format. Pilot operations are where the proof comes from, and they are used to test the original business concept; to test whether the concept can be transferred to other sites and other people; to test the effect that franchising will have on the operation of that concept; to test the effect that franchising will have on the original business; and to test new ideas for subsequent development of the network and system.

TESTING THE BUSINESS CONCEPT

If a business has been operating successfully for some years then there is no need to test the concept because it has already been proven. The existing company-managed outlet *is* the pilot.

If, however, the subject of the eventual franchise is currently no more than an idea, then a business must be created to operate and refine that idea to get it to the stage where it can be judged to be proven. This could take many months, indeed years.

The costs and the other risks associated with the creation of that business *must* be borne by the (prospective) franchisor.

TESTING TRANSFERABILITY

If the existing business already has three or more outlets then there is no need to test transferability because that has already been established. Other outlets have been opened and other people have learned how to operate them.

If the original business has only ever been operated from one outlet, and managed by its creator, then further outlets must be opened to make sure it can be done elsewhere by someone else. Sometimes a business has been successful solely because of its original location, or simply because its creator had special talents or unbounded enthusiasm, and those criteria do not make for good franchising.

The costs and other risks associated with opening a few more branches *should* be borne by the (prospective) franchisor. He could get a partner, or external funding, but the first additional units should essentially be company-owned and managed.

TESTING FRANCHISING

The effect of operating under franchise can only be tested when there are already multiple company-owned units against which the new method of operation can be tested. That figure could be three for a growth franchise, it could be three thousand for a conversion franchise, but however well proven the concept, franchising should be tested slowly, and in no more than two or three units initially.

The costs of testing franchising will *often* be borne between the (potential) franchisor and pilot franchisees. The testing needs to be done by someone with 'skin in the game' otherwise it is not a test of how an independent operator will perform. However it is not fair to ask a third party to take all the risk of proving what someone else thinks will work. It is therefore common for a pilot franchise agreement to be used whereby the franchisee, with full knowledge that this is a test, is allowed to operate an outlet for a specific period of time, maybe up to two years.

If all goes well, at the end of that period the pilot franchisee will be granted a full franchise agreement. If things do not go well, or the franchising project is abandoned, all bets are off, but the pilot franchisee will have had the opportunity to earn an income along the way, possibly even at a minimum level guaranteed by the franchisor.

The franchisor may pay the set-up costs of the pilot units, the pilot franchisee will pay the running costs. Both parties should keep detailed day-book accounts of what happens, both good and bad, as these notes will be used to refine the franchise system, and further develop the operations manual, when preparing it for eventual full-scale launch.

No matter how many branches previously existed, things will change when the operation runs as a franchise. These changes will not necessarily be those that were envisaged when the plan was put together; some will be better, some will be worse, some will be totally unforeseen. Which is, of course, the point of testing them.

Pilot franchisees are inevitably more inclined to take risks, and be more independent and more entrepreneurial, than most franchisees. If they do stay in the network they may well be more difficult to manage than later franchisees, but without them there wouldn't be a network to manage.

TESTING THE EFFECT ON THE BUSINESS

We have previously established that franchising requires a unique culture. Becoming a franchisor will almost certainly require changes in the culture of an existing business. The bigger the business, the bigger the changes, and it is as well to test them, through the pilots, before embarking on a full-scale franchise launch.

Some businesses, no matter how much franchise-awareness training is carried out with their directors and staff, simply cannot get to grips with how to deal with franchisees. If the business cannot adapt then franchising will not work, and should not be continued.

Large-scale conversion franchising is particularly difficult to achieve because large companies have developed their ways of doing things over a number of years and they are slow to adapt. It is particularly difficult when the franchisee used to be one of the employees but is now managing director of one of the company's most important customers.

Serious conversion projects may require that, as one form of doing business is gradually replaced by another, so too should be the board of directors. The old blood needs to be removed, suitably incentivised to engineer a trouble-free transition, by individuals with a more franchise-friendly attitude. After all, the company is in the franchising business now, not whatever business sector its products or services fall into.

TESTING NEW IDEAS

It is much easier to persuade franchisees to invest in new equipment, or change the way they do things, if the new way can be demonstrated to have worked somewhere else. For this reason, many franchisors continue to operate company-owned units, which can be used for training new franchisees, retraining existing ones, and testing new ideas. Those franchisors who choose not to operate owned units often have 'tame' franchisees who are happy to be involved in training or system development in their businesses.

However it is done, the principle remains the same: show a franchisee how a new way of doing things has been tested, and what benefits it will bring to their business, and they are more likely to make the required investment in time and money. Simply telling them to spend thousands on a new IT system may present challenges which are difficult to overcome!

6
Building the franchisor management team

The size of the franchisor's management team will vary greatly from business to business, related not only to the number of operating franchisees but also to matters such as the complexities of the businesses that franchisees operate, and what the franchisor can afford. What doesn't change much are the roles that have to be filled and the tasks that have to be carried out.

The franchisor's job is to recruit, train, monitor and motivate people who want to run their own business. Those people may or may not have had previous experience of selling or providing the product or service which is the subject of the franchise; they may or may not have had previous experience of administering and accounting for such a business; they may or may not have had previous experience of managing staff; they may or may not have had previous experience of running their own business.

The roles that need to be filled are pretty much those that are covered by the chapters in Section 2 of this book. There is no need to list them here, but it is important to realise that all those support functions have to be available to the very first franchisees. If not, they will probably fail and the whole project will go nowhere.

In the early days it will be neither necessary nor possible to have one support person for every role or task – indeed, sometimes the principal of the original business may find themselves doing it all, or various people will be seconded from that business, on a full- or part-time basis, to help with the franchising activity.

An alternative to part-time secondment from within, which inevitably means that the job will not be done as well as it could, or as often as it should, is to outsource the various activities to organisations such as the Franchise Support Centre, until the role has grown to a sufficient size to be worth employing an experienced executive from another franchised network. When that time comes, there are once again specialist franchise executive recruiters at the Franchise Careers Centre who can search for and identify people who will be suitable to join the team in question.

THE TEAM ROLES

Head of franchising

They may be called a director, they may be called a manager, but there needs to be one person who is clearly in overall charge of the franchising project and who is clearly responsible for the implementation and achievement of the Franchised Network Development Plan. This ought to be a full-time, totally dedicated role.

This person needs to understand the original business, and they need to understand franchising. Typically they will come from inside the original business and will therefore need to learn about franchising. Much of this learning will come from working with the franchise consultant who helped with structuring the plan, and who is now involved in assisting with its implementation. On-the-job learning will be supplemented by a formal training programme such as that offered in the UK by the Franchise Training Centre. Indeed all franchise support staff will benefit from taking the modules specific to their roles, and those with longer-term ambitions may choose to enrol on the Diploma in Franchise Management programme. See Appendix E.

Franchise marketing and franchisee recruitment

Until such time as a full-time employee can be justified to fulfil this role it is not unusual to outsource the marketing of the franchise opportunity and the recruitment of franchisees to specialists such as the Franchise Support Centre. Franchisee recruitment is a skilled and demanding role which is not easily learned, but those skills transfer across almost any franchised business. An outsourced executive, even if they are working on behalf of six different clients, will probably do a better job than an inexperienced, part-time employee from within the original business.

Note, however, that such services should only be used to screen applicants down to a short list, which means they meet all the defined criteria in the franchisee profile. The final decision on whether they are accepted as a franchisee should always rest with the Head of Franchising.

Franchisee training

Most franchisors are very good at training their franchisees, both before they start their businesses and continually thereafter, in 'how to run the store'. They are less good at teaching someone 'how to run the business', although the latter is equally important.

The technical 'how to run the store' training is mostly provided by staff from within the franchisor's business as they usually have someone already doing this for the company-owned units. All these staff have to do is to learn the specifics of dealing with franchisees, compared to the way they probably deal with employed staff.

Unless the franchisor has many franchisees he is unlikely to have anyone on the staff who can teach a franchisee 'how to run a business', which includes things like preparing and reviewing business plans and understanding financial information. In addition to training support staff in how to deal with franchisees, the Franchise Training Centre runs generic courses on these subjects which can either be delivered in-house, if a franchisor has enough delegates at one time, or on mixed sessions where a number of franchisors send one or two delegates each.

Franchisee monitoring

Franchisees are subject to varying degrees of qualitative and quantitative monitoring – often just plugging into systems which are used in the original business, although sometimes being enrolled onto outsourced generic franchise management systems, particularly for bookkeeping and accounting.

The outcome of the monitoring needs to be fed back to the franchisees, both individually and as a group, and is best done by someone from within the original business who has had the appropriate franchisee-management training.

Franchisee motivation

Apart from the ubiquitous rah-rah sessions at the annual conference, franchisee motivation comes best from inside the business and can be delivered either by individuals who have been recruited from other franchisors and who have learned the original business; or by those from the original business who have been trained how to deal with franchisees.

Field support and business development

This is the crucial role in franchisee development and support, and the number of staff involved in its supply grows with the number of franchisees – typically one field support manager to between 15 and 20 franchisees, although the ratio varies greatly from system to system.

This role is best compared to that of a GP – the doctor to whom you go to get advice or check-ups across a range of potential ailments. He has the experience to deal with the majority of cases, but if something comes up which needs specialist advice he can refer back to a specialist elsewhere within the organisation.

The common factor for all directors, managers and staff dealing with potential or practising franchisees, whether those staff are outsourced or employed, whether they came from the original business and were trained in franchising, or whether they were head-hunted from franchising and learned about the original business, is a thorough understanding of what makes the franchisor–franchisee relationship work, and what makes franchisees tick.

RECRUITING AND TRAINING THE MANAGEMENT TEAM

Everyone in the franchisor's business who deals with franchisees needs to understand both the business of the franchisor, i.e. what products and services the business delivers to its final consumers; and the business of franchising, i.e. how the organisation supports its franchisees. New members of the team from inside the business will need to learn the principles of franchising; new members joining the company from within the franchising community will need to learn how the franchisor's business works.

Most businesses will have induction programmes in place for new employees, but new franchisors won't know how to teach people about franchising. Similarly, recruiting people from within is relatively easy, but how does a new franchisor find suitable employees with franchising experience?

Fortunately, there are two organisations which can help. The Franchise Careers Centre provides a unique service for matching franchisors seeking to strengthen their management teams with experienced executives looking to further their careers in the franchising community, domestically or internationally; and the Franchise Training Centre provides practical development and coaching for franchisors' management teams, including a series of interactive workshops which can lead to the award of the Diploma in Franchise Management.

A description of the Diploma in Franchise Management programme, and an outline of each of its courses, is shown in Appendices E and F on pages 262 and 264.

7

The franchisee operations manual

Most franchisees do not read manuals – but you still have to give them one.

You'd think that the conscientious franchisee would study your paperwork carefully, having just spent thousands to join your network, but face it; did you read the instructions for the last expensive car, television or coffee maker that you bought?

In fact, it's not such a bad thing that franchisees use your manual for a doorstop rather than for enlightenment. They probably just want to get on with making a success of your business after good training.

WHY IS THE MANUAL IMPORTANT?

So, why bother with all the expense, time and nervous twitches that you will incur writing a manual? The manual you give to your franchisees is actually far more important to you than it is to them, for the following reasons:

1. it reinforces the value of your unique concept;

2. it helps you to 'engineer' your system;

3. it is a reference for franchisee training;

4. it promotes good support office infrastructure;

5. it extends the power and terms of your franchise agreement.

1. It reinforces the value of your unique concept

Not so long ago, many manuals were just 'cut, copy and paste' jobs with a franchisor's name gummed over folders 'borrowed' from other long-established franchisors. Being borrowed, they were often years out of date and already discarded by the organisations that originally wrote them.

Older manuals were masked in legal language so convoluted that even their owners didn't understand them and they often preached more about roasting a franchisee slowly in hell should they dare open late than actually saying much about what they should be doing when they did open.

Using another franchisor's manual isn't going to help you or your franchisees very much, nor is an 'off-the-shelf' manual, because they:

- are obviously generic – especially if you forget to change, for example, 'doughnut' for 'auto car wax' on just one of the 200 pages;

- are overly anonymous – even a good copy and paste job removes so much that made the manual unique to the original franchisor that the document becomes anonymous and reflects none of your own company's philosophy;

- are largely irrelevant – when using someone else's manual as a template it is tempting to leave in a lot of policies that are unnecessary for your own business, just to preserve the weight of the folder;

- include your operation and systems as an afterthought rather than as the heart of the manual – if they aren't written for your business, they tend to shoehorn your operation into the gaps, rather than have it defining and driving the contents of the manual.

If, however, your manual is written from scratch for your business and is comprehensive, it will:

- make it clear to your franchisees that you have put in the effort that they deserve;

- preserve the business philosophy, style and emphasis that made your business successful in the first place;

- underline the value and uniqueness of your concept.

2. It helps you to 'engineer' your system

Properly constructed, the exercise of writing your manual will help you to create the best systems for the smooth operation of your franchise.

Starting from scratch, outlining the aspects of your business that you need to communicate to your franchisees – and thus the eventual contents of your manual – helps you understand and map all the things you need to systemise for franchisees to copy your business successfully.

The best modern franchise systems are 'engineered' around the actual operations of the business and how their first franchisees really learn them and try to copy them.

The best manuals are those that grow with your franchise and systemise those aspects of your business that your first franchisees learn less well, find less than intuitive, regularly fall below your standards in achieving. They help franchisees to perform better in the operation of your business, are efficient rather than bureaucratic, and help franchisees concentrate on sales rather than administration.

In short, you should engineer your systems to drive your business in the *real* world and record their 'blueprints' in your manual. You should not let your business be driven by a poor or theoretical manual.

3. It is a reference for franchisee training

By thinking through all your systems and writing them in your own manual from scratch, you will be better able to train franchisees in full and in sequence. The manual will form a valuable reference tool for your training staff.

Your manual can also be used as a record of training, and you ensure that get franchisees 'sign off' each aspect or chapter as it is completed.

There will then be a written record that you have trained them in each aspect and they won't be able to claim later that 'you didn't tell me that!'

4. It promotes good support office infrastructure

Your role as a franchisor is to provide franchisees with a systemised business that you have already proven to be successful. Nevertheless, knowing how your business works successfully is very different from developing it to support franchisees to do the same.

However strange it may seem, good franchisors often find that the process of engineering their franchise system to serve the needs of franchisees, and recording it in a manual, leads to improvements in their own central infrastructure.

It is also very tempting when writing a manual to preach what you would like to practise but don't. The conscientious, sensible franchisor will then implement the good systems that it has designed for its franchisees at its own branches. A good manual is a valuable component of any business, even before it has any franchisees.

5. It extends the power and terms of your franchise agreement

The reason that old-fashioned 'off-the-shelf' manuals were full of legal gobbledegook and not much in the way of operations (apart from the fact that most of them originated from American systems that operate in a more litigious environment) was that they were conceived as an extension of the franchise agreement rather than as a tool to help franchisees with the day-to-day operation of their business.

Franchise agreements are now quite comprehensive and well tested in themselves, and already contain many of the policies and restrictions that used to be part of manuals, so there is less need to confuse franchisees with legalities in the manual. Franchisees are also more aware now than they have ever been and will not accept a manual that is really just a thinly disguised extension of the legal agreement. They want more operational guidance in manuals, even if they never read them. However, your manual will still be referred to in your franchise agreement, and often cross-referenced to it, as an integral part of that agreement – meaning that anything that you require as a standard or procedure in your manual is as good as a clause in your agreement.

HOW TO GET FRANCHISEES TO USE YOUR MANUAL

The best way to get your franchisees to use your manual is to make it interactive and searchable.

Most franchisees will use a computer daily in their business – whether it is a store or service business. Even those franchisees that have no administration duties will still use a computer as their EPOS till or to receive details of their next job, even if this is via a PDA or smart phone. You may even have supplied those computers in your joining or equipment package.

It is therefore quite bizarre that so many franchisors still hand out their manuals on paper rather than computerising them and making them interactive and searchable.

Many franchisees expect that manuals will now be interactive – either on CD or online – in a format that allows them to type in their question and have it answered. Not distributing your manual in this way can make your business less attractive to prospective franchisees, while making it interactive will give you a competitive advantage.

The simplest way to distribute your manual interactively is to put it up on the internet or your intranet as a 'Wiki'. A 'Wiki' is an online resource that allows users to add and edit content collectively. You can control who is allowed to access or edit any part of a Wiki and moderate any entry – thus allowing some parts of it to grow with the experience of all franchisees, and other parts to remain strictly as you want it.

It is very simple to get your manual online as a Wiki and any good franchise consultant or manual writing professional will be able to help you with this.

Once your manual is in a Wiki format, you and your franchisees will enjoy the following advantages:

- it is easier to use, so everyone uses it more;

- it is less daunting viewed screen by screen than as a weighty printed manual;

- it is interactive, so franchisees can comment on each subject's usefulness or add their collective experience to it (where you allow) and thus want to keep using it;

- it is searchable, so a franchisee can find the answer to their question quickly;

- you can set all or part of it to be unprintable and only viewed on screen;

- you can set it so that it can't be copied and pasted from the screen and so that no-one can download part of it or the entire manual to email to a competitor;

- you can restrict access to parts of it or all of it, so that only your franchisees can see it, so that you need not reveal all of it to all users, and so that you can stop any franchisee accessing it if you are in dispute with them;

- it can grow with collective experience, as your franchisees and support team update allowed sections for you, so that it becomes more useful and stays current;

- it makes it easier to write the manual in the first place because, once you have the contents structure in place, any number of people at your head office can edit those parts that you delegate to them at the same time, rather than you needing to slowly circulate a master copy or coordinate contributions and waste time adding them to the master;

- it allows you to distribute a useful manual sooner. You wouldn't print a half-finished manual but if your manual is online; franchisees can make use of the bits that you have finished before the whole thing is complete.

You should take care to protect any version of your manual that is electronic. If you neglect to lock electronic versions of your manual for access, printing and editing they can be easier to distribute and copy than paper versions. If an online version is too easily hacked and is not placed behind firewalls within your intranet it may also be at risk of being placed in the public domain. The technology to protect you from any of these risks (such as coding manual access to a specific computer) does exist and you should get a good franchise consultant or manual writing expert to help you set it up.

Your main priority is to get your franchisees to use the manual, not simply read it and then forget it in their first week of trading. If you make it easy for them to refer to when they have a question – before they call your support team – you will save yourself a lot of infrastructure time and money. If it's really easy to use and they regularly refer to it, you will also be more likely to ensure that franchisees do things the way you want them done, to your standards (and prevent many misunderstandings into the bargain).

Encourage franchisees into the habit of referring to your manual by ensuring that support team members refer them back to it when they call with a question that the manual answers in detail. The support team member should call back later to ensure that the manual answered the question. Eventually, franchisees will get into the habit of checking the manual before they call.

THE IMPORTANCE OF USING EXPERIENCED MANUAL WRITERS

You may be the only one that truly knows and understands your business but it does not necessarily follow that you would be the best manual writer, any more than you would be the best trainer.

Modern franchise-manual-writing professionals have years of experience of the best format and writing styles to get your message across to your franchisees. A good franchise-manual-writing professional will also know how to make your manual interactive and how to safely put it online so that franchisees use it, but at the same time without assuming that they will ever read it all the way through.

If you have employed the services of a good franchise consultant to help you engineer your franchise system from scratch, they will already have got you to pass on your knowledge to them through questionnaires, existing documents and demonstration, so your role in constructing a good manual need not extend to actually writing it.

More importantly, good franchise consultants have dealt with many other franchisors' businesses and their franchisees. Through that experience, they know how franchisees behave and thus what to include in your manual, what to reinforce and how to communicate it in a way that franchisees will learn and implement properly. If you have never been a franchisor before, you will save yourself a lot of time and money by learning from the experiences of other franchisors with whom your franchise consultant has dealt.

It can take from three months to a year to engineer the systems that need to go into a manual, and from 300 to 1,000 hours to write it all down. Employing a franchise consultant to do it for you can free up that amount of your time which you can then spend on further developing your business.

8
The franchise agreement

The most important document in franchising, alongside the operations manual, is the franchise agreement, since the terms within it underpin the whole relationship.

HOW, AND WHEN, TO CHOOSE YOUR LAWYER

It is important to remember that franchising is not a legal relationship with commercial aspects, it is a commercial relationship with legal aspects, and if you are going to franchise your business, domestically or internationally, the last thing you want is a lawyer!

You will most certainly need one, but not until you have worked out all the commercial arrangements, and completed the franchise development plan, so that you know you have a potentially successful network.

You will also need one who is experienced in preparing franchise agreements – not your normal commercial lawyer, not the one who did your house purchase or divorce, not your in-house lawyer if you are a large corporation, and not necessarily one who deals mostly with franchisees.

Many potential franchisors make the mistake of contacting one of the less experienced, saying 'I'm going to franchise my business, I'll need a franchise agreement, can you prepare one for me?' Typically, the reply is, 'Yes, of course. What would you like in it?'

The problem is that the client doesn't know what he wants in it if he hasn't had expert practical advice – and nor does the lawyer. He may know the matters to be considered, and most of them are outlined below, but he won't know which option to choose.

Regrettably, some lawyers will simply copy a similar document from another franchisor, others will have a stab at recommending the detail. The good ones will ask if the client has prepared a franchise development plan, together with all the financial forecasts, and whether an experienced consultant was involved. If not, they should refer the client back to the consultant first. Beware of those who do not.

While the principles outlined in this book will apply to franchising anywhere in the world, it must be pointed out that we are writing from a UK perspective where we are fortunate in not having to deal with any franchise-specific legislation. Many other countries do have laws which regulate franchising and there may be a greater need for legal advice, although a good consultant in that country will know the legal matters to be considered and will take note of them when structuring the franchise and preparing the development plan.

ITEMS TO CONSIDER

The following are the matters most often covered in a franchise agreement, and some of the options to be considered when deciding the detail, but it cannot be too greatly stressed that the franchise agreement is a document that needs detailed professional advice.

Parties

Who is signing the agreement on behalf of whom. The franchisor may be a subsidiary of the business which originally developed and operated the system; it may be the original business itself; it may a master franchisee of an overseas franchisor.

The franchisee may be a sole trader; it may be a partnership; it may be a limited company set up solely for the purpose of operating the franchise; it may be a limited company already operating an existing business to which the franchise is to be added.

The franchisor will usually decide and control with which type of entity it wishes to be involved. If the franchisee is a limited company it will normally be required to name at least one individual who takes personal responsibility as 'principal' for the franchisee's obligations – thereby removing the protection of limited liability for the franchisee.

The franchisee will be required to make it clear to the public, in a format prescribed by the franchisor, that it is an independent business operating under a franchise agreement with the franchisor, and that it is not an agent of the franchisor and cannot commit the latter's funds or other resources.

Rights granted

Details the rights granted to the franchisee to use the name, system, trademarks, software and other relevant intellectual property owned by the franchisor, in what territory they can be used, and whether or not those rights are exclusive or non-exclusive. There are commercial pros and cons to all the options and they should be considered with an experienced franchise practitioner.

Term of agreement

Defines when the agreement starts and how long it lasts. The term could be anything from two to 20 years for a simple unit franchise – and there are many matters which influence the number of years. EU legislation affects the term for systems where franchisees are tied to products; banks' attitudes to lending to franchisees dictate that any lending should be capable of being repaid by the end of the initial term; franchisors may want to limit the time that must elapse before they can enforce certain changes upon renewal; franchisees may not want to sign the agreement if they don't think they have long enough to take full advantage of the opportunity.

Renewal

The franchisee will normally have the right to renew the agreement at the end of its first term, provided they are not in breach of its terms, and provided they bring their premises and equipment up to date. They will, however, renew on the 'then current' terms, which means they sign a new agreement which is the same as that being signed by franchisees now joining the system – they don't just renew the agreement they already have. There may or may not be a further right to renew at the end of the second or subsequent terms, and the pros and cons again need to be considered as they will vary for every system. There may or may not be a fee payable on renewal but this would normally be much less than the fee payable by a new franchisee.

Fees

All the fees payable to the franchisor by the franchisee – upfront fee, training fee, management services fees, marketing fees, payment for products and services – will be defined, as will the processes for their payment, and the remedies available to the franchisor should they not be paid in full or on time.

Franchisor's obligations

Usually fairly broadly defined, the franchisor's obligations are laid out so that the franchisee can see what sort of support will be provided. The level of support will vary greatly from franchisor to franchisor but the items usually included cover training, marketing, business support, updating the operations manual, managing the corporate website and so on.

Franchisee's obligations

These will be many more in number, and defined in much more detail. What has to be done, how often, who by and how well. They will include marketing, advertising, sales, operational, training, accounting, insurance, compliance, employment, record keeping, reporting matters and approval procedures. There will be a formal link to the procedures and standards laid down in the operations manual, with which the franchisee agrees to comply at all times, and which the franchisor can change at will during the term of the agreement (although common sense dictates that they will not do so in such a manner that will cause problems with, or for, the franchisees).

Premises and equipment

Some franchisors choose to take the head lease on business premises and sublet to the franchisee, but most do not. Those that do may or may not make a mark-up on the rent, or may or may not base the rent on the franchisee's turnover. There is no right answer and the situation must be assessed for every franchisor, and possibly for every site. The franchise agreement and the lease agreement need to be linked, and once a decision has been taken, the technicalities are definitely a matter for the lawyers. Similar considerations come into play if the franchisee is using bespoke equipment – the franchisor may choose to lease, rather than sell, this to the franchisee, therefore maintaining control of it in the event of a dispute.

Selling the business

Franchisees typically have the right to sell their business as a going concern, but only to a buyer approved by the franchisor, using the same criteria as he would for a new franchisee. These criteria will not just consider whether the incoming franchisee has the right skills and attitudes, but also whether they can afford to buy at the price agreed, depending on how the deal is being financed. The franchisor will usually have the right to pre-empt the purchase by acquiring the business himself (either to operate as a company-owned unit or sell on) on the same terms as those agreed with a third party. The franchisor may or may not receive a percentage of the sale price, ostensibly to cover his approval and training costs, and may or may not additionally be entitled to a further percentage if he found the buyer through his normal franchise marketing efforts.

Death or incapacity of the franchisee

If the franchisee is a limited company it cannot die or become incapacitated but its principal can and there will be provisions in the agreement as to what should happen in such circumstances. The directors of the corporate franchisee, or the executors of a sole trader's estate, will be given a period in which to appoint a successor as principal, who must be acceptable to the franchisor, and in the meantime to appoint a stand-in to operate the business after receiving appropriate training. Such a stand-in can be provided by the franchisor, at a cost. Should a replacement not be provided, or the business not be sold, within an acceptable period, say six months, the franchise would be terminated.

Termination of the agreement

Sooner or later all franchise agreements are terminated, either by mutual agreement or force of circumstances. The business fails, or is sold; the franchisee dies, or becomes incapacitated; the franchisor terminates because of non-performance or substantial breach by the franchisee; the franchisee just gives up; or the time simply runs out and there is no further renewal. The circumstances in which the agreement can be terminated by the franchisor will vary with each system and will be made clear in the agreement. The procedures will more likely be defined in the manual, and in all cases it is better to try to achieve an agreed solution rather than get the courts involved. Some agreements may insist that methods of alternative dispute resolution are tried first.

Post-termination provisions

Once the agreement has been terminated, for whatever reason, there will be a number of things that the franchisee must either do, or stop doing. These may include ceasing to use all the franchisor's intellectual property, paying all money due to the franchisor, handing over premises or equipment as appropriate, providing a list of all past and current customers, not being involved in a similar business within so many miles for so many months, not contacting staff or customers, and giving back the operations manual.

The above are the main commercial considerations to be discussed in detail in order to develop a bespoke agreement for every franchisor. The output can then be presented to an appropriately experienced lawyer, either by the potential franchisor or his consultant (although the lawyer will be formally engaged by the client), who will then go on to formalise the wording and add all the necessary boilerplate clauses.

NEGOTIATION

To make life simple, there is no negotiation of the terms of the standard franchise agreement once it has been finally drafted. It is fundamental to practical franchise management, and to successful franchising, that all franchisees joining the system at the same time sign the same agreement and there should be no additions or amendments allowed.

That is not to say, as is often said, that all franchisees in a system are on the same agreement because they will not be. Changes to the standard agreement are made as legislation, good practice or practicalities dictate and the new standard version becomes the 'then current' agreement to which all subsequent new, or renewing, franchisees sign up. Until their next renewal, franchisees will be on the agreement they signed when they joined.

All potential franchisees should be advised by the franchisor to take their own independent legal advice before signing the agreement, but they too should choose a lawyer experienced in such matters. An experienced franchising lawyer will know that negotiation is not an option, but that their job is to explain the agreement and its implications to their client. The client then decides whether or not to sign it.

A contents list for an example franchise agreement is presented in Appendix D on page 260.

A list of specialist lawyers will normally be available from the national franchise association of any country, and a list of such associations and their websites is presented in Appendix H on page 273.

9
International franchising

When a business is nearing capacity in its home market, whether or not it operates through a franchising structure in its home country, cross-border franchising represents a very real opportunity to build a business. The options are either to develop and export an existing business format which you currently own and operate in your home country; or to take on the rights to operate a business from elsewhere which does not currently have outlets trading in your country.

Developing a global brand is now a very real possibility for many successful businesses who would never before have dreamed of it. With it come the advantages of economies of scale in both production and marketing costs, which compound the benefits of the relationship for both franchisor and franchisee. In addition, for the franchisor, there is the benefit of spreading the risk of economic downturn. There is rarely a slump all around the world at the same time so if, say, Europe is having a bad time the chances are economies will still be buoyant in the Far East and the franchisor will have at least some reasonable sales opportunities.

The principles of international franchising are similar to those laid out elsewhere in this book for domestic franchising, but we need to establish some new definitions, both for the parties and for the fees, before considering the opportunities.

The **franchisor** is the company who originally developed the concept which is now to be the subject of the franchise. They may or may not have used a franchising model to develop the business system and brand in their home country.

A **master franchisee** is the individual, or more likely the corporation, to whom the rights to use the system are exported for them to operate in their own country. A master franchisee may originally operate their own company-owned outlets in their country in order to prove and/or adapt the system, but they will sooner or later appoint sub-franchisees to open additional units according to the agreed development schedule.

An **area developer** is the individual, or more likely the corporation, to whom the rights to use the system are exported for them to operate in their own country or region. In this case however they will not be intended to operate through sub-franchisees and will only open their own company-owned units. Area developers can also be referred to as direct franchisees since they are in direct contact with the franchisor, whether they have one or 100 units open.

A **sub-franchisee** or **unit franchisee** is the individual or company which owns and operates the trading outlets which report to the master franchisee in a given country or territory. Their reporting responsibility, and legal agreement, will normally be with the master franchisee, not the franchisor.

The **master franchise fee** is the amount the master franchisee pays to get into the game, and it may or may not cover training, rights to use the name and systems, an amount which enables the franchisor to amortise his international development and recruitment costs, and an amount which reflects the perceived value of the opportunity or territory, particularly if it is being awarded on an exclusive basis. It may also be calculated with reference to what other similar systems are charging, and the general market price for franchises, but it needs to be accurately assessed for each system. As stated in Chapter 3, when discussing franchising in general, just because a competitor is charging, say, $300,000 upfront fee doesn't mean that's the right figure for your business – again, it may not even be right for their business if they didn't research it properly!

Note that the upfront fee is not the same as the total set-up costs; the latter includes all the other necessary purchases and expenses of getting the business opened, most of which may go to third parties.

Note also that a **developer**, whether national or regional, will need to have much more capital available to it than a master franchisee because the developer is committing to opening and operating all the stores themselves whereas the master will eventually be using other people's money (i.e. his franchisees) to build his network. Developers are likely therefore to be much more substantial businesses than master franchisees.

An international franchisor's business should not be about selling master franchises and bringing in upfront franchise fees. The long-term goal should be to generate continuing income from successful franchisees building a recognised brand around the world. Not all international franchisors see things this way, so potential master franchisees should beware.

The **ongoing fees** or **management services fees** include royalties for continuing use of the brand and systems but these fees are mostly to cover the services provided to the master by the franchisor. The range of services, and the level of management services fees, varies greatly from system to system – even for businesses in the same sector – and once again they need to assessed and set by an experienced practitioner. They must be affordable, and good value, for the franchisee; they must be sufficient eventually to pay for the franchisor's support infrastructure and provide them with a reasonable profit, good return on their investment, and adequate funding to further develop the network and the business.

The majority of management services fees are charged as a percentage of the master franchisee's income from their unit franchisees. This will include part of the upfront fees payable by unit franchisees and of their ongoing management services fees. Care must be taken in assessing the appropriate level, as taking too much will leave the master with insufficient funds to grow their network. 'Half of the upfront unit fees, then ten per cent of their ten per cent' is often quoted as a reasonable benchmark, but it needs to be a bespoke calculation for every business.

Where the overseas partner is an area developer, the ongoing fees will be a store-opening fee (i.e. a fixed amount every time they open a new outlet) and a percentage of the retail sales.

Alternatively, **product mark-up** is more appropriate for some franchisors, particularly retailers or manufacturers. Sometimes franchisors charge both, but the temptation to take too much from franchisees in too many ways must be resisted if it affects the viability of their businesses. One of the advantages of being a franchisee is to benefit, not suffer, from being tied to, or part of, a bigger buying group.

A **marketing fee** may also be charged by some franchisors, and this is supposed to go into a pot to help pay for international marketing and branding activity, although one is tempted to question how many international franchisors are truly capable of providing a good-value return. Local country marketing activity is usually a separate expense, paid for by the franchisee.

The chosen structure and fee arrangements will vary from country to country, even for the same franchisor, and they need to be the subject of some detailed research by experienced advisers to get the optimum version. As with all franchise arrangements there is no generic right way to do it. There is simply the right way for the business in question, and this needs to be deduced from all the options and experiences available to specialist advisers.

Generally speaking, a business which does not franchise in its home country would be ill-advised to appoint a master franchisee in another country as it (the franchisor) will have no knowledge or experience of appointing and managing sub-franchisees and will therefore be unable to pass on any such knowledge and experience to the master franchisee. This may not be such a problem if the master franchisee already has experience of running other franchised networks, but then there is the risk of them knowing more than the franchisor and of the tail then wagging the dog.

Therefore the arrangement tends to work best if a business which operates a company-owned chain in its home country appoints area developers abroad. A business which operates a franchised network in its home country can safely appoint either master franchisees or area developers.

So, what about the opportunities for the various parties?

THE FRANCHISOR

A business may have established itself well in its home country, and indeed may even be reaching capacity there. To continue to grow, it has a number of options, not least finding other products or services to supply through its established distribution system (in which case it could even consider becoming a master franchisee or area developer for someone else's system). Alternatively it can look beyond its own shores at the possibilities of duplicating its success elsewhere.

Naturally there are a number of options, including setting up a wholly-owned subsidiary or going into a joint venture arrangement with a business which has appropriate knowledge of the local market. This entity can then open either or both company-owned and sub-franchised outlets. Subsidiaries and joint ventures both carry greater risk than a franchise arrangement, where someone else will be providing the capital and human resources, but of course the more you own the more of the profit you retain.

The advantages are the same as those of choosing to grow a domestic operation by franchising – put simply, you can grow quicker using other people's money and you have less day-to-day hassle because someone else is operating the business. If you can find five different organisations to duplicate your operation in five different countries, you can probably expand at five times the speed you could if you did it on your own. Of course, there are potential problems, but there is now much more experienced professional advice available than was the case even five years ago, so problems can at best be avoided, or at worst anticipated.

THE MASTER FRANCHISEE

For someone who is of the mindset of a typical franchisee, i.e. not too entrepreneurial and looking to be part of a proven system with established support structures, master franchising can offer far greater potential than simply running a single franchised outlet – and in many cases the required initial investment may not be all that different. For example, the master franchise rights for a van-based mobile franchise operation coming in from abroad could be available for around £100,000. To open just one reasonably sized restaurant outlet could cost three times that – even a quick print outlet could be nearly twice as much.

The advantages, compared to starting your own new network, should be similar to those for individual franchisees – proven system, known name, established way of operating, and marketing and training support. Of course, despite what the franchisor will tell you, just because a business works in America or Australia doesn't mean it will work in the UK, or vice versa, certainly not without some local adaptation, but at least it's a start.

As suggested elsewhere, it would perhaps not be a good move to become a master franchisee of a system which is not franchised in its home country unless you already have experience of running a franchised network. Having said that, there are increasing numbers of skilled practitioners who can assist you on either a consultancy, short-term contract or employed basis until you are confident to proceed on your own – and hopefully you'll always have the support of your franchisor.

Being a successful master franchisee requires the same skills as becoming a domestic franchisor – recruiting, training, monitoring and motivating individuals who want to run an independent business outlet. Fortunately these are skills which are increasingly recognisable and definable, and are therefore trainable by experienced training providers. It also brings the same advantages compared to opening company-owned stores – quicker expansion and more motivated local management.

THE AREA DEVELOPER

Area developers need a lot more capital available than do master franchisees because they are going to have to create their own infrastructure and open all their own outlets. Nevertheless, for companies experienced in a particular field – say, food retailing or building facilities management – who have the management expertise but perhaps lack the creativity to develop their own new products or services, or the finance to create a new brand from scratch, taking on a proven system from abroad can present enormous opportunities.

New products for an existing client base or distribution network, or even an opportunity to convert existing stores to a new brand, can quickly transform a business which has perhaps grown tired. Potential conversion works to the advantage of both franchisor and area developer as they can more quickly achieve brand awareness than they would by opening one store at a time.

Having an established network available for conversion is also a good bargaining point for the prospective area developer in reducing the up-front fee on the grounds that income flow from ongoing fees will grow more quickly.

THE UNIT FRANCHISEE

Becoming a unit franchisee for an incoming franchise, through a master franchisee, is no different to joining a domestic franchisor at an early stage of their development, and all the usual caveats apply. On occasions opportunities arise to become a unit franchisee reporting directly to the franchisor, whose support office remains in his home country. This can be a very risky proposition because most likely nothing will have been tested or proven in the destination market, and help could be a long way away and a long time coming. Of course, such a situation could also present opportunities to be in on the ground floor, to negotiate a favourable deal, or even to go on to become the master franchisee, but it should only be considered by someone with a more risk-taking profile than the average franchisee.

The techniques for becoming an international franchisor, or a master franchisee, and finding appropriate partners, are covered in Section 3 of this book.

SECTION 2
PRACTICAL FRANCHISE MANAGEMENT

10
How to market a franchise

Having established the structure of the franchise and prepared yourself to take on your new role as franchisor you will need to begin the process of generating enquiries from prospective franchisees. This is the first stage of bringing all your plans to their fulfilment. The process of marketing is aimed at getting franchisees to communicate with you with a view to finding out more about your franchise. It is a forerunner to your recruitment process and is what drives that process forward.

THE MARKETPLACE

The demand for franchisees

- **There are currently between 750 and 800 franchise systems** operating in the UK and this number has increased consistently over the last decade. Not all will be actively recruiting new franchisees at any one time but you can be certain that you will have many hundreds of systems in competition with you when you launch your marketing and recruitment process. It has been estimated that each year some 60 new franchise formats come to market although this represents a net increase in franchisor numbers of around 30 since each year a number of franchise systems drop out of the reckoning for a variety of reasons.

- **In 2005 2,300 new franchised units began operating** with a further 1,200 units changing hands through a resale process. If all these units were being operated by new franchisees it would suggest a number of around 3,500 franchisees joining UK networks during the course of that year. We know, however, that a significant number would be existing franchisees extending and developing their businesses, leaving perhaps, only 2,500 'new recruits'. Set this against the number of franchise systems operating (in excess of 750) and it would suggest the average UK franchise recruited less than four new franchisees in that year.

- **A random survey of 100 franchisors** identified that they each hoped, on average, to recruit 17 new franchises in the following year. Given the numbers recruited in 2005 this would appear to be a very challenging target.

- **If you are to succeed in competition with these established franchisors** you will need to have a compelling offer which is well communicated to your potential recruits.

> It seems likely that the marketplace for franchisee recruitment will remain challenging for years to come.

THE ECONOMIC CYCLE

- **A healthy economy can be both good and bad news** for a franchisor looking to recruit new franchisees.

- **Good pay rates** for people in employment may deter them from taking the step into self-employment where the salary they are able to earn is totally dependent upon the success of their new business venture. Improving standards of living may make them more risk averse and they may even have committed to a lifestyle that would not be supportable by a start-up business venture. Equally, good rates of pay might provide employees with the opportunity to generate some equity that will allow them to invest in their own business. This equity may come in the form of savings or an increase in value in their house that may be released through downsizing.

- **High levels of employment** and a sense of security in the employment situation may encourage people to 'stay put' in their current job or may be the stimulus that allows them to take the risk of 'going it alone'.

- **A less healthy economy** may increase the perception of possible job losses, and redundancies may provide people with both the incentive and the financial capital to invest in their own business. Beware, however, of the redundant person who sees starting their own business as a way to buy a job. They are unlikely to be focused on developing the business to the full, may feel that it is the only option left open to them, and may be using the franchise option simply to cease being unemployed.

> Whatever the stage and state of the economic cycle, you will not be in a position to influence it. Make plans therefore to develop your marketing and recruitment strategies in a flexible way that can respond to any external changes in the financial environment.

HOW MANY FRANCHISEES DO YOU WANT TO RECRUIT?

- **In developing the structure of the franchise** you will have made some assumptions on the number and size of territories that you will make available to franchisees. This in its turn will determine how many franchisees you need to recruit and when you hope to recruit them. Your first franchisee is often the most difficult to recruit as there will be no-one to endorse your offering to potential recruits. If you have one or more pilots in operation, and these have been successfully developed by franchisees, it will make the recruitment process easier as prospective franchisees will be able to talk to existing ones.

- **Converting enquiries into recruits.** The purpose of your marketing programme is to generate enquires from interested prospective franchisees. However, you should be aware that not all enquiries will result in a recruitment meeting. In fact many experienced franchisors suggest that in order to recruit one franchisee you need to have up to 100 initial expressions of interest. We will look later at how you can get the best conversion rates from enquiries to recruits but we mention the situation at this stage to highlight the fact that in order to recruit, say, three franchisees you may need to generate around 300 initial enquiries.

- **Lead generation** will become critical to the success of the recruitment programme, but the way you follow up those leads in the recruitment process is perhaps more important. (See Chapter 11.)

WHY A FRANCHISE?

A recent survey of franchisees asked why they chose to operate a franchise rather than setting up their own business from scratch. Not surprisingly, the answers included:

- **lower risk** (54 per cent of respondents) While no franchise can ever guarantee the success of their franchisees, all the evidence suggests that following a franchise model is more likely to generate a successful business.

- **marketing/training** (48 per cent of respondents) The existence of the franchise operating system means that franchisees can learn the fundamentals of running the specific business in a relatively short training period. Moreover, the existence of elements of national or local marketing activities by the brand should enable franchisees to grow their business more quickly.

- **long-term ambition** (41 per cent of respondents) The relatively high number of respondents citing this reason suggests that they had done some reasonable levels of research into the options over a period of time.

- **using a known name** (34 per cent of respondents) Trading with a recognised brand name will give the franchisee the benefit of all the successful history behind that brand. Initially your brand may have comparatively low levels of recognition on a national or international stage but your commitment to grow the franchise business will increase the strength of your brand with every new unit you open.

- **potential income** (26 per cent of respondents) The relatively low number citing income potential as a reason for operating a franchise may indicate that they were prepared to sacrifice an element of their income, through paying franchise fees, for the advantages of reduced risk and other support activities.

Knowing the reasons why people choose to operate a franchise rather than setting up a business from scratch gives you some important clues to the messages you will need to use to attract your franchisees. When you know what they are looking for, you can show them how your franchise will deliver it to them.

WHY THIS FRANCHISE?

In a further, more recent, survey, franchisees were asked why they had chosen their specific franchise rather than another system.

Reasons for selection	2004	2005
Growth potential	34%	23%
Affordability	10%	22%
Interest in field	33%	13%
Well-known brand	12%	12%
Available support	0%	9%

The variation of answers between the two years may draw into question the validity of comparing the two years' results, but it does certainly highlight some of the thought processes that franchisees use in deciding on one system as opposed to another. When we come to consider what messages we might want to impart in the marketing materials we will do well to consider those aspects that franchisees say are important to them.

FRANCHISEES' FORMER EMPLOYMENT STATUS

Over 60 per cent of franchisees come from an immediate background of being employed, while just over a further 30 per cent come from a self-employed background, including a small number who are, or have been, franchisees of another system. Only 5 per cent come from a situation where they were unemployed or had recently been made redundant. This perhaps confirms the view expressed earlier that most franchisees had the option of spending some considerable time in researching their options before taking their final decision.

MARKETING FOR FRANCHISEES

Prompting the initial enquiry

In order to attract enquiries from potential franchisees you must make them aware of the existence of the franchise and the potential it offers. Your core business is possibly quite well known within your local trading area but one of the reasons that you will have decided to franchise is to extend the business outside your own locality. This will be virgin territory for you and your brand. Your marketing messages to potential franchisees must therefore contain a clear description of what the business does and what the franchisee will be required to do.

The purpose of this initial marketing exercise is quite simply to attract enquiries from suitably qualified people who will have an interest in operating one of your franchised outlets.

In order to do this you will need to work through a number of processes.

- **Set a time-frame** for the marketing and subsequent recruitment process. During the development period of the franchise system you will have been working to a timed Action Plan. This should have included an appraisal of the target date for the launch of the franchise and a forecast of when your first franchisee would commence trading. It is important that you do not underestimate how long it might take to recruit your first franchisee, particularly if you are relying on income from that franchisee to further develop the franchise. Research has suggested that the average time taken from a potential franchisee's first contact with the franchisor to the commencement of trading is seven months. The process of recruiting franchisees is more complex than that for recruiting employees and sufficient time must be built in for this activity.

So why does it take so long? Let's consider the various elements of the process simply from the point of view of timing.

Your marketing media will be designed to attract applicants to contact you regarding your franchise. Unfortunately, unlike an advertisement for a job, you will not be able to put a closing date to generate a prompt response so you are totally reliant upon the enquirer being sufficiently motivated to respond quickly.

Having received an expression of interest you will need to go through the various stages of the recruitment process (more of which in the next chapter) which might include:

(a) an initial screening over the telephone;

(b) the dispatch of an information pack to give the applicant more information about precisely what it is the franchise does;

(c) the receipt and appraisal of a completed application form;

(d) arrangements for, and conduct of, one or more interviews/meetings;

(e) confirmation from the franchisee that they have sufficient funding available (which might include the arrangement of bank finance) – which, in itself, will prompt the need for a business plan to be prepared;

(f) the completion of the legalities, including the franchisee taking advice from their legal adviser;

(g) the period of initial training of the franchisee before they can start trading using your system.

At each of these stages there is a potential for delay even if the franchisor is driving the process forward as firmly as possible.

Be realistic when establishing the time-scale for the recruitment of franchisees. Remember the average is seven months and the early franchisees for a new system are almost always more difficult to recruit.

- **Set a budget for the marketing process** that is realistic. Whatever media you decide to use there will be a cost implication. It is a good idea to research the costs of the various media you might wish to consider as soon as you begin to think about the marketing process. This should ensure that you are aware of the financial implications of your proposed marketing plan as you begin to structure it.

- **Establish the franchisee profile** – precisely who it is you are looking for and what qualities, skills and experience you wish them to have. Until you have this worked out it will be impossible for you to judge where and how you are likely to find them and how you will recognise them when you do find them. Some of the things you will need to consider are:

  1. Do they need any special formal qualifications or industry experience, or can you provide them with all the skills they need during your induction-training programme? Many franchisors choose not to recruit from within their own sector because they want franchisees who will learn all they need to know from the franchisor. This means that the only way they will know how to do a job is the way the franchisor wants it done.

  2. Will they need sales experience? Every franchise sells something whether it is a product or service – some direct to the consumer, some to an intermediary to be resold to the consumer. In every case the success of the franchisee and therefore the franchisor will be dependent upon their ability to sell and their commitment to selling.

  3. Will they need a commitment to build a business rather than just earn an income that meets their expectations/requirements?

  4. Do they need experience of having run a business previously? If they do, it will considerably reduce the number of potential franchisees who might be able to apply. They will certainly need to understand how to run a business but can this be learned from the franchisor's training programme and system?

5. Do they have, or can they raise, the necessary finance? Without access to sufficient funding there is no chance of them becoming a franchisee of your system.

6. Will the potential income from the franchise realistically meet their income requirements? If they are leaving a well-paid job for a franchise operation that will have limited remuneration available in the early months/years, will they be able to meet any existing financial commitments such as their mortgage and general living expenses?

7. What is their desired lifestyle and will it fit in with the requirements of operating the franchise? A potential franchisee who sees self-employment as a means to spend less time at work will rarely provide the impetus needed to drive a business forward.

8. Do they live or want to trade in an area where there is still a franchise opportunity available? While this is less important during the early days when all areas are available it will become increasingly important as the number of available territories reduces.

9. What is their likely motivation for applying? Do they want to build a successful business or do they simply want to escape from working for somebody else?

10. Do they need to meet any legal criteria for working in the sector? Will they need to pass Criminal Records Board checks before being allowed to work with children or other vulnerable people?

11. Will they need such a simple qualification as a driving licence? It is all too easy to forget those matters that seem commonplace but could be crucial in determining the franchisee's ability to operate the franchised system.

12. Without falling prey to stereotyping, are they likely to be of a particular gender? Not all people who work with children are women although child-centric franchises are often more appealing to women.

13. Are they already likely to be looking for a franchise or will you need to find some way of tapping into the vast majority of the population who have never realistically considered starting their own business but might if the right opportunity confronted them?

This is by no means an exhaustive list, each individual franchise will have specific elements that they will build into their franchisee profile. Once you have developed your own franchisee profile, prioritise the characteristics into 'must-have' and 'nice-to-have' categories. This will allow you to identify those areas of qualification that are most important in your franchisees. This in its turn will assist you once you get into the recruitment process.

The franchisee profile is a crucial element in the process of finding and recruiting franchisees. Without it you will have only a vague idea of who you are looking for and therefore how and where you might find them.

- **Decide what media you will use** to communicate with potential franchisees. Your franchisee profile will tell you a lot about the sort of person you are seeking to recruit and who might be interested in taking your franchise. What you need to consider now is what media are most likely to put your opportunity in front of them. Historically the national and specialist franchise press, along with franchise exhibitions, were predominantly the media chosen by franchisors. More recently, however, the role played by the internet has become critical in franchise marketing. Over 60 per cent of franchisors now use the internet for franchise recruitment purposes compared to 50 per cent using conventional print media (NatWest/BFA Franchise Survey 2006).

You will need to consider the role that each of the following media might play in your franchise marketing process.

The press

National press Most of the national daily and weekly newspapers now have a section dedicated to advertising franchise opportunities. This is, on occasions, supported by franchise-specific editorial in the business sections. When considering whether these should have a place in your marketing mix you will need to think again about your franchisee profile. If you are seeking business-oriented people with financial management skills you may decide that they are more likely to read one of what were traditionally called the broadsheets, *The Times*, *Daily Telegraph* etc. rather than a 'red-top' tabloid. However, the latter could be valuable to a franchisor seeking franchisees from their target readership. You need to assess whether your target franchisees overlap with their target readership.

Local or regional press There is perhaps a limited place for the use of local or regional press when you are trying to establish a national network. However, where a particular region is being specifically targeted, local or regional press could play a role. You will need to establish whether there are relevant sections of the paper that might reasonably accommodate an advertisement for potential franchisees.

Franchise press There are number of publications dedicated to franchising or with a strong franchise bias. Some of these are available for sale on news-stands while others are subscription only. Not all are targeted at franchisees or potential franchisees so care should be taken to ensure that they will deliver your marketing message to your target market. Typically monthly or bimonthly, they have a longer life than a newspaper and are targeted only at the franchise sector.

Trade press If your franchisee profile seeks or simply allows for applicants who have industry experience then advertising in the relevant trade press may prove a useful way of achieving targeted marketing.

Other press options There are a number of publications aimed at those seeking entrepreneurial opportunities of all types. These may well include features on franchising but will almost certainly include a variety of 'business opportunities' where the track record is perhaps not as well defined as in the typical franchise. They may expose your message, however, to a wider audience than those simply seeking a franchise.

Most display press advertising is quite expensive both in terms of design of the advertisements and also cost to place them in the publication. However, you can make clever use of inexpensive classified advertising to drive interested parties to other media such as your website.

Public relations All of the above options use various types of printed publications through paid-for advertising. However, effective use can be made of good PR placements with no direct charge from the publication. A good PR agency, preferably one specialising in franchising, can often get editorial placed in publications at no cost. However, this is largely dependent upon the skill and perseverance of the agency staff, and upon having a newsworthy story that will enhance the publication by being of interest to its readership. It is unlikely that any PR agency will guarantee you placements and so you may end up paying for work to be done that fails to produce a result. If the agency is reputable they will have records to show the level of placements they are typically able to achieve for a given level of activity and corresponding expenditure.

One of the benefits of using a PR agency is that they often have access to unusual placement opportunities including, for example, business-oriented programmes on radio and television. Even a 30-second interview with a happy and successful franchisee could be worth many thousands of pounds worth of direct advertising.

Exhibitions

Franchise exhibitions At present there are a number of franchise exhibitions that regularly take place in the UK. The largest are those in London in the spring and at the National Exhibition Centre, Birmingham in the autumn. While requiring a considerable investment in the design and building of a stand, and the charge from the exhibition organisers for the stand space, they do offer the prospect of face-to-face contact with prospective franchisees. There are specific skills involved in getting the best out of what can be the quite expensive investment of exhibiting, and careful consideration will need to be given to all aspects of stand management if this investment is to provide an adequate return.

Trade exhibitions In just the same way that the trade press might be a suitable medium for some franchise opportunities, trade exhibitions could prove a ready source of potential franchisees. Virtually everyone in the exhibition hall, whether a visitor or other exhibitor, could be a potential applicant.

Exhibitions are likely to be among the most expensive marketing media in terms of the cost of an individual entry. However, they do provide access to many thousands of people who are sufficiently interested in franchising to make the journey to the venue.

The internet

With an increasingly large proportion of the population now having access to the internet, either through their workplace or at home, this method of communication is becoming more and more important to just about every commercial and non-commercial organisation. There are two main areas to consider in relation to franchisee recruitment and the internet – your own website and commercial websites specifically developed for franchisee recruitment.

Your own website You may already have your own website which will have been designed to communicate, as part of your business marketing strategy, with existing and potential customers. It will be important that you have a section of this website dedicated to the franchise opportunity. People who are already your customers or who express an interest in your product or service by visiting the website may well include a number of those who like the product so much that they might like to buy the business, or at least one associated with it.

Whether you have the franchising website as a part of your existing site or whether you make it (or make it appear to be) something totally separate, will be a matter for you to discuss with your website designer. Either way you will need a mechanism for clicking through to the franchise pages. Typically we see websites with 'Franchising' as one of a number of small click-through buttons along with others titled 'Products', 'Services', Location', 'FAQs', 'Contact Us' etc. If you really want to make your home page work for franchise recruitment you will need a much larger area of the page to promote the franchise than just a small click-through button. If you don't make it look an important part of your business then your potential franchisees won't think that it is!

Franchise recruitment websites As recruitment advertising continues to move from the printed page and onto the internet, more and more websites are being established that offer franchisors the online equivalent of both a magazine and an exhibition. You will need to examine what each of these sites has to offer and at what cost. Some allow the franchisor to be very selective about who is able to access their section while for others it is effectively an open house. Whatever route is chosen there must always be the option for the potential franchisee to learn some key information about the opportunity and for them to make an immediate response by requesting further information.

Other linked websites Perhaps the most important website for providing franchisors with a direct link to their own site is the British Franchise Association (BFA) website. This website provides a vast array of information for both potential franchisees and franchisors. Included is a list of all BFA members with, where possible, a click-through link to the franchisor's own site as well as an enquiry facility that forwards enquiries to individual franchisors. Over 80 per cent of BFA franchisor members received enquiries from potential franchisees via the BFA website during 2005 and over a third of these signed up one or more franchisees as the result of these leads.

The internet is becoming increasingly important in all our lives, and its power as a marketing tool for franchisee recruitment is set to grow even further.

Other media

Building the franchise brand should be recognised as being as important as building the core brand of your business. You should consider, therefore, every opportunity to include your franchising messages on any marketing communication to your customers or potential customers. Many of them will have no interest at all in starting a business but they may well know someone who has. In a recent survey over a third of franchisors questioned included 'word of mouth' in their list of the most useful methods of recruiting franchisees.

At least one international fast-food franchisor includes information about the franchise on all the packaging used to serve the food. Other franchisors include the franchising message in adverts they place for their core product or service. It may only be a short message in very small print, so as not to detract from the main message of the communication, but it serves to raise the general level of awareness of the franchise opportunity. Others advertise the opportunity on stationery, vehicles, in fact any medium that could be used to communicate with prospective franchisees.

Finally, it is becoming clear throughout the sector that the requirement for good franchisee applications far exceeds the number of applicants. We must therefore continue to seek new avenues for communicating with potential franchisees, even to the point whereby we try to get in touch with people who have never even considered running their own business but who might be successful at it. Some franchisors are now 'trawling' the many CV websites for people who are looking for a change of employment but might have the qualifications or experience to become franchisees. Some CV posters could take offence at their personal information being used to contact them for a reason other than the purpose intended, i.e. to invite job offers from employers, so care should be taken when drafting the content of any approach letter. You must also ensure that you are not infringing any of the rules or terms and conditions of the CV website.

- **Determine what key messages you will use to attract potential franchisees** in each of your chosen media. Your marketing plan may include a variety of media in order to communicate with everyone who demonstrates key elements of the franchisee profile. The purpose of using a number of different media is that it allows you to target potential franchisees who fit specific qualities identified by the profiling process. It is likely, therefore, that you will need to use different marketing messages to attract these differing applicants.

Until your brand is readily recognised throughout your target market one of the key elements of the message must be to clearly define precisely what it is that your franchise does. It is true that a company like McDonald's is now so well known that it only needs to place the 'Golden Arches' trademark on a page to tell people that what follows is about a fast-food restaurant. In your early days you will need to be much more specific about what your franchise can offer to both the potential franchisee and the consumer of the goods or services that are the subject of the franchise.

In the same way that you will have developed the franchisee profile to determine whom you are seeking, so you must also develop a clearly structured definition of your 'franchise offer'. This should answer a number of questions:

1. What are you selling to your customers?
2. What are you selling to your franchisees?
3. What are your unique selling points?
4. Why should a prospect choose your franchise?

1. What are you selling to your customers?

It may be clearly apparent to you what the nature of your business is – you have been involved in it since its inception – but until your brand is instantly recognisable you will need to explain the product or service to your potential franchisees. As with all selling activities you need to be able to demonstrate not only the features of what you are selling but also the benefits of those features to your customers.

2. What are you selling to your franchisees?

Well, clearly, the opportunity to replicate your successful business in their own territory. However, it is far more than that. What you are offering them is the opportunity to be their own boss, to benefit directly from the financial rewards of their hard work, to follow a proven business system that will enhance the possibility of success and reduce the chance of failure. In fact you need to identify all the reasons that might attract a potential franchisee and demonstrate how your franchise will deliver what they are seeking.

3. What are your unique selling points?

You may be the only business in your industry sector to offer a franchise opportunity, or you may be in direct competition with other franchises within the sector. Either way you will need to demonstrate what it is that makes your franchise system special – and, remember, you need to show the benefits not just the features!

4. Why should a prospect choose your franchise?

Partly this will be down to the features and benefits of your particular franchise opportunity, but do remember to consider what it is the potential franchisees are looking for. Do you have better growth rates and potential profitability than the rest of your sector? Is your brand more strongly recognised? Is your training more comprehensive? Do your existing franchisees say nice things about you? Do you achieve a high rate of customer retention and repeat business? All of these can be possible subjects for inclusion in your initial marketing messages.

The purpose of the above questions is to consider what will make your franchise attractive to potential franchisees. However, part of the marketing message must be used to ensure that the applicant is aware of, and demonstrates, certain 'must-have' elements of the franchisee profile, and so it is important to provide information relevant to them when they consider your opportunity. For most franchises the availability of the level of investment required will be critical for both franchisor and franchisee. If you require an overall investment of, say, £100,000 it is wasteful to attract enquiries from people who cannot find such funds. The messages must be clearly structured to eliminate 'non-starters' without running the risk of putting off good potential candidates. You may decide, however, that in order to generate the largest possible number of enquiries you will limit the 'qualifiers' that you put in your messages and rely on an early personal contact during the recruitment process to weed out the unqualified candidates.

Above all you are seeking to get potential franchisees to make contact with you so make sure that there is a clear 'call to action'. Ensure that your message contains whatever means you wish them to use to contact you, whether it be a telephone call, a visit to your website or an address for written communications.

Month	1	2	3	10	11	12
Target market	Industry professionals looking for a move	General franchisee market	General public with interest in the service	General franchisee market	Industry professionals looking for a move	General
Message	Constrained by company procedures? There is another way!	Lifestyle change with well-known brand	Like our products and service? Could you provide them for others?	Lifestyle change with well-known brand	Constrained by company procedures? There is another way!	Ready for a change in the New Year?
Objective	Offer alternative to employment	Raise awareness of opportunity with the brand	Raise awareness of opportunity with the brand	Raise awareness of opportunity with the brand	Offer alternative to employment	Drive traffic to website
Media	Trade journal advertisement and PR article	Franchise press	Customer database and consumer press	Franchise press	Trade journal advertisement and PR article	Classified franchise sections of national press
Cost £	£1,000 PR plus £500 advert plus internet recruitment sites (IRS)	£1,000 PR plus £1,000 advert IRS	£1,000 PR plus £1,500 direct mail plus £2,000 adverts IRS	£1,000 PR plus £1,000 advert IRS	£1,000 PR plus £500 advert IRS	£1,000 PR plus £500 and sector-specific consumer press IRS
Budget £	£2,000	£2,000	£4,000	£4,000	£2,000	£2,000

Figure 10.1: The marketing plan

Identifying the key messages that will attract a potential franchisee to enquire further about your franchise is critical to the marketing process. No matter what media you choose to use, if the message is unclear, or not compelling, then you won't generate the volume of enquiries that are needed to 'feed' the recruitment process.

- **Develop marketing products and processes** to deliver the messages via the chosen media. You will almost certainly need specialist help here. Writing copy and designing advertisements, websites and brochures are all specialist jobs. You will need to guide the specialist in what you are seeking to achieve but they will have the expertise to help you to produce materials that will achieve the desired results. It will be a waste of money to place poorly designed advertisements in your chosen media. One well-designed communication will produce better results than a dozen 'amateur' efforts. You may believe you can design good advertisements or write compelling copy – in which case, why aren't you working for an agency that does that rather than in your current business?

- **Develop a marketing plan**, using those messages and media, to target potential franchisees. This is the culmination of all the previous pre-marketing activities. Having decided who you are looking for, the timing of the search, the available budget, the various media available to you, the messages that will be used to target different elements of the franchisee profile you will now need to pull all these together in a formal marketing plan. The marketing plan should specify the timing, the media, the target market and the message. You might lay it out in a grid formation, as shown in Figure 10.1. Then confer with your chosen media buying agency to ensure that the timings are suitable and that you are not missing an important time slot, e.g. when a particular section of the press might be running a feature on franchising. The timing of your marketing spend may not correspond exactly with your budget forecast, particularly if a specific media opportunity arises unexpectedly. However you must ensure that your overall budget is not exceeded.

- **Monitor the effectiveness of the marketing activity** and revise it if necessary. You will need to record the sources of all enquiries if you are to make a judgement on the media that produce the best results for you. You will also need to record the number of enquiries generated by any particular piece of marketing, to evaluate the cost of marketing per enquiry. You will also need to be able to track those enquiries right through the recruitment process so that you can see not only which media produced the largest number of enquiries, but also which produced the largest number of ultimate sign-ups. You can then calculate a cost per franchisee.

> The marketing process is aimed at generating enquiries from suitably qualified prospective franchisees. Without these enquiries your franchise will never move on. A well-planned campaign is critical to the future of your franchise.

11

How to recruit franchisees

Your marketing campaign has been designed to generate enquiries from potential franchisees. It is important that, prior to launching the campaign, you have a clear plan of the processes that will be used to deal with those enquiries. Without such processes in place you will run the risk of spending money on generating enquiries and then wasting the results of that expenditure by not making the best use of each lead generated by the marketing activity. Each stage of the process must be carefully thought through and then fully documented so that everyone who has a role to play in recruiting franchisees is quite clear on the desired results from each stage of the process.

> The successful development of any franchise is wholly dependent on finding and recruiting the right number of suitably qualified franchisees.

THE BACKGROUND TO FRANCHISEE RECRUITMENT

- **Recruiting franchisees involves a very different process** from that of recruiting an employee. You will, undoubtedly, have recruited staff for your own business in the past. You had a relatively simple task – to determine whether the various applicants had the skills and experience you sought, and whether they would fit into and contribute to the strength of your current team. By virtue of the fact that they had applied for the job vacancy they had demonstrated that they were prepared to join your company and if you had indicated the salary available they were, presumably, happy with the proposed figure. Any job applicant worth his or her salt would have made sure that they had done some research into your company before applying, to make sure that yours was a company that they would wish to join. During the recruitment interview they are selling their skills and personality to you and you are deciding whether to buy them.

When recruiting franchisees, however, the process is not so simple. The first element of the process may broadly equate to the research being done by the above applicant. They may know little or nothing about how your franchise, or any other business, operates and their initial concerns will be to discover precisely what it is you do and what they will have to do. The whole concept of franchising suggests that a suitably qualified franchisee can learn, from the franchisor, everything they need to know about running an outlet of the franchisor's business. They may assume, therefore, that they need little or no experience in the particular field. It is for this reason that we often see potential franchisees responding to marketing messages from a wide variety of unrelated franchises. Their primary concern is that they want to run their own business, to be their own boss, and a franchise, perhaps any franchise, will allow them to do it.

Once they have made the initial enquiry the whole process potentially becomes an interface between two buyers and two sellers. The franchisor views the franchisee as would any buyer – does this person look as though they will do what I need them to do? However he is also 'selling' the concept of his franchise to this tentative buyer. The franchisee is also forming a buyer's view on what is being offered to him, but once he or she has decided they want to buy they then go into selling mode to convince the franchisor that they are the right person to become a franchisee.

- **Is it franchise sales or franchisee recruitment?** These two phrases are often used interchangeably within the franchising community but they do, potentially, describe very different processes. Selling usually involves nothing more complicated than a transaction between a willing buyer and a willing seller. Providing that the buyer has the financial ability to make the purchase and expresses a desire to do so the seller will happily take their money. There have been, and probably still are, examples of franchisors that have taken this view with regard to their franchisees. All too often they give no consideration to whether the franchisee is right for them, or their system for the franchisee. Result – ill-informed, poorly qualified franchisees who sooner or later are likely either to become disenchanted with the franchise or, worse still, fail financially. The franchisor may even have set out with the specific intention of allowing the franchisee to fail so that they can resell the same territory time and time again. Clearly this is not the action of an ethical franchisor.

It may be, however, that the franchisor has unwittingly sacrificed the long-term prospects of the franchise for the short-term prospect of a franchise fee without fully appreciating the implications of what they are doing. Perhaps, in their anxiety to get the first few franchisees up and running, the franchisor has been less than scrupulous about their selection process. Unless the franchisee meets the franchisee profile (see Chapter 10) there is only a limited chance of their being successful. A franchisee that fails provides a franchisor with a number of problems:

1. the whole recruitment process must begin again to find a franchisee for the territory;

2. it will be doubly difficult to find a franchisee for a territory that has already experienced a failure;

3. potential franchisees for other territories may be put off by the existence of a failed outlet;

4. existing customers could be left without a source of supply during the 'interregnum' and move to another supplier;

5. the source of management services fees will dry up from that territory.

Clearly, while 'selling' is involved, the process must primarily be one of 'recruitment' to ensure that the right franchisee joins the network.

DEVELOPING THE RECRUITMENT PROCESS

Once the marketing process has generated enquiries from prospective franchisees the recruitment process must swing into action.

- **What is the process designed to achieve?** In the very simplest of terms – a flow of suitably qualified franchisees committed to the concept of developing their own business in the franchise format. At each step of the process there will be an interchange of information between franchisor and potential franchisee with a view to both parties satisfying themselves that they are right for each other. It is essential that both parties are able to make an informed decision on this. However, part of the strategy of franchising requires the franchisor to make some of their 'trade secrets' available to their franchisees. The control of this information is therefore critical if franchisors are to protect themselves from misuse of the information. The decision on when and how information is passed on is critical. Strategies must be developed so that this information is released on a 'need to know' basis as the recruitment process progresses.

- **What are the options for the various stages?** A typical recruitment programme will include some or all of the following activities, although not necessarily always in this order:

  1. response to initial contact;

  2. initial qualification on 'must have' attributes;

  3. despatch of prospectus and application form;

  4. follow-up phone call;

  5. review of application form;

  6. 'discovery day' or group presentation;

  7. first meeting;

  8. franchisee accompaniment;

  9. draft business planning;

  10. disclosure documentation;

11. second meeting;

12. franchise offer;

13. receipt of deposit;

14. completion of franchise agreement or 'agreement to agree'.

The franchise system itself, the culture of the franchisor company and the requirements of the franchisee profile, will all influence the eventual structure of the process.

- **The response to the initial contact is critical** – you only have one chance to make a first impression! It is important, therefore, that the recruitment process is fully developed prior to inviting expressions of interest in the franchise. By whatever means the potential franchisee makes contact, and this will largely be determined by the information and instructions that you have given in your marketing materials, the response should be swift and measured. Experience suggests that it is the franchisor who will need to drive the recruitment process forward and a clear time-scale for each section is desirable.

Possible contact options could be:

(a) to visit the franchisor's website and apply online. This will require an enquiry form to be produced using 'obligatory fields' to collect the enquirer's contact data and, possibly, responses to some key qualifying information, e.g. confirmation of availability of funds or specific qualifications. This assumes the enquirer's ability to access the internet, something that is probably not yet universal. However, for those with access it is a quick and easy method of initial contact;

(b) to visit a specialised franchisee recruitment website and register interest in a particular franchise. This would then be passed on to the relevant franchisor;

(c) to enquire by e-mail to the franchisor. For those with access this is a quick and easy method but may produce only the applicant's e-mail address and no other contact information;

(d) to write requesting further information. In this case there may be little opportunity to go through any pre-qualification process prior to the dispatch of a prospectus or other printed information;

(f) to telephone the franchisor or their recruitment agent. This is probably the most desirable of the options, provided that the franchisor has a clear process for accepting such calls. The potential franchisee is in control of when the call is made and the respondent must be ready to deal with the enquiry when it occurs. A dedicated number for franchise recruitment will ensure that the recipient is forewarned that the incoming call is a franchise enquiry and will give them a moment to prepare themselves to receive it. Anyone who is likely to pick up the call, for example a switchboard operator, a receptionist or the franchise recruitment manager must all clearly understand the process to be followed on receipt of an enquiry. No member of staff should be allowed to handle a franchise enquiry who is not authorised to do so and fully conversant with the process. If no one is available to deal with the enquiry in detail, a response should be prepared for the caller to be informed of how the enquiry will be moved forward.

We have learned from anecdotal evidence from potential franchisees that a large number of requests for information go unanswered. To spend money on marketing activities and then to fail to follow up leads generated by those activities would seem to be senseless. However, we do know that a number of franchisors will admit, when questioned, that they do not follow up leads as assiduously as they should. What makes them throw away the chance of contacting a prospective franchisee? A number of things could be to blame:

1. it is often difficult to contact the enquirer by phone unless the recruiter is prepared to make phone calls in the evenings or at weekends outside the normal working day;

2. it is not unusual to have to make a number of contact calls before being able to speak to the applicant. It requires a great level of commitment to keep making the calls until contact is made;

3. all recruiters know that they will be lucky if they recruit two franchisees from every 100 enquiries, so the process is by its very nature time-consuming and potentially frustrating;

4. recruiting franchisees is often only part of the manager's responsibilities and other activities may appear to demand priority attention.

Yet it is critical that all opportunities are persistently followed up if you are to hit even the two out of 100 rate.

> A clear lead-tracking process, carefully monitored by senior management, will assist in making the most of the enquiries.

If you feel that you or your staff cannot give the time or commitment to following up all the leads then consider passing on that role to one of the specialist recruitment or support agencies that exist to provide this service.

One of the ways of making the most of these leads is to encourage the applicants to contact you by telephone within normal working hours. If the enquirer instigates the contact then it will be at a time when they are free to speak to the recruitment manager. All that remains is for the recruitment manager to be available to speak to them!

A recent analysis of all 47 recruitment advertisements placed in a franchise exhibition edition of a specialist franchise magazine showed the following:

	Phone number	Mail address	E-mail address	Website
Total ads showing	46	5	39	27
Preferred contact method*	39	1	7	2

*Preferred contact method deduced from either a clear statement in the advertisement or the prominence given to the contact method.

It is clear that most franchisors have chosen the telephone as the preferred contact method, although, interestingly, the one franchise that didn't include a phone number at all in their advert was a company that operates a call answering service! If your marketing materials include a phrase such as 'Call [Name] for a brief discussion of the franchise opportunity' then the enquirer will at least be prepared to do more than simply ask for a brochure.

- **Ensuring that the 'must-have attributes** of the franchisee profile are met is an important part of the initial contact. If an enquirer fails to meet any of these important criteria it is wasteful to spend any more time with them than is necessary to fulfil the requirement to be polite. Although they may not be suitable as a franchisee they may still be a potential customer for your product or service so be firm but polite in explaining why you feel you can take their interest no further.

- **If they meet your primary criteria** you will need to take them on to the next stage in the process. This may involve sending them a prospectus and application form or inviting them to a group presentation or 'discovery day'. At each stage of the process you are looking for either the applicant or yourself to qualify themselves further or disqualify themselves. Every franchise has its own view on how difficult the qualification process should be. Some franchises take the view that unless the applicant is sufficiently motivated to take the lead in the process then they are not suitable. In such cases the franchisor may take the view that they will not pursue an enquiry any further than the initial contact, leaving the potential franchisee to make all the running and make any further contact. Other franchisors believe that they need to make the most of every applicant and will therefore constantly follow up all enquiries at each stage until either they have satisfied themselves that an enquirer is a suitable applicant or the potential franchisee has withdrawn their interest. Most franchisors would find the former view difficult to justify.

- **The first face-to-face meeting** provides both the franchisor and the applicant with the opportunity to begin to check in some detail whether they are suited for each other. This is the part of the process where both applicant and recruiter will regularly move from a buyer to a seller and back to buyer again. By the end of this first meeting both parties will normally know whether they wish to take the application any further. It is good practice before the end of the meeting for the recruiter to ask the applicant if they are still interested in the opportunity. If both parties are still interested then the process can move on to the next phase.

- **Experience of a franchisee's day-to-day activity** will ensure that the applicant fully understands what they will be expected to do if they join the franchise. Many franchisors insist that applicants should spend some time with an existing franchisee before they move on to the next stage of the recruitment process. It is important that the applicant has a worthwhile experience during this period of franchisee accompaniment so choose very carefully among your franchisees to find the right person to provide this service.

- **The ability and desire to grow a business** will be high among the attributes you will be seeking from your franchisees. All too often we see examples of franchisees who fail fully to exploit the sales potential of their territories because they find that they can make a comfortable living at a lower level of activity. As a franchisor you will want your franchisees to develop their territories fully otherwise they will be limiting your own growth and profitability. By asking a franchisee to produce at least a draft business plan, including financial forecasts, you will be able to judge just how committed they are to growing their new business. Many legal advisers caution against the franchisor becoming involved in drawing up the franchisee's business plan. They are concerned that if a franchisor plays too great a part in this process, for example setting anticipated sales or income levels, they may subsequently lay themselves open to litigation for misrepresentation if the franchisee fails to achieve those levels. However, the franchisor must play some part in providing information to the potential franchisee to assist them in preparing their business plan. Otherwise how will the franchisee discover likely levels of income or expenditure for this new business venture about which they know very little? One solution, which is increasingly being adopted by franchisors, is to appoint an independent third party, who has an understanding of their business, to assist the franchisee.

- **There is no legal requirement for disclosure documentation** in the UK. However, it is considered good practice to disclose voluntarily relevant information about the franchise and the people involved in it. The European Franchise Federation, in its *Code of Ethics for Franchising*, says: 'In order to allow prospective Individual Franchisees to enter into any binding documentation with full knowledge, they shall be given a copy of the present Code of Ethics as well as full and accurate written disclosure of all information material to the franchise relationship, within a reasonable time prior to the execution of these binding documents.'

In *The Ethics of Franchising*, a British Franchise Association publication, Martin Mendelsohn proposes that the subjects for disclosure should cover:

1. the business and financial position of the franchisor;

2. the people involved in the franchise company;

3. the franchise proposition;

4. the franchisees;

5. the financial projections;

6. the contract.

It is at this stage that the franchisee should be asked to take legal advice on the content of the franchise contract and to confirm to the franchisor in writing that they have taken such advice and that they will be willing to enter into the contract. It should be made clear that the role of the franchisee's legal adviser in this instance is to advise them on the content of the contract, not to enter into any process of challenging the terms of the contract, as this will almost certainly be non-negotiable.

- **A second meeting will be an opportunity** for both franchisor and potential franchisee to discuss the proposal in more detail. By this time the applicant will probably be committed to pursuing the venture and the franchisor, besides taking the opportunity for a final appraisal of the applicant, will be looking to ensure that the franchisee is able and willing to proceed, i.e. has the funds in place, is prepared to sign the franchise agreement (contract) and wishes to move the matter forward.

- **If both parties are ready to move forward** the franchisor should make a formal offer to the franchisee. This offer will form part of the contract and should specify the basic terms on which the franchise is to be granted. In particular it should include a clear statement regarding the territory in which the franchisee will be allowed to operate. It is at this stage that the franchisor may ask the franchisee to confirm in writing that they have taken legal advice with regard to the franchise agreement and are prepared to move forward on the basis of that agreement. Some franchisors have a formal 'pre-contract' document that the franchisee must sign at this stage.

- **To reserve their chosen territory** franchisees are often required to make a financial deposit at this stage. This provides not only a sign of commitment but also an indemnity against any expenses that the franchisor might incur in relation to this franchisee if the franchisee is ultimately unable or decides not to move to complete the process. If a deposit is taken it is important that the franchisee fully understands the terms under which the deposit is taken. These should include:

  (a) whether or not it is refundable in whole or in part, and what may be withheld of the deposit if the agreement is not completed. Most franchisors are prepared to return the deposit to a franchisee if they do not complete, less any costs they might have incurred relating to the grant of the franchise between the taking of the deposit and the franchisee's withdrawal;

  (b) a statement to the effect that the deposit will be wholly set against the initial franchisee fee when the agreement is completed.

Some franchisors will retain the whole of the deposit if the franchisee fails to commence trading within a given reasonable period.

- **Once all the preliminaries have been finalised** the franchise agreement is completed by both parties. Both franchisor and franchisee are now bound by the terms of the agreement and have a clear commitment to each other's success.

It is important that whatever elements of the above outline you choose to include in your recruitment process, each step should be clearly documented and recorded.

When franchisors are faced with a poor or failing franchisee they often come to the conclusion that 'we should never have recruited him/her'. This is, more often than not, true. However, it is important that the franchisor should be able to analyse what went wrong in the recruitment process that allowed someone who is now clearly seen as unsuitable to be accepted as a franchisee.

Equally, if a franchisee becomes dissatisfied with the franchise, they will often say that their actual experience was at odds with what they were told during the recruitment process: 'I was promised x or y' or 'I was told that my sales would be far greater than I have achieved'.

In both these circumstances it is important that the franchisor can go back to their original records to check these circumstances.

RECRUITMENT RECORDS

In the same way that a franchisor produces a franchise operations manual to specify the procedures and processes that a franchisee must follow, they should also have a franchisor operations manual that defines the procedures to be followed by the franchisor's staff. In this way the franchisor able to ensure that everyone is using the same procedures to achieve any specific outcome. Perhaps one of the most important sections of this manual will refer to the recruitment process. As has been stated above, when problems arise with a franchisee it is often important to be able to refer back in detail to the time of their recruitment.

> Lead-tracking is an important part of every recruitment process. While there are a number of software programmes aimed specifically at the franchise sector, any database can be developed to provide the necessary information.

- **Every contact from a potential franchisee should be recorded** as the first part of the recruitment process. This first record should include basic information such as their name and contact details and the source of the lead. The latter information is useful for monitoring the results of various marketing activities. It will inform the franchisor of those activities that generate the most enquiries but, perhaps more importantly, it will also allow them to analyse which marketing activities resulted in the most sign-ups.

- **Each stage of the recruitment process** should be identified on the database and completed as each activity occurs. As has been said previously the initial process of contacting a potential franchisee by telephone is often both difficult and time-consuming. It is at this point that enquiries are most vulnerable to being allowed to slip through the net. Monitoring this stage of the process is therefore clearly very important.

- **Define the information** that is to be given and collected at each stage of the process and record that it has been completed. In the same way that a franchisor will have certain key qualifying questions to ask of potential franchisees at an early stage, so also will the applicant have questions to ask the franchisor. First and foremost he or she will probably want to know how much they will need to invest in the franchise and how much income it is likely to generate. The franchisor in his turn will want to know whether the potential franchisee has or will be able to raise the funds needed for the investment and also whether the franchisee is likely to be satisfied with the potential income opportunity. The recruitment manager can satisfy both these needs through judicious questioning and giving of information. The tactic of answering a question by asking another question can be of great use here. In answer to the applicant's question, 'How much will I earn?' the recruiter can respond by asking, 'How much do you want or need to earn?' This will give an immediate insight into whether the franchise is likely to support the franchisee's financial aspirations and allows the recruiter to reply in either a positive or negative way without mentioning specific figures. It is perhaps at this stage that the franchisor is most at risk of making a statement that is later 'relied on' by the franchisee and could later result in an action for misrepresentation. It is important that the franchisor controls the flow of information at every stage, as the need to obtain further information is often a key driver in getting the applicant to move to the next stage of the process.

- **Set time-scales for each element of the process** and then apply them. Those time-scales that relate to the franchisor's activities can be applied rigidly whereas those relating to the potential franchisee are very much in the applicant's control. However, if the time-scales are communicated to the franchisee and then prompts given if they are not fulfilled it will allow the franchisor to drive the process forward at something like his own desired pace.

- **Record the outcome of each and every contact** including details of key information given and received by both parties.

- **Copies of any documentation** given to or received from the applicant should be kept on file. It is important that where a franchisee may have taken information from a website, a copy of the contents of the website should be archived each time changes are made to it.

PREPARING TO START TRADING

Once the franchise agreement or a pre-contract has been completed, what may be considered the final stage of the recruitment process must commence – the preparation to start trading.

It is good practice to provide the franchisee with a detailed checklist of all the activities that need to be completed before trading can commence. This ensures that nothing gets missed in what can be a hectic and sometimes fraught period of time. This checklist may form part of the operations manual or may be a separate document given to the franchisee at a late stage in the recruitment process. It should include not simply a list of tasks to be completed but also, whenever possible, details of how best to go about completing them and any useful information that will make the process easier for the franchisee. This checklist might include activities such as:

- procurement of property from which to trade, including specifications on size and location;

- purchase of vehicles and equipment if not provided in a package by the franchisor;

- registration with relevant authorities, e.g. HM Revenue and Customs for taxation and VAT issues, local authorities or regulatory bodies;

- opening bank accounts, credit facilities etc.;

- staff recruitment;

- pre-trading research;

- launch marketing programmes;

- franchisee and staff training.

A well-planned and executed pre-opening phase will ensure a smooth and hopefully successful launch of the business, which is the final stage of the recruitment process.

Being unable to recruit sufficient, well-qualified franchisees is probably the most critical limiting factor in the growth of any franchisor's business. A well-prepared and implemented marketing and recruitment process will enhance the chance of success for both the franchisor and their franchisees.

12
How to get the best results from franchise exhibitions

If exhibitions have a place in your marketing plan, and like most other potential media they will not be right for every franchise opportunity, you will need to develop a strategy that will ensure you get best value out of them. They represent an opportunity for a short burst of face-to-face marketing activity to a self-selected target audience. This in itself presents particular problems and requires careful planning if those problems are to be converted into opportunities.

THE DECISION TO EXHIBIT

The decision to exhibit, like the decision to use any other media, should be the result of careful appraisal of the opportunity and an analysis of the role to be played by an exhibition in your marketing mix. Information is available from exhibition organisers on the numbers of visitors who have attended previous similar exhibitions and they also have information collected from registration data that can be used to gain a clear idea of the number of visitors that might potentially match your profile. Perhaps one of the clearest indicators here will be the amount of money individual visitors have available for their investment. It would not be surprising to discover that there will be relatively large numbers of visitors looking to invest up to £20,000 and relatively small numbers with the ability to invest, say, £200,000 plus.

In deciding whether franchise exhibitions ought to form part of your marketing media portfolio, consideration should be given to a number of issues:

- Are there likely to be a sufficient number of visitors who might match your franchisee profile?

- Are your direct competitors likely to be there?

- Is an exhibition environment suitable for you to deliver your marketing messages to potential franchisees?

- Are you able to take full advantage of the additional opportunities offered by exhibiting?

- Is your offer sufficiently strong to stand out among the highly concentrated grouping of other franchises?

- Have you the personnel, and have they got the skills, to make the most of what could be a large number of five-minute encounters with potential franchisees?

- Are there any other benefits to be derived from a franchise exhibition that might help justify the decision to exhibit?

- In comparison with other activities is it likely to be cost-effective?

Let's consider each of these issues in more detail and see how they might influence your decision on whether or not to exhibit.

- **You have developed your franchisee profile** in which you have identified the skills, experience and other attributes that you will be seeking in your potential franchisees. Research into the information available from the exhibition organisers will give you the opportunity to match the profile of visitors to the franchisee profile. If there appears to be little match in the two profiles you should seriously consider whether the exhibition fits into your marketing plan. If there is a good degree of match you should continue your decision-making process by considering other criteria. A study in the late 1990s suggested that about 75 per cent of visitors to franchise exhibitions were first-timers but that people who visited more than one exhibition were more likely ultimately to buy a franchise. This was said to suggest that franchise exhibitions featured strongly in the early stages of potential franchisees' investigations into franchising.

- **If your direct competitors will be there** will your offer stand up to side-by-side scrutiny? Will your presentation be dwarfed by big-spending competitors or will your message shine through? Remember big is not always beautiful but in an exhibition environment it is more easily noticed. Getting noticed, however, is only a small part of the story. What matters is how you deal with the attention that you create.

- **Will your chosen marketing message** benefit from the bustle of an exhibition or will that bustle make it difficult for your message to come across to visitors as they pass your stand?

- **Many of the benefits to be derived from exhibiting** come from activities outside the exhibition hall. Are you in a position to take full advantage of these add-ons? During the period running up to the franchise exhibitions the exhibition organisers and organisations like the British Franchise Association (BFA) will mount a PR campaign aimed at raising awareness not only of the exhibition itself but also of franchising. Riding piggyback on this PR activity by providing these organisations with interesting and usable articles about your franchise can substantially improve your market visibility if any of the press choose to feature your press release.

Virtually every element of the franchise-specific press will have exhibition features that will concentrate on the franchises taking part in the exhibition. Whether dedicated magazines or simply part of the business section of newspapers they all provide an opportunity for additional exposure at little or no cost.

If you are to get the full benefit of exhibiting you should be prepared to make what extra effort is needed to provide press release material to the relevant organisations.

- **The exhibition will feature perhaps hundreds of stands**, which will be offering franchises, or services to franchisees or franchisors. You will need to consider whether your franchise offer will be able to stand out among the competition. This will, very often, depend on the budget that you have available for both the exhibition space and the stand that you present in that space, but it will also depend on the attractiveness of your offer in comparison with the other franchises. If you have a clearly unique product or service, or if you are the best-established or leader in your sector then your offer should happily stand alongside the rest of the exhibitors. If, however, you are the most recent newcomer into an already well-established sector, with little to differentiate you from the competition, then giving potential franchisees the opportunity for direct comparison with others may be counter-productive.

- **If your stand and your franchise offer is attractive** you may well generate a large number of enquiries from visitors to your stand. It is important therefore that you should have sufficient staff to deal with these or you risk part of your marketing spend being wasted. Equally the staff need to have the ability to appraise the enquirer quickly and judge whether they are worthy of an extended conversation or a brief discussion with the potential for a later follow-up.

- **Your presence at a franchise exhibition** may have additional benefits for your business over and above that of recruiting franchisees. If your franchise provides a product or service direct to the consumer your stand may raise awareness of that to all the visitors, irrespective of whether they are interested in your business as a franchise opportunity. There is little doubt that many of the visitors seen watching a demonstration of a product or service are interested not in the franchise but in what it offers. This may therefore generate additional business for you and your franchisees and thus make a direct contribution to the cost of exhibiting.

- **As with any marketing activity** you will need to make a judgement on the cost-effectiveness of the proposal to exhibit in comparison to other alternative media. This may be difficult to do in theory and it may only be after you have exhibited at least once that you can make an informed decision on cost-effectiveness.

PREPARING TO EXHIBIT

You will need to make careful and extensive preparations if you are to get the full benefit from the exhibition.

- **Having taken the decision to exhibit**, the first step in the process is to decide on the size of stand that you will need and to book the space with the organiser. You will need to decide whether you wish simply to buy space on which you will erect your own stand or whether you will need a 'shell', i.e. space enclosed by walls separating you from the adjacent stands. These walls can then carry your marketing messages or act as a backdrop to other marketing materials and structures.

- **The marketing messages that you will choose** to convey to the exhibition visitors will need to be carefully thought through. On the basis that 'a picture is worth a thousand words', seek to make use of photographs of franchisees at work that will quickly convey to the passing visitor what the franchise offers. These, linked with short messages, will make the best use of the five or ten seconds that a potential franchisee will spend looking at your stand. The messages should both grab the visitors' attention and also convey the benefits to be gained by joining your franchise. These benefits should be selected to attract those visitors who will best match your franchisee profile.

  Demonstrations of the product or service offered by the franchise will always generate interest. The size and configuration of your stand will dictate whether these can be actual demonstrations or video presentations.

  You should consider carefully whether you wish to make any marketing materials available for distribution to potential franchisees at the exhibition. Those who have exhibited already will know that, in the same way that there are people who collect stamps or train numbers, there are also people who collect brochures and other marketing materials and will wander from stand to stand picking up anything that looks as though it might be free, whether it is of interest to them or not. These collectors are most easily recognised by the number of carrier bags they are carrying and a listing gait as they lean towards the side with the heaviest bag. You may find the cost of the exhibition rising by hundreds of pounds if your expensive marketing materials are simply left on a stand at the mercy of these collectors.

- **Allow yourself plenty of time** to have your stand materials designed and produced. When developing the materials try to avoid anything that might date them and thus mean that they cannot be reused for subsequent exhibitions. Equally consider whether there might be future occasions when your franchisees might want to use some of the materials locally to promote their services. By making them multi-purpose you will get more value from what can be a considerable production cost.

- **Developing a clear exhibition strategy** and communicating it to everyone who may be working on the stand will ensure that you get best value from the exhibition. The target visitors identified by your franchisee profile and the number of enquiries you hope to generate will dictate how you deal with visitors to the stand.

If you have a low-entry-cost franchise that could appeal to a very broad cross-section of the population you will need to be able to deal with a large number of enquiries. This may result in your deciding to take contact details of everyone who comes onto the stand so that you can follow up with marketing materials and a personal contact at a later time. There may be little time available to qualify these enquirers at the exhibition so decide what the key qualifiers are, then confirm that the enquirer may have an interest, take contact details and explain the follow-up procedure. Do not assume that if the enquirer is serious they will subsequently contact you. Those that are very seriously interested might, but experience tells us that you will need to drive the recruitment process for the vast majority of potential franchisees.

If your franchise requires a substantial investment or is likely by its nature to generate only a few enquiries you may choose to have a strategy that allows for more detailed discussions with the visitors to the stand. If this is the case the stand management team must clearly understand what subjects can be discussed in those initial conversations and what subjects will only be discussed at a later formal meeting. There may be an opportunity to collect some of the information normally sought on an application form or, where an enquirer seems particularly suitable and interested, they can be encouraged to complete a full application form at that stage prior to arranging an initial meeting.

- **To maintain the impetus of the enquiry process** you may wish to arrange 'open days' or group presentations within, say, two weeks of the exhibition and encourage potential franchisees to book a place on one of them. Those who are seriously interested will find a way of making themselves available for such a presentation and will, therefore, self-prioritise themselves for your interest. This is not to say that you should then ignore the other enquirers but it will allow you to focus your attention on the hottest prospects.

- **Can you drive people to your stand?** By their very nature exhibition layouts can be confusing, with the aisle grids not always following through lines from one end of the exhibition to the other. It is possible that a proportion of the visitors might never find themselves passing your stand. Among these could be potential franchisees who may never have the opportunity to seek your marketing messages. You may wish, therefore, to consider using additional means to raise interest in your stand and cause visitors to seek it out. These methods might include some form of additional sponsorship that ensures that every visitor receives a leaflet about your franchise in their 'welcome bag', or the use of high-level banner advertising in the roof area of the hall, or leaflet distribution by a team inside the hall. You should check with the exhibition organisers which of these possibilities are available and allowable.

- **Inviting existing franchisees to help man the stand** can be a powerful confidence builder for potential franchisees. Having the opportunity to discuss the business with someone who has already taken the plunge can do much to reinforce a potential franchisee's belief in the franchise system. Clearly you will need to choose carefully the franchisees you invite to help in this way, ensure that they will give an articulate and positive view of the franchise while not misrepresenting it in any way.

- **Maintain a to-do/ideas list** from the day you first decide to exhibit. Give everyone associated with the project open access to this list so that they can add to it as ideas come to them. Having such a list and then cross-checking against it will ensure that you are arrive at the exhibition with all the equipment and information that you need.

- **Whether this is your first exhibition** or the latest of a long series consider whether you and your team might benefit from some training in exhibition stand management. There are, undoubtedly, specific skills related to getting the best from the short period that you are exposed to your potential franchisees, whether these relate to interpersonal communication or simply sound stand management/etiquette.

THE RUN-UP TO THE EXHIBITION

- **Make the most of pre-exhibition PR opportunities** by both supplying the organisers and the bfa with suitable information about your franchise and also making your own PR approaches to the media. Prepare a press pack to be made available in the exhibition press office, ensuring that it includes information about the franchise, some human interest stories including photographs, and contact details should a feature writer wish to follow up for further information.

- You will receive clear instructions from the stand organisers regarding set-up and knock-down times prior to and following the exhibition. You will need to make sure that you have sufficient staff and transport available to ensure that you can get this work done within the parameters laid down by the organisers. The existence of a check-list for all the equipment you need will make these final days and hours easier for all concerned and make sure that you arrive at the exhibition fully prepared.

ON THE DAY

- **Exhibitions are hard work!** They are also an activity in which your stand team will have had very little experience or practice. If you are to get the most out of the exhibition everyone associated with the stand needs to be alert, fresh, well-informed as to strategy and committed to the cause. A 'liquid' team-building event the night before is therefore ill-advised!

- **Ensure that you have sufficient team members** to be able to allow rest periods throughout the day without leaving the stand undermanned. This will ensure that the team can get a coffee or a bite to eat without having to eat and drink on the stand.

- **Maintain an 'open stand'** by ensuring that team members are welcoming to potential enquirers. Even if everyone is already committed to an enquirer make sure that new visitors are at least acknowledged, if only with a smile. Avoid passers-by being confronted by a wall of backs as the stand team holds discussions between themselves or with other visitors – even when in conversation with a visitor aim to remain outward facing. If you are seeking a large number of enquiries (see exhibition strategy above) develop tactics to encourage passers-by at least to stop and consider your offer.

- **Safeguard the fruits of your work.** Make sure that contact information is collected from all enquirers and that it is then kept securely, ready for further action after the exhibition.

- **Take time to view the other stands.** Look for ideas on how you might improve your own stand for subsequent exhibitions. Has another franchise got a great idea for delivering a message that you could adapt to your own use? Watch the visitor-flow. Could you have been in a better location? Take the opportunity during quiet periods for networking with others in the franchise community, whether suppliers or other franchisors, but avoid taking up precious time if they are busy, even if you aren't.

AFTER THE EXHIBITION

- **Have an early review of successes and failures** with the stand team. What worked well? What could be improved or altered? At this stage it will probably be too early to determine whether the exhibition has been a successful recruitment medium although you may have some raw criteria to assess, such as the number of enquiries generated. Review the total spend, including the cost of the exhibition itself, all materials used, travel and accommodation costs for the stand team and the time–cost implications. You will then be able to use this information to generate a cost per enquiry figure and also, eventually, a cost per sign-up. This can then be compared to other marketing media to assist in the decision about whether to attend future exhibitions.

- **Set the recruitment process in chain.** Make sure that full use is made of every lead. If you have generated a large number of leads this may involve drafting additional staff onto the process or using the services of a lead follow-up service provider. Make every lead count.

Franchise exhibitions can play an important role in the marketing mix for many franchisors. They will, undoubtedly, not be a valid medium for all franchises but where they form part of the mix, careful planning and execution of the exhibition strategy will assist the franchise recruitment process.

13

How to help franchisees to prepare and review their business plans

Business plans form an integral part of any business's development process. Without a business plan a business has little chance of success. In many small businesses the plan resides in the mind of the business owner or manager and is often vague and lacking in clear thinking. The very process of putting the plan down on paper presents an opportunity, or even a requirement, to produce clearly developed strategies for the growth of the business.

WHY HAVE A BUSINESS PLAN?

The franchisee's initial business plan has a number of objectives:

- it may be required to present to a bank or other source of finance to help fund the franchisee's investment;

- it confirms to the franchisor that the franchisee has realistic objectives for the franchised outlet;

- it focuses the franchisee's mind on what has to be achieved in the new business;

- it provides a series of markers against which to monitor the progress of the business.

All too often small business owners produce an initial business plan for the first of the above objectives and once finance has been approved the document goes into a desk drawer, never to see the light of day again. The wise owner, however, sees the business plan as an integral part of the business development strategy and continually reviews, revises and rewrites the plan.

It is almost impossible to read any book, article or other document about business planning without seeing some version of the old adage 'To fail to plan is to plan to fail'. However, Sir John Harvey-Jones had a much more thought-provoking view when he said 'Planning is an unnatural process; it is much more fun to do something. The nicest thing about not planning is that failure comes as a complete surprise, rather than being preceded by a period of worry and depression.'

- **When presenting a business plan to a bank** or a possible investor it is important that the reader can see that the business has a clear strategy that should result in sufficient profitability for the funder to get its capital repaid, in addition to an adequate return on the capital. Clearly set out goals relating to both the activities of the business and the financial consequences will give confidence to any lender.

- **During the franchisee recruitment process** the franchisor may require the prospective franchisee to produce a draft business plan that will demonstrate the franchisee's objectives for the business. If the franchisee's goals fall short of the franchisor's expectations for the territory being granted it may prompt a discussion about the level of commitment required by the franchisee to develop the business fully.

- **The franchisee, while writing the business plan**, will have to set out both his goals for the business and also what will need to be done to achieve those goals. This could be the final opportunity for the applicant formally to reappraise whether the business opportunity offered by the franchise is right for them.

- **During the early months of the business** the actual results of the business, both in terms of financial and developmental achievements, can be checked against the objectives laid out in the business plan.

The initial business plan has often been likened to the planning that goes into an expedition. The objective is set to reach a certain destination or achieve a certain result, the resources needed to get there are measured, the personnel who will be involved are identified, the methods of transport to reach the destination are chosen and time-scales are developed to ensure that all the objectives can be met within the limitations of the resources. All this planning, however, will be of little avail if the progress of the expedition is not monitored against the plan.

ANNUAL BUSINESS PLANNING

Any franchisor that does not require their franchisees to produce a business plan at least once a year is failing those franchisees. Most franchisees, when they first set up their business are quite naive in business matters. Even those who have held management positions in the corporate world may have little or no idea of how a business is run or what plans need to be made to ensure its success. Part of the franchisor's role is not only to provide the disciplines the franchisee must follow in operating the system but also to provide good advice on general business management issues. It is not sufficient that the franchisee knows how to 'do the job'; they need to know how to run a business that does the job. Business planning is an integral part of this process.

If a franchisor does not receive copies of the franchisees' business plans it is difficult to see how they can make meaningful plans for their own business. They may hope to increase turnover by say 15 per cent during the coming year but if all his franchisees are aiming for only 8 per cent their hopes are bound to be confounded.

Within most businesses the growth of the business is almost entirely in the hands of the business managers. They set the objectives and then develop the strategies needed to meet the objectives. Yes, they rely upon their employees to implement the strategies but they do have the ability to manage and motivate their staff on a daily basis. A franchisor, however, is totally dependent upon the performance of their franchisees, over which they have little direct influence. Franchisees who fail to develop their businesses fully have a direct and detrimental effect on the profitability of the franchisor and the development of its brand. We discuss in Chapters 16 and 17 respectively the importance of monitoring franchisees' performance and of motivating them to develop their business. The business plan is a key instrument in both of these processes.

WHO WRITES THE BUSINESS PLAN?

Ideally it is the franchisee. However, at the point that the initial business plan is written, the franchisee will have no direct experience of the business to inform what goes into the plan. Moreover, they may have little or no knowledge of what a business plan is or how to write one. There is a clear role for the franchisor to play in providing some assistance with the writing of the initial business plan.

The franchisee will need information for financial forecasting on many or all of the following:

- potential sales levels;
- sales profiles in a start-up situation;
- sales profiles with regard to any seasonality of the business;
- purchase and profit margins;
- sales per head of staff;
- anticipated expenditure levels;
- customary credit arrangements for both purchases and sales;
- anticipated start-up costs including equipment and fixtures and fittings;
- stock levels required.

However, the franchisor must be wary of providing any financial information that could be considered in any way a guarantee of performance. Many legal advisers will warn their franchisor clients of the potential hazards of becoming involved in assisting franchisees to develop their financial forecasts lest the unsuccessful franchisee should later come back to the franchisor and make the claim that 'You said I would achieve x sales and y profitability and I haven't.'

In reality the franchisor will need to provide guidance based on the achievements either of its own outlets or those of the pilot and other franchisees or both. It is then up to the franchisee to make their own forecasts based on this information. The franchisor will, however, wish to satisfy itself that the financial forecasts are realistic and in line with the actual performance of other units. Franchisors are increasingly using the services of independent third parties to assist their franchisees in producing their business plans. These advisers will need to have a clear understanding of the business, its operations and the key information needed to guide the franchisee.

When writing the narrative of the business plan the franchisee will need access to various information from the franchisor:

- the franchisor company's trading history;

- the number of franchisees operating;

- any national or local marketing instigated by the franchisor;

- details of any recommendations from the franchisor regarding local marketing to be instigated by the franchisee;

- details of the support structure of the franchise.

This information may be provided as 'bald facts' for the franchisee to incorporate within their business plan, or they may be provided as part of a template produced by the franchisor with the franchisee filling in the 'local' sections. Either way all these topics will need comment in the business plan.

WHAT SHOULD BE IN THE INITIAL BUSINESS PLAN?

The franchisee's business plan should contain all the information normally found in a business plan but should also contain in many of the sections additional information regarding the franchisor's business.

Typically it will contain, although not necessarily in this order:

- vision/mission statement;
- details of key employees;
- company history;
- list of company products or services;
- details of target market;
- the growth opportunity;
- competitive climate;
- SWOT analysis;
- details of planned marketing activities;
- company services or products, including any unique aspects;
- revenue/profitability history;
- financial forecasts;
- capital requirement and provision.

- **A vision/mission statement** developed by the franchisee will provide a positive, focused starting point for any reader of the business plan. This vision/mission will be based on the franchisor's vision or mission statement but will be adapted it to the franchisee's local business situation.

- **Details of the franchisee's work background and experience**, linked with those of any other key employees, for example partners who will be involved in the business, should show in what areas there is experience that will benefit the new business. Where there is no relevant experience comment should be made on the training that the franchisee has undergone, or will undergo, to equip them to run the business. It is often helpful also to include information about the franchisor's key personnel, as it will be they who will be providing guidance and support for the franchisee.

- **In an initial business plan** there will be no company history available for the franchisee unless they have had a previous trading company and the new franchise is an extension of that. It would be useful, however, to include a small section on the trading history of the franchisor as this will demonstrate that there is a proven business system behind the franchise.

- **Details of the company's products or services** should be included in sufficient detail to provide the reader with an understanding of the way in which revenue will be generated. Where it is considered useful some of the franchisor's own product or service literature could be included as an appendix.

- **The target market should be identified** both in terms of the local market for the franchisee and also the national market for the franchisor. Where, due to local circumstances, these two markets differ, comment should be made on the reason for the difference.

- **The growth opportunity** should be quantified as far as possible, again for both the franchisee and the franchisor.

- **Information on the competitive climate**, both locally for the franchisee and also nationally for the franchisor, should be discussed. Details of market research by the franchisee should be included to demonstrate his or her knowledge of its local competitors and their relative strengths and weaknesses.

- **A realistic SWOT analysis** outlining the Strengths, Weaknesses, Opportunities and Threats relating to the franchisee's business should be included. This will demonstrate that the franchisee has thought through the proposed venture and identified the areas where it may need most support or guidance from the franchisor.

- **Any marketing activities** proposed by either the franchisor or the franchisee to raise awareness of both the brand and also the individual franchisee's operation should be detailed. In many franchises local marketing is critical to the success of the operation. While a retailer with a dominant brand such as McDonald's or Clarks Shoes may immediately attract customers as soon as the outlet is open, many franchises rely totally upon continuing marketing activity to find customers.

- **A brief description of the company's products or services** and details of anything that makes them unique in the sector should be included.

- **Where the franchisee has previously traded**, details of their revenue/profitability history should be included along with basic information about the franchisor company.

- **Sales/profitability and cashflow forecasts** should be included for at least three years, including a detailed month-by-month analysis at least for the cashflow. This will determine the level of funding required both for the start-up investment and also for working capital.

- **Finally, information should be included on the capital requirement** and how it will be provided. This should include a clear indication to investor/funder what the funds will be used for and how it is proposed that they will be repaid. It is likely that the franchisee will have already received an 'in principle' indication from their bank regarding the level of borrowings that will be available and the terms on which they will be lent.

> The preparation of a fully detailed business plan for presentation to a bank that probably already has a clear understanding of the franchise may seem over-detailed. However, the very activity of preparing such a plan forces the franchisee to address all the issues involved in starting and running a successful business.

WHAT SHOULD BE IN SUBSEQUENT BUSINESS PLANS?

After the initial business plan, which often has funding as one of its objectives, subsequent plans can be less detailed. The franchisee should be encouraged to produce sales/profitability and cashflow forecasts for the coming 12 months and a narrative section that addresses the activities that will need to be completed in order to generate the forecast level of sales. This might include the identification of new target customers or new marketing activities that will attract new customers.

Subsequent plans should also address other development issues, for example staff training and identifying the franchisee's own training needs. It may be that if new marketing and sales strategies are planned new skills will need to be learned by the relevant personnel.

They should also include a review of the previous 12 months' trading in comparison to the forecasts within the earlier business plan. This self-appraisal should produce a similar result to the type of appraisal that a member of staff might receive from his or her manager and may go on to form the basis of an annual review meeting with the franchisor.

MONITORING PERFORMANCE AGAINST THE BUSINESS PLAN

The role of the business plan in monitoring performance is discussed in Chapter 16. However, it is important to stress that a business plan is of little use if it is not used as a marker against which to monitor current performance.

A system should be established, therefore, for the franchisee to produce regular, simple management accounts that report on the key indicators within the business. Perhaps the most important of these is cashflow. It is well known that poor cashflow results in the failure of many profitable businesses as generating profit is not necessarily a guarantee of generating cash.

If it becomes clear that either temporary or permanent additional funding might be required during the coming months it is important to arrange this funding as soon as the requirement is identified. A banker will be more prepared to consider additional funding if given good notice of the requirement than if they are asked at the point that the funding is required. The banker will certainly wish to see the forecasts that identify the need for the funding and will need to know why it is required. It is clear that the application for additional funds is more likely to be successful if it is to fund growth within the business rather than fund losses!

FINALLY...

Earlier we likened the business plan to the preparations for an expedition. It could equally be likened to a map that must be followed if that expedition is to be successful. It lays out the route to success and shows how the business can steer clear of risks and obstacles while taking the optimum route to its final goal of profitability.

This business plan map is essential to every business because without a map how will you know when you are lost?

14

How to write the franchise operations manual

DEVELOPING A GOOD MANUAL

There are nine steps in developing a good manual:

1. outlining the system;
2. creating a system questionnaire;
3. engineering the system;
4. indexing the manual;
5. structuring the manual;
6. manual writing style;
7. responsibility for policies and procedures;
8. appendices and forms;
9. review of the documented system.

1. Outlining the system

First, consider all the aspects of your business that you need a franchisee to copy or to understand.

Arrange them first by operational function such as set-up, operations, marketing, etc., then, within each function, arrange systems in the order that a franchisee would naturally use them so that the manual is easy to refer to.

For example, under 'set-up' you might start with 'Finding premises', then 'Acquiring premises', 'Building works and decoration', 'Installation of equipment', and so on. The last chapter in such a section might be 'Opening your doors to the public for the first time' and the first chapter in the next section, if it was 'Day-to-day operations', might be 'Greeting customers'.

Then create the sub-systems under each chapter. For example, under 'Finding premises', you might list the subjects 'How to search', 'Specifications of approved premises', 'Premises appraisal checklist', 'Creating a shortlist', 'Headquarters visits to appraise your shortlist', 'Getting our approval for your selected premises', etc.

You should end up with what looks like a list of contents for your manual, probably some 40 to 60 pages long.

In fact it's more important than just an index to your future paperwork; it is a list of all of the elements of your business that you must:

- design systems for (if they don't exist);

- refine in your own business to meet the standards that franchisees expect;

- learn and create – because you didn't need them before franchising;

- support in your new role as a franchisor.

Don't worry if you have to change or add to this list as you develop your new systems or refine existing ones. Manuals should be 'living documents' and it is normal that your outline will change.

An example of a good outline is shown on page 120.

2. Creating a system questionnaire

As you should now have a fairly comprehensive list of the aspects of your business that you need to include in your system – and eventually in your manual – you will be able to start delegating the completion of different sections to your staff and your franchise consultant.

One of the most efficient ways of doing this is to create a long questionnaire based on your outline. This helps you ask yourself and your team the right questions and makes it easier for others to get back the information you really want.

1. SECTION C – CORPORATE IDENTITY AND USAGE

1) Overview

2) The image

   a) Overview

   b) The brand

   c) The brand image and brand values

   d) The ethics we follow

   e) Products

   f) Customer-facing elements

      i) Service in the store

      ii) Service in the delivery business

      iii) In the community

   g) Code of honour

   h) Standards and uniformity

   i) Customers and their influence on our brand

3) Logo and trademarks

If any part of the questionnaire is left blank or comes back with the answer '...don't know', then you probably need to create a system or policy that does provide an answer.

The following is an example from such a questionnaire that you might send to your marketing department:

*		Level						Question/answer
Who	Section	0	I	II	III	IV	V	Question/answer
								SECTION F – MARKETING, SALES AND COMMUNICATION
M	F	4						What is our marketing philosophy for the network?
M F	F	6						Who pays for marketing and advertising? Please list by every type of marketing activity that we are involved in.
								Are there any marketing or promotion activities that we would ever ask contractors, recruiters or end clients to participate in?
								How much of their revenue do you expect franchisees to reserve for local marketing? (Irrespective of any advertising levies that they may pay us.)
								What national advertising do we actually do? (Or plan to do?)
								Etc.

M = Marketing department; F = Finance department.

3. Engineering the system

The manual itself is less important than the systems that it documents. You should engineer your systems around your experiences with your first franchisees and what they really need.

The aim of the best franchise systems should be to create working practices, policies, procedures, tools, and training that help your business and the businesses of your franchisees 'run by themselves' without anyone ever needing to refer to the manual.

Creating the manual is an inherent part of engineering a good system because it helps you map out what you need to get done, and what you need to train and support franchisees. It then documents those things, so that you know what you have implemented or planned.

4. Indexing the manual

When putting together a manual it is important (if it isn't automatically updated and interactive) that you index every page. This is so that you can easily instruct franchisees what pages to replace when you send them updates.

An example of a page-header index might be:

FRANCHISOR NAME			Subject:	Franchisee Operations Manual	
Date:	01/2007		Issue/Rev:	01	03
Section/Title:	B	Concept	Responsible:	AB/ CD & EF	Page 49 of 579

5. The structure of a good manual

A good franchise consultant has the experience to help you design your manual to cover all the subjects that a franchisee would expect or need to be advised on and those subjects that require policies for effective franchisee management.

A modern franchise manual might contain all of the following:

SECTION A MANUAL CONTROL AND CARE
The administrative and document-control paperwork that precedes the contents pages of any manual.

SECTION B INTRODUCTION TO THE CONCEPT
A section that hopes to provide franchisees with an overall understanding of the concept, rather than launch them into the detailed operations sections.

SECTION C CORPORATE IDENTITY AND USAGE
This section documents the importance of the brand and the policies and procedures that are in force to protect it for the benefit of everyone involved in the network.

SECTION D PRE-TRADING MANUAL
This section assists franchisees through the process of starting up as a new franchisee in your concept and launching their new business.

SECTION E OPERATIONS (THE SYSTEM)
This section forms the 'meaty middle' of any manual and documents

the way that you work, and the way franchisees are expected to work, to serve your customers properly and to help ensure franchisees' profitability.

SECTION F MARKETING, SALES AND COMMUNICATION
This section documents how to use marketing and communication effectively to increase sales, and details the sales processes and standards that franchisees are expected to use.

SECTION G QUALITY AND CUSTOMER CARE
This section documents the importance of delivering the system's products or services to the required standards.

SECTION H GENERAL ADMINISTRATION
This section contains the detail of running the administration of the franchise and dealing with office management, records, accounts and banking, compliance and so on.

SECTION I HUMAN RESOURCES AND RECRUITMENT
This section shows franchisees when and how to recruit and manage staff and handles their contracting, induction training, payment, treatment and discipline.

SECTION J TRAINING
This section documents the training programmes and policies and often replicates the induction-training programme that you gave franchisees for their use in training their future staff.

SECTION K FRANCHISE COMMUNICATIONS
This section documents policies and procedures that are imperative in maintaining a good relationship for mutual success between franchisor and franchisees.

SECTION L REALISING THE VALUE OF YOUR INVESTMENT
This section documents the pros and cons of franchisees selling their franchise in the future, how to build it into an asset that is worth something, typical calculations for valuation and the process that must be followed should they ever wish to sell.

APPENDIX 1 STANDARD FORMS
This is an appendix holding copies of all the forms, letters and

standard documents contained within or referred to by the manual. It is used both as a reference and as a master document to make copies from as and when franchisees need them.

APPENDIX 2 EMPLOYEE HANDBOOK
Herein franchisees should find a copy of the handbook that they are to give to every member of their future staff.

APPENDIX 3 DIRECTORY OF CONTACTS AND PNS
This details all the useful contacts at your head office, among the network and at large. It also details any *preferred nominated suppliers* (PNS) that you prefer franchisees to use, and the specifications of supplies that they are already authorised to make available to franchisees.

6. Manual writing style
Manuals should be written in plain language that is clear, concise and unambiguous.

The manual writing style needs to be professional but it should reflect the attitude, character, philosophies and values of the business.

7. Responsibility for policies and procedures
There are aspects of your franchisee's business that are just that – their business.

If you suggest in your manual that your franchisees adopt certain tax, data protection, health and safety or employment practices and they turn out to be inappropriate for their size of business in their location, you might end up in a questionable position over who is responsible for their actions should their implementation of those policies end up in criminal prosecution or legal action.

It is often better to outsource advice on these matters to relevant professionals who will be aware of these sorts of issues and how to avoid them. A list is available from the Franchisee Support Centre.

8. Appendices and forms

Franchisees, like most of us, hate administration. They want to get on with making money not filling in forms.

A good manual probably won't need more than ten forms, especially if you ask for formal communication on most issues requiring approval by a simple letter or e-mail.

9. Review of the documented system

Once your manual is complete it is important to review it in the following ways, for the following reasons:

1. Read through it carefully yourself, so that you can:

    -   understand what you have promised to franchisees in the manual;
    -   see what elements would benefit the rest of your organisation if implemented there;
    -   mark the systems that are as yet untested and that you will monitor to ensure their effectiveness.

2. Pass a copy to every department in your organisation (confidentiality permitting) so that they can:

    -   confirm that the contents are accurate for their function;
    -   agree that they can do or supply what the manual requires of them;
    -   implement new systems that are promised in your manual.

3. Test it with initial or pilot franchisees, so that you can:

    -   fine tune it to work with future franchisees;
    -   roll it out as a proven system;
    -   develop further or discard the aspects that were a 'good idea at the time' but really don't work in practice.

4. Periodically review the manual, so that you:

    -   can keep it up to date.

HOW TO PROTECT YOUR MANUAL

Once you have completed a comprehensive manual, it should cover all aspects of duplicating your business successfully – *including* all of your trade secrets, tips and tricks. Unfortunately, this will also mean that any competitor that gets hold of the manual could use it to reduce the gap of competitive advantage between you and them.

Of course, you shouldn't keep your trade secrets from your franchisees because these secrets are part of the reason that they have bought into your franchise. On the other hand, there are several ways that you should consider protecting your most important trade secrets.

- **Copyrights** – you should make your copyright clear on every page of the manual and lodge one copy with a solicitor so that they can verify when it was authored. Unfortunately, the sheer volume of most manuals, the fact that much of what they contain will be in the public domain anyway and the ease with which they can be transliterated all reduce the power of protection that you will enjoy by copyrighting. Anyway, once your ideas are out, a copyright does more to protect the way in which the ideas are written down than to prevent someone else implementing them.

- **Registration** – you should register each manual with its own serial number on every page, so that you will know which franchisee had allowed it to be copied. If the serial number is preserved on the copies, you will know which franchisee allowed it to be copied.

- **Watermarking** – you can physically or electronically watermark each page so that it is clear that you were the author of any copies. To be a little more devious, you might subtly change one or two words on each page and register who was given which version.

- **Distributing the manual in unprintable versions** – if you distribute your manual electronically you might want to make it unprintable (except for forms). You should also make it locked for editing, so that there is less risk of someone else changing it and passing it off as their own. Be careful, if you lock a document for editing in Microsoft Word, one still may be able to 'copy and paste' from that document to a new document and retain all formatting and structure – Adobe Acrobat Writer makes this more difficult. Properly hacker-protected online interactive versions of your manual will also be less easy to copy and edit.

- **Recording interactive access to the manual** – if your manual is online and interactive through your intranet or extranet, you could record who accessed what and when. By doing this you can monitor, or get your systems to flag up, abnormal access to the manual.

- **Signing up franchisees' staff to non-disclosure agreements** – make sure that a franchisee's staff are contracted not to reveal the contents of the manual or to copy it.

- **Giving the manual at the right time** – never hand out your manual to a prospective franchisee who has not signed up to your franchise agreement and paid their joining fee. To go one step further, it may also be advisable only to hand the manual over to a franchisee once they have successfully completed each section of training.

- **Disseminating some trade secrets outside the manual** – if you believe that some of your trade secrets are so valuable that they shouldn't be recorded in the manual, you might pass them on to your franchisees in other ways – verbally through training, for example.

- **Protecting some trade secrets in systems** – some of your trade secrets may be so sensitive that you want to guard them from franchisees. You might be able to find ways to protect such secrets through your system by managing them centrally. For example, if you had a secret recipe sauce, you might supply that sauce to your franchisees, rather than have them make it from scratch in their store. Or, to give an example in a service business, if you had a loans business and your competitive advantage rested on your relationship with lenders, you might take on the underwriting role at your head office and forbid franchisees from dealing directly with those lenders.

15
How to develop and deliver a franchisee training programme

The fundamental principles of franchising are based around the franchisor's willingness to allow their franchisees to replicate the business system developed and successfully proven by the franchisor. This involves the transfer of all relevant information needed to replicate the system. While no guarantee can ever be made that the franchisee's business will be successful it is accepted that there is more likelihood of success if the system is followed. It is implicit therefore that the transfer of the relevant knowledge in how to operate the system must be timely and complete. Effective franchisee training is therefore fundamental to the whole process.

DEVELOPING THE TRAINING PROGRAMME

The training programme must be suitable for any franchisee who might join the franchise network irrespective of their previous experience and existing skills base. It must comprehensively cover all aspects of the operation of the franchisor's system. While the franchisor may have specified certain existing skills or experience in the franchisee profile it is not sufficient to rely upon the franchisee's apparent ability to complete parts of the activity without further training from the franchisor in their methods.

In preparing to develop the training programme the franchisor must therefore:

- identify all the core skills needed to operate the system;

- produce detailed processes for each of the business's activities;

- select the most appropriate methods of imparting this information through training;

- develop a timed programme for the delivery of this training while considering the skills requirements at various stages of the business's development;

- ensure that each franchisee receives the relevant training and is competent in all the activities of the business.

> The process of transferring the necessary knowledge and skills that the franchisee will require to run a successful business is critical to the likelihood of success.

- **In identifying the core skills needed** to operate the business the franchisor must be wary of assuming that the franchisee has even the most basic experience and skill base or that the existing skills will be relevant to the operation of the franchise system. It is important therefore to identify in each area of the operation all the skills required. These operations may include some or all of the following:

1. marketing activities;

2. sales processes including associated administration;

3. product/service knowledge;

4. product/service delivery;

5. customer care.

All of the above are likely to be specific to the franchise system. In addition the franchisee will need to understand the activities and the skills required to run a successful business. These will include some or all of the following:

1. an understanding of business profitability;

2. an understanding of the importance of cashflow;

3. an understanding of basic administration and accounting;

4. an awareness of relevant legislation, both industry specific and general, relating to employment, health and safety etc.;

5. where staff are employed, the principles of management and leadership including training and development, performance appraisal, selection and recruitment processes etc.

It is easy for a franchisor's management team to assume that incoming franchisees possess experience and skills in these areas, or to consider that they are all 'common sense', forgetting that they themselves may have unconsciously developed these skills and practices through long exposure to running the original business.

- **The detailed processes involved** in the operation of the franchise will have been documented in the franchise operations manual. While this will be useful during the training process it is not sufficient simply to hand over the manual saying, 'this contains everything you need to know to run the business.' Although it may be useful as a training document the real value of the franchise operations manual is as a reference document to which the franchisee can turn to refresh their memory following training.

- **Appropriate methods of delivering** this knowledge and information must now be considered. Some aspects might best be delivered 'on the job' with the new franchisee accompanying an existing franchisee for a period of time. Other aspects will require a more theoretical approach initially and therefore be more suitable for a 'classroom' situation, perhaps followed up by some practical experience. Others may require an initial period of 'self-study', perhaps using the operations manual, prior to more formal training delivery. General business management training may be better delivered by external specialist providers.

- **Timing the delivery of the training is critical.** Too much, too quickly and the franchisee may not be able to absorb it all: too little, too late, and the franchisee will not possess the skills needed for a successful launch. There will almost certainly be some activities in which the franchisee is unlikely to become involved until the franchise is well established. For example they will not need to do a year-end stocktake until the end of the first year's trading. Training related to this can reasonably be delivered at a later, more appropriate time.

- **Training is not simply about appropriate delivery**, it must also involve some process of examining the trainee's understanding. In some areas an examination-type assessment may be appropriate while in others, observation of the franchisee in action may provide the best guide as to whether the training has been effective. The adage 'If the pupil hasn't learnt, the teacher hasn't taught' must be applied to results of this assessment.

TRAINING TOPICS

Marketing and sales

By definition, the core business, around which the franchise has been developed, is a successful business. This will often be as the result of the business owner's innate skills in sales and marketing. It is often difficult for such skilled people to understand that few others possess these skills naturally and that many find the acquisition is difficult. Equally the 'natural salesperson' may find it difficult to encapsulate just what it is he or she does that makes them so successful at selling.

Every franchised business sells something, whether a product or a service, and no profit can be made until a sale is concluded. Selling skills and the marketing that precedes the sales opportunity are therefore critical to the success of the franchised business. However, sales and marketing are perhaps the two business activities that cause the greatest concern to franchisees in general. It is this concern that leads many 'business opportunity' providers to lead their marketing programmes with the phrase 'No selling involved!' and yet is difficult to see how any business can be successful if it doesn't sell something.

Franchises that are particularly susceptible to these issues include those where a degree of cold-calling is required to generate sales opportunities. Anyone who has ever been involved in this marketing activity will know how frustrating it can be to spend hours on the telephone or making visits to potential customers, only to be rebuffed within the first few minutes of the conversation. It is important that the franchisees remain positive and confident under such circumstances and an understanding of this will need to form a key part of the marketing and sales training.

Most people learn best when they understand the reasons underlying the various processes they are being asked to undertake. It is not sufficient, therefore, simply to give trainees a list of activities they must fulfil or scripts that they must follow without also imparting an understanding of why those activities or scripts will produce positive results.

While the franchisor may know the marketing and sales techniques that work best in its business the whole subject of marketing and sales is one where an understanding of the core principles involved is invaluable.

Knowledge of the product or service

Part of the sales process will involve describing the product or service to the customer and showing how it can provide the benefits the customer is seeking. To do this the franchisee will need to be fully conversant with the details of the product or service offered.

Delivering the product or service

This is perhaps the area in which franchisors are most accomplished in their training. It is, naturally, critical that they should ensure that their franchisees know how to deliver effectively the subject of the sale, whether it is a meal in a restaurant or a business coaching programme. Equally this is the area that is often of most interest to the franchisee. After all it was the opportunity to deliver the product or service that probably initially attracted them to this franchise rather than another. They often, mistakenly, believe that it is the uniqueness of the product or service that makes the franchise successful whereas in reality it is often the marketing and sales activity that leads to the delivery that drives the success.

Customer care

Most businesses rely on or offer the possibility of repeat business from satisfied customers. It is generally acknowledged that it is substantially easier to sell to an existing customer than to find new customers. However, ensuring that customers are more than simply 'satisfied' will greatly enhance the chance of further sales or referrals to new potential sales opportunities. Customer care strategies will increase the opportunities for business development.

All of the above topics will most likely be delivered by the franchisor, their staff or other franchisees who have been developed as trainers. However, there is an opportunity to use specialist external providers to enhance many of the above subjects especially in the fields of sales and marketing and customer care.

Business management

Most potential franchisees will have little knowledge about, or experience of, running a business. It is important, therefore, that the franchisor ensures that they learn not only 'how to do the job that the business does' but also 'how to run a business that does the job'.

Many owners of small or medium-sized enterprises (SMEs) will have learned these skills from the experience that they gained from developing their own business and may have learned, in some instances, as the result of mistakes they made. Franchisees, however, see a franchise as an opportunity to build a business based on the franchisor's experience and thus avoid making the mistakes that the franchisor might have made. Franchisors must, therefore, ensure that the franchisees possess all the skills, understanding and information they need to run a successful business.

This knowledge includes:

1. an understanding of how a business generates and keeps profit. This will include the principles of pricing to produce a margin sufficient to generate a realistic gross profit and the control of costs to leave a net profit providing an adequate return on investment;

2. an understanding of the importance of cash flow with particular reference, where relevant, to the credit control function;

3. an understanding of the basic principles of business administration and accounting including any administration and reporting requirements that the franchisor might require from their franchisees;

4. an awareness of relevant legislation, both industry specific and general, relating for example to employment, health and safety etc. While the franchisor should not put themselves in the position of acting as legal adviser to their franchisees it is desirable that they ensure that the franchisees are aware of the various obligations that the relevant legislation places upon them;

5. where the franchisee has to employ staff they should be aware of the principles of staff management and leadership including training and development, performance appraisal, selection and recruitment processes etc. As has been stated previously, many franchisees will have had no experience of running a business and these are among the skills they may lack.

Training on all of the above topics may best be delivered more practically and more cost-effectively by an external training provider that can supply a generalised, non-franchise-specific context for the learning.

DELIVERING THE TRAINING
Having decided on all the topics to be covered in the training, consideration must be given to the timing and method of delivery.

- **Timing the delivery of the training** will often depend upon the lead-time available between completing the recruitment process and the franchisee commencing trading. It is a fact of life that when a franchisee is learning they are not usually earning and many franchisors therefore try to reduce the amount of time spent on training to a minimum. This is, more often than not, a false economy. An extra week or two added to the training timetable may well produce a better trained and more effective franchisee who will make up for the additional period of not earning by higher levels of sales in the initial trading period.

Thought should be given in developing the training process as to what knowledge needs to be imparted during the initial pre-trading training and what can be left until a later date when it can become part of the ongoing training. Providing in-depth training in the key areas prior to trading is far better than trying to deliver all the training at this stage.

Where timing allows, it may be possible for the franchisor to train a number of franchisees at the same time. However, with typical levels of recruitment, these opportunities are rare during the initial training process. Most initial training is, therefore, delivered on a one-to-one basis. Group delivery may be more suitable for later elements of the ongoing training programme. This greatly influences the options for the method of delivery.

- **It is important to have a variety of delivery methods** for the training since different people learn in different ways. Some will respond well immediately to practical activities, others will learn best when they understand the theory of the activity before putting it into practice.

Time spent working alongside an existing franchisee can be useful provided that the tutor franchisee sticks rigidly to the franchisor's operating systems and is efficient at the task being taught. Experience tells us that when training is done in this way it can tend to reduce the productivity of the tutor since he or she has to spend time explaining the processes and even allowing the trainee to practise delivery skills. This may well reduce the tutor's earning capacity and the franchisor should seek ways of directly compensating for this loss while at the same time rewarding the tutor for their efforts.

Classroom-style training may be appropriate for some subjects. In normal training processes this would involve the preparation and delivery of a formal 'lesson plan'. It is important to have such a plan even when training on a one-to-one basis to ensure that all the relevant topics are covered. The trainer must also be careful not to allow the particular interests of the franchisee to divert the training from its planned programme. Only in this way can it be guaranteed that the training has been completed across the full subject matter.

There may be subjects in the training provision which the franchisee can learn away from the formal training process by periods of self-study. This is a particularly relevant process where factual information needs to be learned, for example developing knowledge of the properties of certain cleaning chemicals and the circumstances in which they should and should not be used. The franchisee can be encouraged to learn these subjects in their own time and at their own pace with the franchisor simply having to check that the learning has been completed.

The increasing use of distance learning using the internet allows trainees to learn in the comfort of their own homes and in their own time. While this is not an ideal delivery method for all aspects of training, it is particularly useful where factual information has to be learned and then tested. This method allows the franchisor to monitor the trainee's progress through the training programme and, by online testing, to ensure that all the necessary knowledge has been acquired.

In the same way there may be elements of the training that can be delivered by video or DVD rather than in person. This is particularly useful where there is a largely visual element to the learning outcome. For example, a restaurant operation may use this method to show how to present a particular dish on the plate or a training company may provide a recorded example of a particular training module.

By using varied delivery methods different learning styles can be catered for. Not all methods, however, are suited to all training topics.

DOCUMENTING THE TRAINING PROCESS

The operations manual has a clear role to play in supporting the franchisee training activity. It may be, however, that additional training materials need to be developed to complement the instructions laid out in the manual. After use the franchisee should retain a copy of these materials, including any personal notes they have made during the training, as a supplement to the operations manual.

As franchisees receive each element of their training this should be documented and signed off by both trainer and trainee. This primarily confirms that all the modules in the training programme have been covered. It also ought to allow for either trainer or trainee to identify areas where additional training may be required in order to ensure total competency. The completion of this training record can also act as a prompt to initialise or set up a timetable for the next stage in the training process.

The core concept of franchising is based upon the franchisor delivering to the franchisee the systems and knowledge required to replicate effectively the franchisor's business system. A well-planned and delivered initial and ongoing training programme will enhance this knowledge transfer and improve the franchisee's chance of success.

16
How to monitor franchisees' performance

One of the key differences between business format franchising and other methods that can be used to help individuals start businesses, such as licensing or what has become known as 'business opportunities', is the existence of the ongoing franchisee–franchisor relationship. An integral part of this relationship is the provision of continuous support and guidance by the franchisor and a continuing commitment from the franchisee to operate under the franchisor's brand in accordance with the franchise agreement and operations manual.

However, it cannot be assumed that simply because the franchisee has signed such an agreement he will always fulfil his obligations within that agreement. There is, therefore, a clear need for the franchisor to monitor the franchisee's performance continually.

WHY MONITOR PERFORMANCE?
It's about protection...

- to protect your brand;
- to protect your income;
- to protect your customers;
- to protect other franchisees;
- to protect franchisees from themselves!

- **Your brand, and what it stands for**, is one of your most important assets. It is effectively your promise to your customers. It tells your customers and potential customers everything about what you stand for and what you do. It is, after all, what has attracted your franchisees to you; it is what they have paid to share. It is important, therefore, that your franchisees are powerful proponents of your brand values and demonstrate complete commitment to them.

- **Your income, in common with most franchisors**, is likely to be largely or totally dependent upon your franchisees. Whether you receive a management services fee based on sales, or simply rely for your income on mark-up on products that you sell to your franchisee for subsequent resale or for use in the delivery of your service, you will need to satisfy yourself that the franchisee is declaring all their sales upon which they must pay a fee and is purchasing products only from you or other authorised suppliers.

- **Your customers are your most valuable asset.** One simple definition states that what businesses do is 'to strive to find and keep profitable customers'. It's as simple as that and it is difficult, if not impossible, to think of a business format that cannot be reduced to that simple definition. You must ensure, therefore, that *your* customers and every customer of your brand is *your* customer, whether served directly by yourself or indirectly by your franchisees – receive the level of service and quality of product commensurate with your brand promise.

- **One of the advantages for franchisees of trading under a common brand** is that, right from the first day of their business, customers know what it is they do and what they stand for. True, it takes some time for a brand to become so well established, but this is ultimately what every franchisor and franchisee hopes for in the relationship. However, any failure to deliver the brand promise by an individual franchisee can have a detrimental effect on the brand and the customers' perception of other franchisee businesses.

- **The majority of franchisees are totally naive in business matters** when they first apply to become a franchisee. Although they may have had experience of the business sector in which they are going to trade they rarely have experience of *running a business* in that sector. Left to their own devices they are likely to make poor decisions about how to manage the business and will eventually feature among the long list of businesses that fail to get past their second or third year of trading.

PROTECTING YOUR BRAND

Have you got clear brand values? Do your customers think of you in the way you think they think of you? By having clearly defined brand values and brand positioning you make life easy for those customers who wish to trade with you and for you and your franchisees who wish to trade with them.

So what are your brand values? They probably relate to:

- the objective quality of your product or service;

- the value it offers in relation to the price charged and the quality of the offer;

- the ethical stance of your business;

- the position you hold in the market in comparison with your competitors.

Each business will have a different set of brand values but it is important that everyone involved with the business is committed to operating by those values.

When deciding what you will wish to monitor in relation to your brand it is useful to make a list of the many ways in which your brand, as opposed to your business, might be damaged. Certainly if your brand is damaged your business will be damaged, but not all things that will damage your business will be the result of damage to your brand.

So what might damage your brand? Clearly it will depend upon what your brand promise implies:

- For any restaurant or other provider of food products, any instance of poor hygiene or association with food-related illnesses will potentially damage the brand;

- for any franchise that involves the care of potentially vulnerable people, whether they be the young, the old or the sick, any instance where the level of care is seen to be below the level demanded will potentially damage the brand;

- for any franchise where the service is one of cleaning or restoration of a customer's property, if due care is not taken of that property, or the property is in some way damaged or lost, this will potentially damage the brand;

- for any franchise that provides a product or service to other businesses any failure in that product or service will quickly be communicated around the business community, resulting in potential damage to the brand;

- for a franchise that has to operate under strict rules imposed by statute or professional bodies, any failure on the part of a franchisee to meet compliancy standards will potentially result in damage to the brand;

- for any franchise where the brand values refer to 'value', or the relationship between quality and price, if franchisees fail to give value either because of delivering poor quality or over-pricing, it will potentially damage the brand.

Make a list of all the ways that your brand might be damaged and you are well on the way to identifying those activities that you will wish to monitor in relation to your franchisees' performance.

In the same way, consider what other things, related to your relationship with your franchisees, might damage your business. These might include:

- loss of income resulting from under-declaration of sales, or purchasing not-approved products;

- poor franchisee profitability, credit control or cash flow resulting in the franchisee's inability to pay management services fees or invoices for product on time;

- the failure of an individual franchisee resulting in damage to the 'franchise brand' and loss of income, even if only temporarily, for the franchisor;

- relationships with key suppliers being damaged as a result of franchisees not meeting supply and payment conditions;

- relationships with key customers or national accounts being damaged as a result of poor performance by franchisees.

The above issues may make you begin to wonder why you are considering franchising in the first place if it is fraught with so many potential difficulties. It is fair to say though that most franchisees are, in general, compliant with the franchise agreement in all areas. However, you do need to have monitoring systems in place to spot the odd one who may not be.

PROTECTING YOUR INCOME

Given that many franchisors' income is dependent upon a proportion of the franchisees' income, their income stream is at risk if the franchisees under-declare their own income and therefore their liability to pay the franchisor's proportion. Most franchisors would say that by and large they believe they are victims of only minor instances of under-declaration from a proportion of franchisees. In fact there is a view in franchising circles that 'if your franchisees are not trying to rip you off they are not entrepreneurial enough!' While not necessarily subscribing to this view, we feel it does indicate that franchisors almost expect a degree of under-declaration. The key issue though is deciding what is an acceptable level and what is unacceptable. It is arguable that to introduce monitoring systems that would identify even the smallest level of under-declaration would be prohibitively expensive to install and manage. It is necessary, therefore, to provide a balance between protection of your income and the cost of such protection.

While structuring your franchise offer you will have given considera-tion to these monitoring systems and introduced relevant checks and cross-checks to identify instances of loss of income.

PROTECTING YOUR CUSTOMERS

To ensure that you protect your customers from 'rogue franchisees' you will need to have a clear understanding of the principles of customer care that you wish to have applied in your business. You will then need to ensure that all franchisees and, where appropriate, their staff, understand and subscribe to these principles. This could well form a section within your operations manual or may be documented separately as a customer care process.

The two most significant areas of customer care relate, firstly, to the standards of delivery of the product or service and secondly – if those standards aren't applied, leading to customer complaints – to the recovery process to guarantee a satisfied customer. It is perhaps the second of these that needs most careful consideration.

Within your own business you will have procedures and processes to be followed in the event of customer dissatisfaction. In many cases these may include putting the matter right, to the customer's satisfaction, even if you believe that their complaint is unjustified. You may well follow the principle that 'the customer may not always be right but they are always the customer!' You will have recognised that although it may cost you money it is a small price to pay for having resolved a complaint and retained a satisfied customer.

You will wish your franchisees to follow similar principles but experience suggests that franchisees who do not understand and subscribe to the basic principle of 'finding and *keeping* profitable customers' may be reluctant to spend their 'hard-earned money' on an 'unreasonable customer'. It is important, therefore, for franchisees to understand that giving a refund or replacement product is a small price to pay for keeping a customer while a refund given with bad grace is likely to aggravate the situation further.

It will be important to develop a process whereby adherence to your customer care policy can be monitored.

PROTECTING OTHER FRANCHISEES

We have already discussed how any damage to the brand can potentially affect everyone who trades within that brand. Any franchisee who fails to deliver the brand promise completely is indirectly damaging every other franchisee's business. Even though they may be in a different territory it is well accepted that bad news travels fast and a long way.

PROTECTING FRANCHISEES FROM THEMSELVES

We have said previously that most franchisees are very naive in business matters when they first establish their business. Initially, they will follow the franchise system to the letter. However, as they become more knowledgeable about the business many will be tempted to introduce variations which they will consider as 'improvements' to the system. What they forget is that when they joined the franchise it was because it had a proven business format that was likely to deliver them a successful business. They now believe that they can improve on that system in spite of having only a few months' experience in comparison to the many years' experience offered by the franchisor.

It is at this point that they need to be protected from themselves and monitoring processes put in place to identify non-adherence to the system principles.

MONITORING PERFORMANCE AGAINST STANDARDS

Monitoring performance is not simply being aware of what the franchisee is doing. It involves checking the franchisee's actions and activities against a series of previously prepared standards. These standards are typically defined in three key areas:

- the business plan, which identifies what is planned to be done;

- the franchise agreement, which states what must be done by both parties;

- the franchise operations manual, which states how it should be done.

It is important, therefore, to identify the standards that are contained within these documents that relate to the areas previously identified as requiring monitoring.

The business plan

The business plan contains two specific types of information that can be identified as possible standards for the purpose of monitoring performance:

- financial forecasts, with which actual financial performance can be compared;

- proposed business development activities such as marketing, identifying new target markets, asking for and following up referrals etc.

Perhaps the easiest and most productive of these to monitor are the financial forecasts.

Financial forecasts and achieved results

In the past, franchisors often had to rely on franchisees submitting a variety of reports before the franchisor had a clear picture of what was happening in the franchisee's business. Now, with the increasing use of information technology, the franchisor can often have access to detailed information about a franchisee's financial performance on a day-to-day or even hour-to-hour basis.

Typically the key financial information to be monitored with be:

- gross sales/income;
- achieved gross margin;
- costs/expenses;
- net profit;
- the level of the franchisee's salary or drawings;
- stock or purchase levels;
- cash flow.

By regularly monitoring these areas the franchisor can often identify potential problems long before they might become a danger to the business. The financial performance can also act as an indicator to what other activities possibly need closer scrutiny.

- **Gross sales/income**. Perhaps the simplest and most crucial measure. If the franchisee is failing to achieve the sales forecasts contained within the business plan it is almost certain that they will not achieve the level of profitability originally forecast. Where sales are below those forecast it should give rise to further investigation to determine the cause for the discrepancy. This might highlight, for example, that the business development activities, marketing etc., are not being completed in the way outlined in the business plan and/or the franchise operations manual. If these marketing activities are lacking it provides the opportunity for the franchisor to investigate with the franchisee why they are not taking place. If all the marketing requirements are being fulfilled it may indicate that the franchisee is not as competent in sales techniques as he needs to be to make full use of the leads or enquiries generated by that marketing. It may be that the original forecasts simply prove to have been too optimistic for the territory. It may be that the franchisee is failing to record accurately all the sales he is making because his administration is not up to date. Or it may be that sales are being fraudulently under-declared. I put this possibility as the last in the list to emphasise that it is perhaps the least likely cause although a cynical franchisor might choose to believe this is the most likely option and spend time investigating that at the expense of time better spent considering the other possible causes.

In any of these circumstances it is not sufficient simply to identify what the problem is: action must be taken to rectify it where possible. If the lower sales levels are the result of some form of inactivity on the part of the franchisee then the franchisor must encourage greater activity. If they result from the franchisee lacking skills then further training must be undertaken. If it appears that the forecasts were optimistic then consideration must be given to the forecast for the rest of the period and amendments made to the business plan. This may, in itself, then produce a need for further action to adjust other outcomes of the forecast, particularly in relation to cash flow and funding requirements.

- **Achieved gross margin**. Where the achieved gross margin, relative to the level of achieved sales, is lower than anticipated it may suggest that the franchisee is discounting the price of the product or service in an effort to increase sales. Where this is the case it immediately calls into question whether the sales levels being achieved, which might meet or exceed forecast, are commercially realistic or will fall when the product or service is sold at full margin. A reduced margin may also indicate that the franchisee is suffering from an unacceptable level of wastage or stock loss. In a restaurant or food service situation it may suggest the portion control is inadequate. Each franchisor will know from their own experience where these reductions in margin are most likely to be occurring and should start their investigations there. Once the reasons have been identified actions should be taken to rectify the situation.

- **Cost/expenses**. The profitability forecast will have identified likely and acceptable levels of each area of cost in the business as well as the profile of the timing of those expenses. These should be compared item by item with the amount and timing of the actual expenditure and where necessary remedial action be taken.

- **Profit**. Problems in any of the above three areas will produce a reduction in net profit. Not only will this have an effect on the return on the investment and the possible viability of the business but it might also have a detrimental effect on cash flow and therefore on the ability of the franchisee to pay their creditors and service any loan.

- **Franchisee salary or drawings**. I have stated previously that most franchisees are financially unaware or naive in business matters. I have seen examples of franchisees who, suddenly finding that they have substantial cash funds available in their bank, choose to increase their levels of drawings, or purchase that Porsche they have always wanted. They have clearly been unaware of (or have chosen to ignore) the fact that, for example, a large amount of the cash in the bank belongs not to them but to HM Customs and Excise for VAT, and is due to be paid in a few weeks' time.

In working with franchisees I have often encouraged them to distinguish between their salary and the profitability of the business. Their salary should be commensurate with the job they are doing. If they are managing a retail shop they should earn the going rate for such a manager. If they are selling directly business to business they should have a salary related to that of an employed salesperson in the same sector. This policy ensures that the profit generated by the business can be clearly identified and measured against the investment involved. While both profit and salary may belong to the franchise, the business should have first call on the profit.

- **Stock or purchase levels**. Where the franchisee purchases stock for resale to customers, if the levels of stock held and the purchases made vary from the norm, this can have a detrimental effect on the business. Insufficient stock and the business may not be able to satisfy the requirements of all its customers; too much stock and there will be a detrimental effect on the cash flow.

- **Cash flow**. This is perhaps the most critical item to be monitored, and the one which most often first raises awareness of issues in other areas. Cash availability falling below the forecast should immediately give cause for concern. It may result from reduced sales levels, lower margins, increased costs, increased drawings, overbuying – all the problems identified above. It may result from poor credit control where sales are made on credit. Equally it may result from the franchisee not having put the planned investment into the business or having withdrawn some of it at a later date. Poor cash flow provides probably one of the greatest risks to franchisee and franchisor.

Most franchises make provision in their franchise agreement for their franchisees to submit financial information in the form of regular management accounts and annual audited accounts. However, our experience tells us that they often fail to insist on the submission of this information in the early days of the franchise. They may fear alienating franchisees by requiring access to what they see as their personal financial information. They may not understand the importance of monitoring the financial performance of their franchisees, or worse still not be able to recognise the warning signs that such information could produce. They may simply be too busy trying to recruit more franchisees to worry much about those they have signed up. However, sooner or later, perhaps after a franchisee has got into financial difficulties, they recognise that they need the information to monitor the franchisees' performance. At that point they almost invariably find it difficult, if not impossible, to get full compliance in this area as many of their franchisees will be reluctant to pass on the information when previously it has apparently not been needed.

Monitoring the detailed financial performance of franchisees is probably the most efficient way to identify areas of non-performance or non-compliance. Failure to do so will put both franchisee and franchisor at increased risk of financial problems or even failure.

Business development activities

In growing their core business franchisors will have identified those activities that produce the best results in terms of business growth. These will all have been systemised and included in the operations manual. In many cases there may be proven measures that can be applied to these activities. In businesses where sales are initially generated by cold-calling potential customers there are likely to be known ratios to measure this activity. For example x number of phone calls will produce y number of sales meetings that ought to produce z level of sales. In these types of business the failure to achieve forecast sales levels can almost always be identified as the result of insufficient activity at the first stage of the process.

One UK franchise has a key measure that gives them a clear indication of the activity of the franchisees and their likely levels of sales. Key to their marketing activity of winning new customers is to provide potential customers with a free sample of the product and then follow up with a call to see what the customer felt about the product. Their experience tells them that such activity results in a certain percentage of those trying the product becoming a customer and there is a high level of repeat business generated from each customer. They require their franchisees to report on how many free samples they have given in each trading period. This gives them a clear indication not only of the activity that the franchisee is putting into building the business but also the level of sales they are likely to achieve in the coming months.

Such a simple measure but a powerful indicator of success.

The franchise agreement

The franchise agreement, like virtually all legal contracts, is written in a style and language that most people other than lawyers find hard to understand. Yet it is important that everyone connected with the franchise support team should know, in detail, what is contained within the agreement since it is one of the documents that contains standards against which you will wish to monitor performance. Equally you must remember that the agreement also contains details of the franchisor's obligations to the franchisee and is therefore the standard against which your franchisees will monitor your performance.

Most of the day-to-day obligations of the franchisee will be contained within the franchise operations manual. Where performance issues need to be discussed it is, generally, far better for them to be discussed in the context of a franchisee not performing according to the manual rather than the fact that they are in breach of the agreement.

The agreement will contain details of the action to be taken if the franchisee breaches any aspect of the agreement. This may vary from their being given a number of days' notice to remedy the breach where it is less serious, to an immediate dissolution of the contract for serious breaches. It can therefore be seen by the franchisee as a very authoritarian document, which imparts potentially extreme powers to the franchisor including the right to terminate the relationship.

The franchisee–franchisor relationship is such that any failure to perform should first be tackled by a process of persuasion and encouragement rather than by invoking the obligations contained within the agreement. Only where this process of persuasion has failed to produce a change in the franchisee's performance should the franchise agreement be taken out of its drawer and dusted off. It is commonly agreed that by the time the franchise agreement is invoked the relationship with the franchisee has either broken down already or is about to do so.

The franchise operations manual

Whereas the franchise agreement is a document written in legalistic language and embodies a long-term, unchanging contract, the franchise operations manual should be written in a user-friendly language and is able to be revised and updated from time to time. It fulfils a number of purposes.

It is, first and foremost, the blueprint for how the business is to operate. It should contain detailed instructions and information about all aspects of the business. As such it becomes the operational guide and reference book for the franchisee. In doing so it also lays down standards against which the franchisee's performance can be measured and provides the franchisor with the means to encourage the franchisee 'to do the job properly'.

As with the franchise agreement, all of the franchisor's staff who have any role in monitoring performance should be fully conversant with the contents of the operations manual.

HOW IS PERFORMANCE MONITORED AND BY WHOM?

It is important to establish clearly and unequivocally who, within the franchisor's business, has the responsibility for monitoring performance. It is a key part of the franchise support function since it identifies those areas where a franchisee may be failing to deliver and so needs more guidance, support or direction. It is preferable, therefore, that the support manager allocated to any individual franchisee is responsible for the whole monitoring process, even if data for that process is generated by other sections within the franchisor's business. For example the accounts department may collect and summarise financial data from the franchisee but it should also be passed to the relevant support manager for analysis and subsequent communication to the franchisee. This ensures that the information obtained from one monitoring process can be considered in the light of all the other information known about the franchisee and thus prioritised for action.

Each franchise will use different processes to monitor performance but some of the key procedures may include:

- reporting systems;
- field visits;
- customer satisfaction surveys;
- levels of customer complaints;
- levels of customer retention and repeat business;
- levels of referrals and recommendations;
- mystery shopper activities.

Reporting systems

Franchisors may set up a variety of reporting systems to assist them in monitoring franchisees' performance. On the financial side these may range from simple reports on the levels of sales achieved to full monthly management accounts. Other reports may include details of marketing activity, a full list of current customers including the number of new customers generated within the period, sales detail by individual product or service etc.

This information will allow the franchisor to monitor the performance of individual franchisees but will also allow them to produce aggregated reports of the whole network's activity. This will enable them to identify where franchisees are operating outside normal parameters and, if issued to the franchisees, will allow them to check their own performance against their peers'. Performance outside the norm may identify areas where a franchisee is failing but perhaps more importantly where a franchisee is overperforming against the norm. This then enables the franchisor to investigate what it is that the high-performing franchisee is doing, and to communicate the successful strategy to the rest of the network.

Field visits

Field visits by support managers allow the franchisor to see the franchisee in action in the workplace. (See Chapter 18 on getting the best from field visits.)

Customer satisfaction surveys

The results of customer satisfaction surveys can be a powerful way of identifying whether a franchisee is performing to the standards laid down in the franchise. Carefully worded surveys that seek information on the key attributes of the franchise are critical to the process. Bland questions such as 'Was the service good?' give no points of reference for the customer to provide an objective judgement. (See Chapter 20, page 197 for more on customer satisfaction surveys.)

Levels of customer complaints

Complaints from a dissatisfied customer will normally be addressed in the first instance to the franchisee. This may mean that, without a formal procedure requiring the franchisee to inform the franchisor of all customer complaints, the franchisor only hears about those complaints that the franchisee fails to resolve to the customer's satisfaction. This will, hopefully, be only a fraction of the total number of complaints but that may hide the failures of a franchisee who continually underperforms in the eye of the customer but who nevertheless later puts the matter right to the customer's satisfaction. It is a useful process, therefore, to require the franchisee to report all instances of dissatisfaction and also details of how the matter was resolved.

Levels of customer retention and repeat business

Analysis of customer records can produce information on customer retention and levels of repeat business. Both of these measures are powerful indicators of the quality of service, product and customer care. They are particularly easy to measure where the customer is clearly identified at the point of sale, for example by the issue of an invoice. However, even retailers can identify the number and level of purchases made by a customer if some form of loyalty programme is developed. The loyalty cards given by many of the large supermarkets may return a proportion of the purchase value to the customer although by its very nature this 'discount' will have to have been considered when setting the basic price of a product. The real value for the supermarket, however, is not the aid that it provides to customer retention but rather the information that can be gathered on the extent and type of the customer's purchasing that might allow more direct marketing activity to that particular customer.

Levels of referrals and recommendations

In many businesses referrals and recommendations are a key way of generating new business. The simple process of asking existing customers for referrals and asking new customers about how they heard about the business can provide useful information on the standard of service provision and thus customer satisfaction.

Mystery shopper activities

While there are companies that specialise in providing mystery shopper services it is often possible to do such surveys in-house by the use of company staff with whom the franchisee or his staff may not be familiar. Visits to the franchise outlet will allow the mystery shopper to experience not only the service offered but also the ambience of the premises. Are they clean and attractive to the customer? Are the branding or promotional materials being used properly?

Regular, comprehensive and consistent monitoring of franchisees' performance is critical to the success of any franchisor's business. The performance of the franchisor's business is directly related to the performance of its franchisees. By identifying instances of both good and bad performance the franchisor will provide itself with the information needed to encourage and support the franchisees to achieve higher levels of sales and profitability, thus ensuring increased sales and profitability for itself.

17

How to motivate franchisees

One of the most often-quoted benefits of developing a franchise network is that it provides the franchisor with a team of local business owners who will be dedicated to growing their own business for the personal rewards that it offers. The assumption is that they will be more highly motivated than an employed manager whose only financial interest in the business is the salary that it provides. It therefore often comes as a surprise to franchisors when they discover that franchisees are often not as totally self-motivated as they might have supposed.

It is important for franchisors to understand that part of the support that it will need to give to its franchisees will be providing continual motivational activities.

The annual NatWest/bfa franchise survey continues to suggest that the biggest bar to the development of a franchise is finding the right number and quality of franchisees. Franchisors generally suggest that the second biggest barrier is when franchisees reach their 'comfort zone' and fail to develop fully the territory that they have been allocated. This is a particular problem if the franchisee has been granted an exclusive right to trade in the territory; a right which in today's practice is more rarely granted. Franchisors are therefore always looking for ways to motivate franchisees to continue to develop their business.

WHAT MOTIVATES FRANCHISEES?

The assumption spoken of in the first paragraph rests on the premise that financial success is what will motivate a franchisee. Moreover it assumes that having invested an often large sum of money in the business the franchisee will wish to get the best possible return on that investment.

As stated in Chapter 4, however, both experience and some recent research suggest that money, while being important to provide for a certain standard of living, is not in itself a very strong motivator. The research suggests that franchisee motivation is driven by success, satisfaction and freedom. Sixty per cent of franchisees questioned claimed to be motivated by the goal of running a profitable business and making money for themselves in the process. It is interesting to note the response identifies the goal of running a profitable business as the motivator, with the money it generates as a secondary factor. Other key motivational factors included 'being your own boss' and 'job satisfaction'.

It is clear, therefore, that the ability to increase the amount of income generated by the business is not a prime motivator, and this would appear to tie up with franchisors' comments about franchisees reaching their comfort zone.

If we are to motivate franchisees to bigger and better things it is clear that we must find some motivational activities that do not simply concentrate on profitability and potential income.

A THEORETICAL APPROACH TO MOTIVATION

Mazlow's Hierarchy of Needs suggests that once the basic requirements of life are met, that is to say the physiological requirements of food and drink and a safe environment in which to live, man has other more social rather than physiological needs. These include the need to belong to a social grouping or society, the need to achieve a degree of esteem within that society and ultimately the opportunity for 'self-realisation' or 'to be the best that he can be'.

The above research among franchisees suggests that this theoretical situation prevails in practice. Once sufficient income is generated to meet the franchisee's lifestyle needs the ability to generate additional income becomes less important. Franchisors must, therefore, seek to discover what other motivators could be used.

THE FRANCHISEE LIFE CYCLE

Most franchisors will be aware of and recognise the concept of the franchisee life cycle. The theory uses the life cycle of a human to demonstrate various stages through which a franchisee is likely to progress during the term of the franchise.

- **The child**

  In this phase, the early months or years of the franchisee's business, he is totally dependent upon the franchisor for help, information and assistance. He recognises and accepts that the franchisor knows far more about the business than he does and accepts and acts upon advice and guidance.

- **The adolescent**

  The child-like state was never going to last for ever, was it? As the franchisee begins to feel more confident and has a better understanding of some parts of the business there is a temptation for them to think that they not only understand everything there is to know about the business but also understand it a lot better than the franchisor! This is the point at which the franchisee is most likely to try a little 'muscle-flexing' to see just how far they can go in the relationship. Just as in families the adolescent stage may be almost non-existent or may appear to last well into middle age!

- **The adult**

  Hopefully the franchisee achieves this level of maturity without too much conflict with the franchisor during the adolescent period. This is the beginning of the period when the adolescent who thought his parents knew absolutely nothing suddenly discovers that they seem to have learned an awful lot in a very short period of time. The relationship has matured. The franchisee once again accepts the role of the franchisor and will often seek out the very guidance and help that was resisted during the adolescent stage.

- **Middle age**

  This is potentially the period that is most likely to correspond to what the franchisor describes as the franchisee's comfort level.

Appropriate levels of earning have been reached and perhaps the golf course seems to beckon more strongly.

- **Early retirement**
  It is at this point that the franchisor may introduce the concept of 'early retirement' to the franchisee perhaps by introducing a potential purchaser for his business or even suggesting that he sells part of his territory. Equally, at this point the franchisee may reject the proposal and either be stimulated to develop the business further to achieve a better ultimate sale price or may slip even deeper into semi-retirement. This is possibly the worst of all results for the franchisor.

- **Death**
  Not, it is to be hoped, the end of the franchisee's life but certainly the end of his life as a franchisee. The franchisor may invoke the right, provided they have it, not to renew the franchise agreement at the end of the current term. The franchisor's ability to do this and the process that must be followed to do it will be contained within the franchise agreement.

So why is an awareness of the franchisee life cycle important? Because at each stage of the life cycle the franchisee is likely to be motivated by different things and be receptive to different approaches. Given that at any point in the life of a franchised network there are likely to be franchisees at each stage of the franchisee life cycle, the franchisor needs to develop an awareness of each individual's situation and the strategies that are most likely to achieve results.

> There is no one answer to how to motivate franchisees but there are a number of strategies that do appear to work.

KNOW YOUR FRANCHISEES

Spend time learning about every one of your franchisees. Find out what makes them tick, what interests them, what excites them, what they like and dislike doing. You will have to get to know them on both a business and a personal level and by doing so you will begin to fulfil some of the social needs outlined earlier. If you are interested in them as a person, rather than an as opportunity for you to make more money, they will begin to feel part of the society that is your franchise. Moreover as you learn about them you will begin to identify what 'buttons you will need to press' to encourage them to develop their business further. These 'buttons' will change from time to time and the intensity of their reaction to a 'press' will also vary.

Unless you develop a strategy to recognise these motivators and then concentrate your activity around them you are unlikely to be able to effect any change in behaviour.

DEVELOPING MOTIVATIONAL STRATEGIES

Earlier in the chapter we discussed research into franchisee motivation in which franchisees identified that what motivated them were success, satisfaction and freedom. Strategies need to be developed, therefore, that address these issues.

- **Success**

  The concept of what is a successful business will undoubtedly alter from one person to another. For one, a successful business is one that makes sufficient profit to accommodate the owner's lifestyle financial requirements. For another, the measure of success may be a level of profitability that produces an adequate return on the investment. For yet another, success may mean owning the biggest business in the network. For another, success might be having a business where husband and wife can work together and thus spend more time together.

  Perhaps the most important contribution a franchisor can make here is to identify what the franchisee's definition of success is and then help them to achieve it or recognise it when it has occurred. The salesperson's mantra of 'Find out what the customer wants and then show them how you can provide it' is equally relevant within the franchisee–franchisor relationship.

The concept of success centres on the achievement of a goal. Helping franchisees to identify their goals clearly is a key function in the motivational process. These goals may be financially based even though they are not financially driven. That is to say a franchisee may be encouraged to move the business to new levels even though the opportunity for additional earnings is not a key motivator. Most people will respond to a challenge, especially if it is one that they have set themselves.

- **Satisfaction**
  When people refer to 'job satisfaction' they often talk about 'having done a good job', and 'enjoying what I do'. By definition, therefore, lack of job satisfaction can come from a feeling of not having done a good job or not having enjoyed doing it. Within any franchisee operation there will be functions that a franchisee will enjoy and others that they find frustrating or uninteresting. By knowing your franchisees' likes and dislikes you may be able to help them identify potential solutions to the uninteresting or frustrating activities.

- **Freedom**
  This is perhaps the most difficult area for a franchisor to meet their franchisees' objectives. By the very nature of the franchise the franchisee has only limited freedom to operate. They must follow the franchisor's systems in the territories they have been allocated. However, there may be opportunities to enhance the feeling of freedom within the confines of the system.

SOME PRACTICAL MOTIVATIONAL IDEAS

Over the years many practical strategies have been developed by franchisors to help to motivate their franchisees. The most effective of these concentrate upon the notions contained within the theories of motivation relating to social situation, esteem and self-fulfilment linked to the concepts of success, satisfaction and freedom.

Success

Identifying the individual's definition of success
A simple but powerful question in helping to identify a person's definition of success is 'What is important to you?' Once the franchisee has identified these issues the franchisor can help them to concentrate on achieving them. The ability to coach franchisees to recognise both what they wish to achieve and how to go about achieving it is critical in the motivational relationship. Coaching is a process of helping someone to recognise their goals, to take responsibility for achieving them, to identify how they might achieve them and finally, given their commitment, to do whatever is necessary to achieve them. It is not a process of introducing the coach's own goals for the franchisee.

Recognising success
It is not sufficient to assist the franchisee to set and achieve their goals. Once those goals have been achieved or partly achieved the skilled motivator will recognise that achievement. Franchisors traditionally use a variety of strategies to recognise success.

- **League Tables.** Publishing league tables of franchisee performance is probably one of the most commonly used motivational strategies. These league tables recognise the achievements of the best performing franchisees. They can also be motivational for those franchisees who aspire to climb the league tables. It must be recognised, however, that they can also be demotivating for some, especially those who see no opportunity of ever achieving any level of recognition. It is important, therefore, to set different criteria from time to time for the production of the league tables. They could reflect performance in:
  – sales levels;
  – increase on previous year;
  – sales of a new product;
  – new customers won;
  – sales : costs ratio.

In each of these instances different franchisees will be better placed to achieve a leading place in the tables. The new franchisee with a small territory may never feature very high on the sales league table but may have a good chance of featuring in the year-on-year increase category.

- **Awards and prizes.** Many franchisors will operate a system of awards that might include 'Franchisee of the Year', 'Best Newcomer', 'Best Business Builder' or simply awards for achieving certain milestones in business growth. In all of these situations it is important that the judging is objective and it is preferable that the franchisees know and understand the criteria used in making the selections.

- **Mentioned in despatches.** A franchise newsletter is a useful tool not only for communicating information to franchisees but also to recognise individual franchisees' achievements.

- **PR opportunities.** A press release about an individual franchisee's achievements will often be accepted by a local newspaper if there is a good 'human interest' story. Not only will this raise the profile locally of a franchisee's business but it will also provide them with local recognition – a clear step up the 'esteem' ladder. The same article featured in the national press could be even more motivational.

- **ABCD award.** A national, non-franchised, retailer has an ABCD award in its motivational toolbox. This is awarded to any member of staff who is deemed to have performed 'Above and Beyond the Call of Duty'.

- **Recognition cards.** A number of franchises whose franchisees employ teams of staff, e.g. retailers, personal care providers, etc. have adopted recognition cards as a motivational tool. These are simply small slips of card or paper headed 'Thank you to . . . For . . . '. Staff are encouraged to recognise examples of helpfulness from colleagues or particularly good performance of some aspect of their role. At the end of the week the cards are passed to the relevant staff who see that their efforts have been recognised by their colleagues.

- **Letter from the MD.** A simple, short, handwritten note from the MD of the franchisor recognising a particular achievement by an individual franchisee can be a powerful motivator. By the same token a 'Well done' phone call from a franchise support manager can have similar effects.

- **Franchisee conferences/regional meetings.** A well-planned national conference or regional meeting can be an excellent opportunity to motivate franchisees. A proportionate mix of business and pleasure at a conference will remain in the mind for a considerable period of time and will enhance any message that the franchisor may have delivered. Regional meetings where franchisees can meet their peers and exchange ideas and experiences can also be a useful mechanism. In both cases the opportunity should be taken to recognise the success of individual franchisees.

Satisfaction

By recognising success in your franchisees' business you will also be reinforcing in their minds that they 'have done a good job', a key element of the concept of job satisfaction. It is then important to try to help the franchisee to find ways of 'enjoying what they do'. This will involve finding out what they like and dislike about their roles and then trying to find ways of eliminating what they dislike.

Where a franchisee dislikes, for example, the administration involved in the business it is likely that they will firstly neglect it and secondly find it even more dislikeable when they finally have to catch up with a few months' admin. If the franchise system suggests that they should do their administration themselves and the majority or all of their peers do this they may not feel empowered to consider employing someone to do the admin for them. Yet if they did this it would produce more timely and complete administration of the business and also allow the franchisee to spend more time doing what they most enjoy, which might be selling or relationship building. If the franchisor were to suggest this course of action the overall effect on the business and on the franchisee could be considerable. There may even be an opportunity to 'buddy up' two franchisees who have complementary skills and preferred activities. A day spent completing another franchisee's admin could be swapped for a day spent cold-calling on the telephone to try to arrange sales presentations to new customers.

Freedom

While control ensures that a franchise network operates to certain standards it is good practice only to control where necessary and to allow the franchisee freedom to choose, perhaps within clearly defined boundaries, wherever possible.

An example of an opportunity to allow franchisees an element of freedom might come in the choice of vehicle that they must use to deliver the franchise service. A franchisor may believe that it is important that all franchisees operate the same brand of vehicle but is this really necessary? Provided that the vehicle carries the franchisor's livery and is fit for purpose in terms of size, capacity etc. does it really matter whether it is a Ford, or Vauxhall or Mercedes Benz? Most customers of the franchise will only ever see the vehicle operating on their territory and even if they regularly saw other franchisees' vehicles it is more than likely that they would notice only the branding and not the make of vehicle. However, the demotivational effect of a 'Ford man through and through' having to drive a Vauxhall may be considerable.

The success of a franchised network depends totally upon the success of its franchisees. No matter how good the system or product or service, the business will never achieve its full potential if its franchisees are not well motivated. It is a key function of the franchisor and their support staff continually to find ways of motivating their franchisees to strive for success. They will only be able to do that effectively if they know what each individual franchisee defines as success.

> Every franchisee is an individual with individual goals and priorities. The successful franchisor will seek ways of attuning those goals and priorities with those of the network as a whole and must employ a variety of motivational strategies to encourage their franchisees to achieve their mutual goals.

18

How to get the best from field visits

If monitoring franchisees' performance and motivating them to improve their performance are two key functions of the franchisor then the field visit provides an important tool in each of those processes.

Key to the franchise relationship is the ongoing contact and support provided by the franchisor to the franchisee. It is through this support that the franchisor can help the franchisee to develop their business and, therefore, the franchisor's business. This contact and support is delivered through a variety of media ranging from a simple e-mail or telephone call to the visit by a member of the franchisor's support staff to the franchisee's outlet.

A recent survey of franchisees showed that 45 per cent reported having contact with the franchisor at least once a week with a surprising 20 per cent claiming daily contact. The majority of this contact will, more than likely, be on a group basis through e-mails, newsletters, etc. The same survey shows 70 per cent of franchisees describing the support they receive from the franchisor as either good or excellent. The field visit provides an opportunity for this support to be delivered on a face-to-face basis and provides a vehicle for discussions about various aspects of the franchisee's business and the franchise relationship in general.

THE FRANCHISE SUPPORT TEAM

Research suggests a large variation between franchisors in relation to the number of support team members per franchisee. This will depend on a number of factors including the complexity of the franchise operation, the budget available from the franchisor's income and the maturity of the network. In the early years of network development the ratio of support staff to franchisees is likely to go through a 'wave' formation as the first support manager initially has only a small number of franchisees to support, then this number increases to the point where an additional member of staff is required, at which point the number per support staff member declines sharply, only to begin the upward climb again. Equally, in a well-established network with mature, successful franchisees some of the support functions needed in the early years will no longer be required and ratios may be allowed to increase. However, the nature of the role is so key to the development of the franchisee–franchisor relationship that both the quality and quantity of the support must never be allowed to slip below the level where the quality of the support is compromised.

Perhaps the most important members of the support staff are those field support managers who regularly visit the franchisees at their outlets. The role played by these support managers varies greatly from one franchise to another and this is sometimes reflected in the titles given to them. These range from the all-encompassing 'Franchise Manager' to the slightly more specific 'Business Development Manager' or the even more specific 'Technical Support Manager'. Even the titles given to these members of the franchisor's staff can influence how they are viewed by the franchisee and may influence the relationship between the support manager and the franchisee.

- 'Franchise Manager' may be taken to imply that the role is to manage the franchisee. If this is truly the purpose of the role it is likely to cause resentment from the franchisee who may have left employment for the franchise in order to become master of their own affairs and escape aspects of being closely managed that so often go with being an employee;

- 'Business Development Manager' may imply that the support staff member's role is to build the franchisee's business for them. Unless this is clearly the case the franchisee may mistakenly feel that they can rely on the Business Development Manager to provide all the development function needed and may abdicate all responsibility for marketing and sales development;

- 'Technical Support Manager' is perhaps least open to misinterpretation as it is a clear statement that the role is to provide technical support to the franchisee provided, of course, that that is what the role really is.

Arguably, the all-encompassing 'Franchise Support Manager' or 'Field Support Manager' provides the best description of the typical role. Most franchise support managers have very varied roles that come into play to greater or lesser degrees depending on the franchisee that is being visited.

THE ROLE OF THE FRANCHISE SUPPORT MANAGER

The role of the typical franchise support manager will be varied and will be both franchisee and franchisor facing. It is likely to encompass the roles of messenger or communicator; business consultant; system expert; business builder; trainer and coach; and, finally, compliancy officer.

- **As a messenger/communicator** the support manager will play a key role in communicating new ideas, strategies and policies from the franchisor to the franchisees. While these may often be communicated by other media like newsletters or changes to the operations manual the opportunity for a face-to-face discussion with the franchisee on these issues will provide the chance to ensure that the franchisee has both received the earlier communication and understood it, both in terms of the desired outcome in changes of behaviour and the reasons for the proposed changes. It is simply not enough for the franchisor to say 'We're now going to do it this way so get on with it.' The franchisee (and for that matter any employee) is more likely to respond positively to proposed changes if they can clearly understand the reasons for those changes.

This communication must not simply be one way. The support manager also has a role to play in communicating both ideas and possible concerns from the franchisee to the franchisor. It is at this point that the support manager may sometimes feel something of a 'piggy-in-the-middle', being pressured from both sides. If he has an open, positive relationship with both franchisee and franchisor he should be able to fulfil both elements of this communication role honestly and ethically.

- **Acting as a general business consultant** to the franchisee the support manager has an important role to play in both educating the franchisee and identifying areas for business improvement. Although it may not take much knowledge to have a better understanding of business matters than the new franchisee (who, as stated already, typically has only a limited understanding of what is required to run a successful business) it is important for the support manager to keep himself fully abreast of the changes and potential changes in the way the franchisee's business can be developed. The franchisee's limitations need to be compensated for by the knowledge and understanding of the support manager.

  Whether in the areas of sales development, margin improvement, controlling expenses, or monitoring cash flow, the knowledgeable business consultant can make a great contribution to both the franchisee's and the franchisor's businesses. Information on Key Performance Indicators or benchmarking with other franchisees will provide both a focus and also an incentive for changes in the level or direction of activity. However the support manager should always demonstrate that their efforts are directed towards developing the franchisee's business. The benefit for the franchisor will become an outcome of this rather than simply a driver for it.

- **Being an expert in the franchise system** is perhaps less important than having expertise in it. By this I mean that the support manager does not need to have expert skills in every activity of the business. He or she does though need to understand what is required to drive those activities successfully and be able to give advice from a position of knowledge and understanding. The support manager is more likely to gain the respect of the franchisee if they can demonstrate in a practical way that they can contribute to the growth and development of the business in a particular area of expertise. This can best be demonstrated during a field visit by taking some active part in working with the franchisee or their staff on a particular project or issue.

- **Identifying ways of building the business** with the franchisee and then making practical efforts to implement them will enhance the relationship between franchisee and support manager. If the franchisee sees that the support manager is genuinely interested in and committed to the success of their business they are more likely to listen to any advice offered or suggestions made.

- **The role of the support manager as trainer and coach** will develop over the lifetime of the relationship with the franchisee. In the early stages of the relationship the support manager will be responsible for much of the ongoing skills training required by the franchisee. This may be to reinforce aspects of the initial induction training or to introduce new skills and procedures that were omitted from that training. As the relationship develops and the franchisee becomes proficient in the core skills the personal development role of the support manager may move more towards that of a business coach. While training may be relevant to subjects where the franchisee has low levels of competency, coaching becomes more relevant where the franchisee has competency in an area but perhaps lacks motivation.

The support manager may also be able to add value to the business by acting as a trainer for the franchisee's staff. This must be done only with the agreement of the franchisee. It is generally recognised that an external third party can often have a greater influence on changing behaviour than someone closely associated with a business.

- **The role of compliancy officer** often appears to be paramount in the view of some franchisors. It is true that the very nature of franchising requires compliancy with the systems and thus consistency of product or service for the consumer. However, it is important that compliancy should not be seen as an end in itself. If this is the case the franchise support manager will be required to concentrate most of their activities on what will be seen as a negative issue by the franchisee and will reduce the time that can be spent on some of the positive activities listed above. Compliancy is rarely an issue where franchisees are well motivated and successful. It is the natural outcome of such a state.

There will though always be some requirement for monitoring compliancy especially where there is a double requirement to be compliant not only with the franchisor's system but also with the requirements of an external regulatory body. In both cases it is far better to encourage the franchisee to make their own compliancy checks on a regular basis. In this way compliancy will become an everyday issue rather than something that is just checked during a field visit.

THE ROLE OF THE FIELD VISIT IN THE FRANCHISE RELATIONSHIP

The field visit provides a great opportunity to enhance the relationship between the franchisee and the franchisor. By their very nature though they are relatively infrequent. It is important to ensure, therefore, that when they do occur full use is made of the opportunity. This will be achieved only if the visits are well planned and well structured.

During the field visit there can be a number of opportunities to enhance the franchise relationship by:

- identifying ways to improve franchisee profitability;
- providing a forum for open and honest communications;
- bringing an external view on all aspects of the business.

These will best be achieved when the franchisee has complete confidence in the relationship with the support manager.

- **Advice that will help improve profitability** should be irresistible for any franchisee. The astute support manager should have such a clear understanding of the franchise system and its benefits that they can always find an opportunity to suggest ways of improving the business. They will be aware that franchisees can often dismiss such advice if it is based solely on improving sales, as they may feel that the sole purpose is to improve the franchisor's revenue. Where advice focuses initially on improving profitability at the current level of sales it will be apparent that the immediate benefit is to the franchisee.

  This advice might include ways of improving margin by, for example, encouraging the franchisee to look for other ways of closing a difficult sale other than by offering a discount. There may be an opportunity to improve the return on investment by helping the franchisee to operate with lower levels of stock. Benchmarking business expenses levels against those of other franchisees may highlight areas where savings could be made. Examining levels of stock losses through either waste or pilferage may identify further opportunities to improve profitability. The list is almost endless and support managers should consider this function as a key part of their role.

- **By providing an opportunity for open and honest communication** the support manager will often be able to recognise potential areas of conflict between franchisee and franchisor and seek ways of resolving the issues before they become major stumbling blocks. In providing this forum, support managers must have the confidence of the franchisees otherwise the latter may be reluctant to raise areas of concern. They must be able to empathise with the franchisee while also remaining loyal to the franchisor. Where sensitive issues are raised, the support managers must be confident in their ability to communicate the issues back to the franchisor in a positive and unedited format. In order that they are able to do this, the franchisor needs to be prepared to listen to such issues even though they may feel that they are unfounded or unreasonable. Above all else the support manager needs to be confident that there will be no attempt to 'kill the messenger'.

The field visit allows the support manager an opportunity to witness at first hand what really happens out in the field and to report back to the franchisor on the practical application of theoretical aspects of the franchise system. While all modifications or improvements to the operating system should have been tested in pilot outlets it sometimes happens that when they are introduced to the rest of the network operational issues arise that were not recognised in the testing stage. It is important that such issues are reported back to the franchisor so that further modifications can be made where necessary.

- **Familiarity with their local situation** often means that it is difficult for a franchisee to look objectively at their business. The support manager, however, can bring an objective, external view to the business and can often recognise or observe situations that are no longer visible to the franchisee because they have lived with them on a day-to-day basis. These may range from basic physical aspects like light bulbs that need replacing or premises that need redecorating to more serious examples of staff 'cutting corners' and not providing the level of service for customers dictated by the franchise system.

Support managers can also help franchisees identify and come to terms with situations that the franchisee is perhaps shying away from because of personal relationships. Where a staff member has become a personal friend of the franchisee but is now not performing to an acceptable level the franchisee may be reluctant to acknowledge or rectify the situation. The support manager, who has no such personal involvement, can be instrumental in helping the franchisee come to terms with the situation and guide them towards a solution to the problem.

PLANNING THE FIELD VISIT

Announced or unannounced?

There are franchisors that believe all field visits should be unannounced. They believe that only in this way can they be certain of seeing the franchisee's operation the way it operates from day to day rather than in the way it might operate when the franchisor's staff are present. While this may be true the unannounced visit has a number of disadvantages.

- It can appear to the franchisee that the sole reason for unannounced visits is to try to catch them out. By its very nature this eliminates any element of trust, as it seems to assume that the franchisee will not be operating the franchise system correctly. This lack of trust will do little to enhance the franchise relationship and may even result in the relationship becoming adversarial rather than co-operative.

- There is a possibility that the franchisee might not even be present at the time of the visit or may not have sufficient free time to engage with the support staff in a meaningful way because of other commitments. This will prove to be a waste of the support manager's time and will result in a missed opportunity to add value to the franchisee's business. In the absence of the franchisee it would be unwise of the support manager to continue with any element of the visit.

- The franchisor may wish to discuss some particular aspect of the business, for instance comparing actual financial performance with the business plan but the information needed to support this discussion may not be available at the premises being visited.

There is clearly a role for the unannounced visit where the franchisor reasonably suspects the franchisee of being in breach of some aspect of the franchise agreement, such as using unauthorised products or practices, and needs to collect evidence of this. However, in most cases more benefit will be derived from the visit if both franchisee and franchisor have an opportunity to plan for it.

Where a franchisor nevertheless wishes to include unannounced visits as part of the support programme it is important that their rationale should be explained to the franchisees so that they understand the positive elements of such visits. If no positive elements can be found then serious consideration should again be given as to whether they should be part of the process.

Planning the visit

The activities involved in planning and preparing for the visit include:

- booking the visit;
- setting an agenda;
- preparing any information needed;
- reviewing previous action plans.

Time spent on planning and preparing will ensure that the most effective use is made of both the franchisee and franchisor's time.

- **A mutually convenient time should be agreed** for the visit both in terms of the date and also the amount of time that is likely to be involved. Support staff should always be conscious of the fact that time spent by them on a visit is time spent doing their job, whereas time spent by a franchisee on a visit may be time spent keeping him away from doing his job. Visits, therefore, should not involve more time than is absolutely necessary. Where there is an option of different venues, consideration should be given to which venue will be more suitable for the purpose of the meeting or more convenient for the franchisee.

  The franchisee should be encouraged to ensure that, where necessary, staffing levels are such as to enable him or her to be available for the meeting without prejudicing customer service. Consideration should also be given to whether any other member of the franchisee's staff or any other person involved in the business, for example the accountant, will be required to join the meeting. This will obviously be dictated by the agenda for the visit.

- **An agreed agenda** will allow both parties to get the fullest benefit from the visit. The support manager may have specific matters that they wish to discuss during the visit but should always offer the franchisee the opportunity to add any subject to the agenda that he or she wishes to form part of the visit.

  As with most business meetings the first item on the agenda is likely to be a review of any action plan agreed at a previous meeting. This may be followed by a number of core tasks such as a review of sales, profitability and cash flow against financial forecasts; elements of performance benchmarking; marketing and promotional activities etc. There may be a need for the support manager to communicate and discuss new or modified operating systems and check that the franchisee is conversant with the changes.

Where a franchisee wishes to add a subject to the agenda, care should be taken not to relegate it to a position where it always follows the franchisor's agenda items. Firstly, this gives the franchisee the impression that their items are considered less important; secondly, if the franchisee's subject involves any aspect of discontentment with the franchisor, they are unlikely to be responsive to any other matter until they have had a chance to raise their own concerns.

- **Both parties should prepare for the visit.** Where specific information is required to support discussions the franchisee and the support manager should agree who is to prepare it. This can then be forwarded to both parties prior to the visit.

- **Reviewing previous action plans** prior to the visit will give both the franchisee and the support manager the opportunity to finalise any unfinished activity before the visit.

The day of the field visit

The timing and likely length of the visit will already have been determined. It is important, therefore, to make every minute count once the day of the visit arrives.

- **Punctuality is one of the simplest common courtesies** and it goes without saying that the support manager should arrive at the agreed time: better still they should arrive sufficiently early that they have some time to make a final review of the agenda and prepare themself mentally for the visit. This is particularly valuable if they have already spent a long and possibly frustrating time behind the wheel of the car. This period of mental preparation will allow the manager to ensure that he is in a positive frame of mind for the start of the visit.

- **Always seek a positive opening to the visit.** The support manager should look to find some aspect of the franchisee's business about which they can make a positive, perhaps congratulatory, comment. A recent good week's trading, a recently won new customer or contract, an attractive product display can all provide opportunities to get the visit off to a positive start.

- **While always being conscious of making the best use of time**, some time should be allowed for 'settling in' rather than moving straight to the agenda for the visit. The support manager may have allowed themself some time for mental preparation, the franchisee may not be so well prepared.

- **As the formal element of the visit begins** it is a good idea to take a moment to confirm the agenda and check whether the franchisee has any other matters they wish to include. Some pressing matter may have arisen that should override all other agenda items. If this is left until the end of the visit there may be insufficient time to deal with it properly.

- **The second courtesy** that the support manager should afford the franchisee is to give him or her their total attention. For most people the key to this will be firstly to switch off their mobile phone! While now considered an invaluable business tool, the mobile phone has become one of the most intrusive items in modern life. By making a point of switching off the phone in the presence of the franchisee, the support manager will not only signal that the franchisee has his full attention but will also provide an explanation of why their phone might go to voice-mail if the franchisee calls them on a subsequent occasion.

- **As the various agenda items are dealt with** it can be helpful to try to break up the day by changing location, perhaps by dealing with some items over a cup of coffee in a local coffee shop. This may also provide an opportunity to visit a competitor's outlet or to meet one of the franchisee's customers.

- **By looking for an opportunity to do something practical** for the franchisee the support manager can demonstrate not only that they know how to do the job but also that they have an interest in helping the franchisee to develop their business. While a franchisee may not be able to mystery shop a local competitor the support manager, who will be unknown to the competitor, could do it for them.

- **If the support manager needs to provide feedback** to the franchisee about some aspect of the business they should take care to ensure that it is not personal. If criticism is required it should be directed towards the situation or performance rather than the person.

- **Making a written record** of the issues discussed during the visit provides both the franchisor and the franchisee with a useful reminder of the meeting. This may also include any elements of an action plan that has been agreed.

- **The final exit**, like the entrance, should be on a positive note.

After the visit

The support manager should forward a copy of the relevant part of the visit record to any member of the franchise team who may need to be made aware of any issues or who needs to be part of the action plan. They should then follow this up with whatever discussions are necessary to complete the process of communication between franchisee and franchisor and ensure that any elements of the action plan that depend on other people's activity are completed in a timely manner.

The field visit is an important tool in the franchisor's management system. Used well it can enhance the franchise relationship and provide varied benefits to both franchisee and franchisor. Used badly it can permanently damage the relationship, leading, ultimately, to its possible breakdown.

19
How to manage franchise unit resales

'As franchising as a business format continues to mature, it is understandable that greater numbers of retirements and investment realisations will occur.' (NatWest/bfa United Kingdom Franchise Survey)

One of the benefits of franchising is that, although the franchised outlet forms part of the franchised network and has a close relationship with the franchisor, it nevertheless is owned by the franchisee who retains the right, subject to certain conditions, eventually to release the capital value of the business by selling it. This is the process that is known as a franchise resale. Once a franchised network is complete, that is to say all territories have been allocated, the only way that a potential franchisee can join the network is by buying an existing business from a franchisee.

Research work completed in 2004 suggested that within five years over half the franchisees entering the sector for the first time would be buying an existing business. In reality this situation was virtually reached by 2006. This increase in resales has both influenced and been influenced by a subtle change in attitudes towards the resales process.

A NEW WAY OF THINKING
For some time the concept of resales was seen as a somewhat negative process particularly by new franchisors. Resales often resulted from a failure of a franchisee or a discontented franchisee opting out of the

network. Neither of these outcomes would be seen as good news by a franchisor hoping to recruit a relatively large number of franchisees to complete its network. There would be additional pressure to recruit a new franchisee for the territory as existing customers were to be serviced, and it would probably be more difficult to find such a franchisee because of the difficulties encountered by the previous incumbent. In addition, all the activity surrounding this recruitment would be simply in order to maintain the status quo, as the total number of outlets was not being increased. To some degree this negative attitude still prevails with new franchisors that are just beginning to establish their network.

However, as the number of resales taking place has increased, franchisors have begun to have a more positive view of the process.

- **There is recognition that maturity of the network** will inevitably increase the number of resales that occur. As a network matures so will its early franchisees, and retirements are inevitable.

- **As resales occur they demonstrate** to prospective franchisees the level of capital value that can be built up in a successful business.

- **A new franchisee taking over an existing outlet** almost always improves sales substantially. This is probably as a result of a number of factors. The new franchisee will probably come into the business with a level of enthusiasm and verve that the previous franchisee had long since lost. They will presumably only have bought the business because they thought they could improve its performance. Finally they will need to ensure they generate sufficient profit to make a return on what will normally have been a much higher initial investment level than for a green-field opportunity.

- **A resale can provide the opportunity for a franchisor** to split the territory between two new franchisees. This is often a useful option where the initial territory planning resulted in territories that were too large for a franchisee to be able to fully maximise the potential. This split can be achieved either by the franchisor buying the business itself and then selling it on or by introducing to the outgoing franchisee two buyers, each prepared to buy half of the business.

- **An alternative solution for too large territories** is to negotiate with the existing franchisee to release part of their existing territory and sell it along with the goodwill of existing customers to an incoming franchisee. This would allow the existing franchisee to concentrate their efforts on a smaller area to try to develop the level of sales and income previously achieved on the whole territory. At the same time the new franchisee would have the benefit of some existing business but would also need to seek out new customers to bring the outlet up to a viable trading level.

- **On the basis that 'any business is up for sale'** provided that the price is right, a franchisor might use a resale opportunity to negotiate out a poorly performing franchisee whom they would like to terminate but who has not breached the franchise agreement.

THE RESALE PROCESS

Many franchisors tell us that their first resale opportunity occurred earlier in the life of the franchise than they had expected and, moreover, that they were poorly prepared for it. While it may be the last thing you wish to think about when you are establishing your franchise you will need to give some thought to the resale process before the first opportunity occurs.

In just the same way that you will have systemised your business in preparing it for franchising and you will have produced a systemised process for many of the franchise management activities, including recruiting and monitoring franchisees, so you should have a system in place for your first resale.

Once the system has been developed you should ensure that all your franchisees understand at least the basic requirements for starting a resale process.

Why should the franchisor involve itself in the resale process?

The franchisor will have to be involved in the process to some extent, if only in approving the purchaser. However, having a clearly defined process that can be brought into play as soon as a franchisee expresses the wish to sell can make life easier for all parties concerned and contribute to the smooth takeover by the new franchisee. It is a common occurrence that vendors have an inflated view of the value of their business. One of the roles of the franchisor must be to manage the franchisee's expectations right from the outset as to what price is likely to be achieved. This can more easily be done if there is a clear sales process that includes formulae for certain elements of the valuation.

Franchisors must also be aware of the areas in which the prospective purchaser is likely to seek their advice or perhaps rely upon them for information. It must always be remembered that it is extremely difficult and arguably undesirable for a franchisor to distance itself completely from the sales process. However, the more a franchisor is involved the more it must ensure that it acts as an 'honest broker' for both parties to ensure that it cannot be accused of having acted in bad faith either by action or omission.

What is involved in the resale?

In structuring the process consideration must first be given to how the sale is likely to be achieved. Where the outgoing franchisee is a sole trader or partnership it will involve a simple purchase of the assets of the business. However, where the franchisee is a limited company there will be the option of a purchase of the company or simply a purchase of the assets. In many cases the vendor will prefer to sell the company while the purchaser will wish to purchase only the assets. This will obviously be part of the sales negotiation but you will need a process in place that can deal with either option. There is little doubt that a sale of assets is more easily completed than the sale of a company with all the problems and expense of a due diligence investigation.

This is not the place to discuss the due diligence process that a purchaser of a company should instigate. Suffice it to say that they should take independent professional advice. However, some of the activities listed below will undoubtedly form part of a due diligence process as well as being key in a purchase of assets.

Franchisors should be wary of 'guaranteeing' any information that is outside their direct experience or control. For example a purchaser may ask the franchisor to confirm the revenue levels stated in the vendor's accounts. All a franchisor can do in these circumstances is to confirm what information they have received from the vendor. It is not safe to assume that just because a franchisee pays a management services fee based on sales they are more likely to have understated rather than overstated sales figures. When a business is being sold a degree of 'window dressing' may have taken place in order to achieve an enhanced goodwill payment.

What is being sold?

Whether a company is being purchased or simply the business assets, consideration must be given to identifying those assets in order to value them effectively. In many cases a franchisor may need to become involved to a degree in the valuation process, as the incoming franchisee will wish to ensure that the figure being sought by the vendor is reasonable. The process of valuation is, again, not a subject for discussion in this book although there are some comments on reasonable valuations later in this chapter.

Typically a purchaser may be purchasing some or all of the following types of assets:

- stock;
- equipment, vehicles, shopfitting etc.;
- property or leases;
- goodwill;

and in many cases they will be legally bound to take on existing staff under the TUPE regulations.

Each type of asset will bring with it different aspects in which the franchisor may wish or need to be involved.

- **Where stock is being purchased** there are a number of issues to consider. These are broadly covered by the headings, 'Quantity', 'Condition', 'Location' and 'Valuation'.

  - **Quantity.** As in many areas of the sales process the vendor and the purchaser will have different views. The vendor will wish the purchaser to buy all his existing stock as he will have no use for it after the business has been transferred. The purchaser, however, will only wish to buy the minimum needed to continue the business in order to reduce the level of his investment. Either way there will need to be a realistic valuation of the likely level of stock at takeover in order to ensure that the purchaser has sufficient funds in place. It may be necessary to include some process for deferred payment for any stock that remains in the business at the point of sale over an agreed figure.

  - **Condition.** The incoming franchisee will wish to satisfy themself that the stock being purchased is in good condition and suitable for subsequent resale to customers. Areas of potential concern here might include seasonal stock that is out of season, fashion stock that is out of fashion, perishable stock with a limited 'life' and stock which is no longer in perfect condition.

  - **Location.** Where stock is held in a number of locations arrangements will need to be made for contemporaneous stocktakes. However, where these locations are numerous, for example where goods have been placed in a number of retail outlets on consignment invoicing, special arrangements will need to be made for the transfer of ownership of both the stock and outstanding payments.

  - **Valuation.** The incoming franchisee will clearly not wish to pay more for stock than the franchisor's current supply price and, given the potential for downward valuation highlighted above, may well wish to pay considerably less. The franchisor will need to supply the purchaser with current supply prices to assist the valuation. In many cases the franchisor may recommend a valuation formula that is fair to both parties and allows for the variations detailed above.

- **Where the sale will involve the purchase of equipment** the franchisor may again need to be directly involved in providing information to the prospective purchaser. Many franchise agreements will specify the frequency at which equipment needs to be renewed or updated. If the franchise is premises-based there may be a requirement to refit the premises to the then current format before a new agreement is granted or after a certain period of time. This may mean that the existing shop-fit has little or no value if it has to be renewed within a short period of the purchase being effected. The franchisor must be prepared, therefore, to give a clear undertaking to the purchaser about the potential 'life', under the terms of the franchise agreement, of the assets being purchased.

- **Premises-based franchises** have the additional complications relating to the sale of a freehold or the transfer of a lease. Anyone who has ever had to deal with the transfer of a lease will know that it can be both time-consuming and difficult. The incoming franchisee will wish to satisfy themself that there is a sufficient term left in the lease for them to fulfil their obligations under the franchise agreement and also make an adequate return on their investment. If this involves seeking a renewal of a lease before the original term has expired it is possible that the landlord will make attempts to make the new lease more onerous or seek an increase in the rent payable. Whatever difficulties might arise they will be certain to extend the amount of time between finding a willing buyer and being able to complete the sale. It goes without saying that the purchaser must take full legal advice relating to any property matter, particularly relating to any ongoing liability that they may incur relating to the condition of the premises.

- **The valuation of the goodwill attributable to a going concern** is perhaps the area where the vendor and purchaser will have the greatest difference of view! Numerous volumes have been written on this subject and sometimes it might seem that there are as many views as there are volumes. In many sectors there is a 'rule of thumb' that allows a simple initial valuation to be done e.g. one and a half times gross sales or three times adjusted net profit etc. but ultimately the value of any business is what someone is prepared to pay for it.

However, this raises additional issues for the franchisor. If the vendor finds a purchaser willing to pay a price that the franchisor is aware is in excess of the true value of the business what are they to do? To advise the purchaser that the price is unreasonable will result in the vendor being unhappy; to allow the purchaser to pay over the odds may result in the new franchisee failing as a result of the poor returns on the investment. While the franchisor might not be able to tell the purchaser directly that the price is unreasonable they do have the right to refuse to transfer the franchise to an applicant they deem unsuitable. They may feel, therefore, that a purchaser who is prepared to overpay for the franchise does not have the business acumen that the franchisor is seeking. Informing the vendor that they are not prepared to move forward on that basis may result in the outgoing franchisee understanding that they need to accept a more reasonable offer if they are to get the franchisor's agreement to transfer.

If a franchisor allows a franchisee to overpay for a resale they may find that their new franchisee takes the view that the franchisor did not fulfil their obligations to their new franchisee in terms of providing the franchisee with a business opportunity where they had expected to rely upon the franchisor to help them to be successful. Irrespective of whether this might lead to litigation it is hardly the ideal starting point for a new long-term relationship between franchisor and franchisee.

The final acquisition that a purchaser might make is the requirement to take on any existing staff on the same contract as they are currently enjoying with the vendor. TUPE regulations are clear and may sometimes be onerous for the unwary purchaser. The franchisor would be well advised to ensure that the prospective franchisee has taken legal advice on these regulations and the implications for them on the purchase of the business. This could be particularly important where a franchisee has been employing one or more members of their own family in the business.

Having considered the variety of subjects in which the franchisor may become involved during the resale process it is clear that the more a franchisor can develop a structure for this process the better it is likely to be.

Structuring the resale process

The resale process is a tripartite activity involving the vendor, the purchaser and the franchisor. In developing the process, therefore, consideration must be given to the activities in which each party will be involved.

- **The vendor**, the outgoing franchisee, must:

  1. inform the franchisor of his wish to sell. Franchisees should understand that from the point when the decision is made to sell their franchise the process could take many months, if not years to be completed if they are to get the best price for their business. Planning an exit strategy should, therefore, be a long-term process, not something done on a whim. From this point onwards the franchisor will have a role to play in managing the vendor's expectations as to the likely value of the business;

  2. prepare for the sale by gathering together all the information that will need to be provided to a prospective purchaser. If the franchisor has a standard form for the sale prospectus it will ensure that all the relevant information is made available;

  3. set a realistic price. Where a franchisee has clearly unrealistic expectations of the value of the business it can sometimes be useful for the franchisor to encourage them to look at it from the point of view of the purchaser. Suggest that the

franchisee prepare a business plan as if they were the purchaser seeking finance from a bank and see if they feel that the bank would realistically lend against the plan;

4. seek and negotiate with prospective purchasers. In many cases the franchisor may be able to introduce a possible purchaser from applicants that they have already interviewed for a franchise.

- **The Purchaser**, the incoming franchisee, must:

   1. fully investigate all aspects of the purchase. It is essential that the prospective purchaser take independent advice on the purchase. Their financial adviser/accountant will ensure that they investigate all the areas that are relevant to the purchase and seek assurances from relevant sources as to the veracity of the information included in the prospectus;

   2. negotiate a suitable price for the business and satisfy themselves that they can raise the necessary finance;

   3. be acceptable to the franchisor. Where the vendor has introduced the prospective purchaser the franchisor will need to satisfy itself that the prospective franchisee meets their normal recruitment criteria.

- **The Franchisor** must:

   1. manage the vendor's expectations. Getting the franchisee to take a reasonable view on the true value of the business will both speed up negotiations and remove the potential for dissatisfaction at the final price achieved;

   2. approve the buyer on normal recruitment terms including the provision of an initial business plan;

   3. approve the buyer's financial status and the availability of funds as required in the business plan.

   4. offer assurances regarding the vendor's business only where it has verifiable information;

5. facilitate the resale process by having a clear structure available.

- **The Franchisor** may:

  1. introduce a potential purchaser from the applicants for the franchise;

  2. manage the whole process... or stand well back. Where the franchisor does get involved in managing the process it is more likely to proceed with fewer problems although the franchisor must ensure that it does not overstep its responsibilities or leave itself open to litigation for misrepresentation or poor advice;

  3. provide voluntary information on the condition and suitability of any assets being purchased and provide an estimated 'replacement timetable';

  4. act as an 'honest broker' to try to ensure a fair result for both parties;

  5. act as holder of any monies paid as deposit or any monies retained as part of the sales contract against future obligations.

Documenting the process

Once the process has been determined it is important to document it so that each party knows in detail what they are required to do.

Some franchisors will detail the resale process in the franchise operations manual, others will maintain it as a separate series of documents. Whichever route is taken the contents of the process should be communicated to all franchisees at the earliest opportunity.

The documentation could include:

1. an introduction to the resale process for the prospective vendor that encourages them to plan well in advance of any proposal to sell;

2. a standard outline sales prospectus that details what information should be prepared for the potential purchaser and the associated documents e.g. audited accounts, customer lists and details of their most recent purchases etc.;

3. a standard contract of sale;

4. formulae related to the valuation of different types of asset;

5. a timetable outlining the likely time-scale for the completion of all the activities leading to the sale.

A similar set of documents could be prepared for the prospective purchaser. These could include:

1. a copy of the franchise agreement whether or not the purchaser has been approved by the franchisor. If the purchaser has not been approved the process will not need to begin if the prospective purchaser is not prepared to accept the conditions contained within the franchise agreement;

2. details of the approval process including, where necessary, formal application form, details of any checks to ensure the probity or financial standing of the purchaser, the outline timing of meetings with the franchisor and the content of those meetings, the requirement to produce a formal business plan including the capital requirement and how it will be provided;

3. a copy of the standard contract of sale;

4. formulae related to the valuation of different types of asset where applicable;

5. a timetable outlining the likely time-scale for the completion of all the activities leading to the sale;

6. all other standard disclosure documentation as outlined in Chapter 11 'How to recruit franchisees';

7. a formal statement that the prospective purchaser is responsible for taking suitable professional advice related to the proposed purchase and the franchise agreement.

Once this documentation has been prepared it should be regularly reviewed by both the franchisor and its legal and other professional adviser.

RECRUITING FOR RESALES

In Chapter 11 mention was made of the importance of identifying, in a franchisee profile, those skills and attributes that a franchisee would need to possess. The franchisee profile for a resale opportunity is likely to contain most of the original characteristics but may differ in some strategic points.

There is a likelihood that the investment required to purchase a resale opportunity will be considerably larger than that for a start-up, particularly where the outgoing franchisee has built up a successful and profitable business that commands a significant goodwill payment.

At the same time the resale opportunity with its 'guarantee' of the existing levels of profitability may be more attractive to a more risk averse individual. However, the franchisor will wish to assure itself that the prospective purchaser is not simply buying the business to enjoy its current level of activity but rather wishes to build on the present business to achieve even greater levels of sales and profitability.

At the same time it may be that the role of the incoming franchisee will be more about relationship management with existing customers and less about developing new customers than would be the case in a start-up enterprise.

MARKETING THE RESALE OPPORTUNITY

Perhaps the most obvious route for marketing a resale opportunity is to offer it to existing franchisees. Whether this is done by a direct approach to appropriate franchisees or simply by making it known that a resale opportunity has occurred in a particular region and inviting expressions of interest will depend upon the individual situation. However, franchisors must be confident of being able to handle the delicate situation of refusing an existing franchisee permission to take over another, perhaps adjacent, territory. Not all franchisees will have the skills and motivation to develop a multi-outlet business but many may think they have!

Where no suitable internal candidate exists consideration must to be given to whether the existing marketing messages and media will be relevant for the resale opportunity given the possible changes in the franchisee profile. Whereas marketing messages for a start-up opportunity may emphasise the attractiveness of building a business from scratch and the personal satisfaction to be gained from that, the messages aimed at a resale candidate may concentrate on the skills required to take an existing business to new levels of activity.

While one medium may be right to attract candidates with the initial franchisee profile it may be that entirely different media are appropriate to a resale opportunity. Consideration should certainly be given to placing the details with the Franchise Sales Centre, which specialises in franchise resales.

As the resale is specific to a particular geographic location consideration could be given to using local media. While this is not generally a good source of franchisee enquiries when recruitment is aimed at filling a network across the whole country it could be relevant for such a localised sale.

THE MATURE NETWORK

Initially a franchisor will be recruiting only for start-up opportunities. However, as the network matures there will be an increasing need to run a two-track recruitment process, one aimed at start-up franchisees, the other aimed at candidates attracted to and suitable for resales.

Once a franchise network is fully subscribed and resales are the only way of joining the network the process again becomes single track but with the added complication of finding purchasers for a variety of businesses trading at different levels and requiring different levels of investment and management skills. At this point recruiting the right franchisees is perhaps even more critical as the growth of the franchisor's business is totally dependent upon finding franchisees that can substantially increase the turnover of what is now a finite number of businesses. The franchisor can no longer achieve growth by opening new outlets; it is now totally dependent upon the development of the existing outlets.

Sooner or later all franchisors will need to be involved in a franchise resale. The process can be complex and time-consuming. Preparing a structure for the resale process in anticipation of its first being needed will ensure that all three parties to the process, the outgoing franchisee, the incoming franchisee and the franchisor itself, all understand their role in the process.

20

How to monitor your performance as a franchisor

We looked at various ways of monitoring franchisee performance in Chapter 16, but what about monitoring how you are doing as a franchisor? You will want to know how your operation stacks up against your competitors, and against current good practice. You will also want to know how you are doing in the eyes of your franchisees.

There are few things more valuable to a franchisor when building and managing its network than knowing what its franchisees are thinking, for example about such things as the profitability of their franchised outlet, the quality and quantity of the support provided by the franchisor, and how they would like the business to develop into the future.

Similarly, there are few things more valuable to existing and potential franchisees than knowing what existing members of a network think about the franchisor, and all parties want to know what the network's end customers think of the service provided by the franchisees.

Finding a format through which such information can be gathered simply, accurately and cost-effectively has traditionally been difficult, but thanks to modern technology the problem has now been solved and a number of products which can quickly and confidentially measure franchisee, staff and customer satisfaction are available, through the Franchise Support Centre. The results can then be used to identify or anticipate problems, for which solutions can be found, to the benefit of all concerned.

THE FRANCHISED NETWORK HEALTHCHECK

Most businesses that use essential plant and machinery adopt a planned maintenance programme to anticipate and avoid break-downs; most car owners have an annual MOT check done on their vehicle; many consumers have their domestic heating and security systems given an annual once-over; and more and more individuals have regular, planned check-ups to identify potential problems with their health.

The aim of such procedures is to have a specialist assess the situation against either a defined standard, or against the average, and to advise on what actions should be taken to ensure continued optimum operation of the system concerned.

So it is with franchised networks, and conscientious franchisors are increasingly having bespoke checks carried out on their systems every three years or so. An experienced franchise consultant will agree the terms of reference with the franchisor, possibly working from a template which covers all the options and selecting those of particular concern to the network in question. This can include a review of any or all of the following:

- the franchise agreement;
- the operations manual;
- marketing materials and plans;
- competitor analysis;
- recruitment procedures;
- training programmes;
- business plan reviews;
- monitoring systems;
- reporting processes;
- communications programmes;
- financial performance;
- cash flow forecast;
- record keeping;
- support team structure.

Many franchisors will swap information about such matters informally with each other at National Franchise Association or Third Wednesday Club meetings but a confidential review by someone who knows the franchising sector and is aware of recent developments, with a number of bespoke recommendations for improvements, can help to keep an individual franchisor ahead of the game.

Certain industry-wide statistics such as the best media sources of franchise enquiries, total numbers of franchisors and franchisees, and average failure or churn rates are available from the NatWest/British Franchise Association Annual Survey of Franchising; and more confidential matters such as recruitment targets, enquiry conversion rates, ratios of support staff to franchisees, and franchisor staff salaries and rewards come from the Howarth Annual Survey of Franchisors. Bespoke surveys of a particular franchised network are now easily carried out, and these are described below.

FRANCHISEE SATISFACTION SURVEYS

Franchisors have often tried to measure the opinions of their franchisees using traditional paper-based or telephone surveys. The results have always been useful but paper-based surveys tend to get a poor response, and are time-consuming to administer, whereas telephone surveys are expensive and respondents worry about confidentiality.

Internet technology can be used by the franchising sector to measure not only franchisee satisfaction but also that of staff and customers. It was originally used within our business to provide benchmarks of performance among franchisors, by measuring such things as the effectiveness of franchise marketing methods and franchisor staff reward structures. That test went well so we moved on to preparing a franchisee satisfaction survey which can be used by just about any franchisor, anywhere in the world.

If the client goes for the standard package of 30 generic questions the project can go from start to finish of the entire process in about six weeks. The franchisor provides the e-mail addresses of all the people they want to take part in the survey, and these people receive an initial message notifying them that a survey is about to be done, and the opportunity to take part will soon be upon them. This message also assures them that all responses are completely confidential and there is no way that an individual response will be identified to the franchisor.

They then receive another message a day or two before the survey 'goes live', then a final one telling them how to log on and complete the survey. They will then be given a 'window', say seven days, in which to complete the survey, which typically takes about 15 minutes. Although we cannot identify individual responses we do know who has responded so non-respondents receive maybe two reminders before the deadline is up to encourage full participation. Responses are then processed and the survey report is ready for presentation and discussion within about a week.

Of course, there's no point in carrying out a survey if you do nothing with the results, and there are a number of benefits to be gained:

- A survey shows that the franchisor cares about what their franchisees think, and is willing to listen to their opinions. If the results highlight areas of concern then actions can be taken to improve things, and hopefully the results will become apparent when the survey is repeated the following year. What better way of demonstrating that the two parties are working together to improve the business?

- Just as important could be the benefits in recruiting new franchisees. As recruitment becomes ever more competitive, it is another sign of professionalism if a franchisor can demonstrate to their prospects that they carry out regular surveys. Not only that, but if their results are better than those of their competitors, or if their competitors just don't carry out surveys at all, they can use that as a positive feature of their marketing and recruitment process to recruit more franchisees.

STAFF SATISFACTION SURVEYS

The technology can also be used to improve franchisees' businesses.

Some franchisors, and indeed some franchisees, have a large number of employees. Everyone says the people are the most important part of their business but how many franchisees take the time to find out what their staff are thinking? Exactly the same system as that used for the franchisee satisfaction survey can be used to develop an employee survey, and the benefits should be the same in terms of recruitment and retention of good people.

Just as with the franchisee survey, it is possible to base the survey on a generic questionnaire but to add some network-specific questions, or to remove those questions that are not relevant. The skill comes in the preparation which ensures the survey asks the questions – and gets the answers – that are most relevant to the business at the time. Again, an annual repeat can track progress and hopefully demonstrate continued improvement.

CUSTOMER SATISFACTION SURVEYS

The final area where the new technology can help is in customer satisfaction surveys.

For franchisors whose system provides goods or services to business clients a similar system to that already described would typically be used. For those whose franchisees work directly with consumers, the system is less practical but there are some other options. For example, a device can be installed on the shop counter, or the franchisee can carry a mobile version if working on customers' premises, which enables the customer to answer a few simple questions just by pressing the relevant buttons. Responses are transmitted to a central point for processing and evaluation.

Not only are such surveys invaluable in recording overall customer opinions and satisfaction levels but they can highlight those franchisees who are underperforming, and therefore need help, or identify those who doing brilliantly and may have something worth disseminating to the rest of the network.

Any business needs to measure its levels of internal and external effectiveness to make sure its systems, products and services are aligned to staff and customer needs. It also needs to check how it is perceived by its customers, particularly how it rates against competitors.

New technology makes all this easier, cheaper and more effective than ever and franchised networks will benefit greatly from taking advantage of these opportunities. They can help franchisors to recruit more franchisees, to keep their existing franchisees happy, to retain better staff, and to improve customer service.

Further information about surveys can be found at
www.franchise-surveys.com

21

How to avoid legal problems for yourself and your franchisees

This chapter does not seek to offer legal advice – that is the role of your solicitor – but it aims to raise your awareness of areas where either you or your franchisees might put yourselves at risk of litigation or prosecution, and suggest ways of avoiding those risks.

As more and more regulation is imposed on businesses, and individuals appear to become increasingly litigious, the opportunities increase for both franchisor and franchisees to become involved in legal problems. By careful appraisal and assessment of these risks procedures can be put in hand to reduce them.

WHAT COULD BE THE CONSEQUENCES OF PROSECUTION OR LITIGATION FOR YOU OR YOUR FRANCHISEES?

Any legal process, whether litigation between two parties or defending a prosecution, will undoubtedly have both financial and other implications.

- **The financial implications** of responding to a prosecution or litigation can be significant. The legal fees involved in responding to such cases can be substantial, and costs awarded to the other party can increase these considerably. Moreover, if a prosecution or litigation is successful the fines or awards involved will further add to the financial burden.

- **Whether it is the franchisor or a franchisee** that is the object of such actions there will almost certainly be the potential for damage to the brand. If, for example, a franchisee is taken before an industrial tribunal for a breach of employment law any reference to the case in the local press will almost certainly refer to the franchisor's brand name even though it is the franchisee, not the franchisor, who is the object of the action.

- **Where a franchisee is found to be in breach** of some law or regulation it may result in all other franchisees being subject to an investigation. For example, if a franchisee fails to administer his VAT records correctly, resulting in inaccurate VAT returns, this could well result in time-consuming VAT inspections for the other members of the network. Not only will this be an unnecessary distraction from the activities of running their businesses but it could also generate disquiet in the network if it was felt that the franchisor could have avoided the situation by better training or monitoring.

While each individual franchisee will be responsible for all aspects of legal and regulatory compliance the franchisor can do much to ensure that they are aware of the various potential pitfalls.

WHAT ARE THE POTENTIAL PROBLEM AREAS?

Some issues relate to both franchisee and franchisor while others relate only to the franchisor.

Issues for both franchisee and franchisor are the same as for all businesses and might include:

- directors' duties;
- company law;
- accounts and reporting;
- employment law;
- health and safety;
- Tax, NI, VAT, etc.;
- data protection;
- contracts with customers;
- sale of goods legislation;
- the internet and e-mail;
- trademarks;
- sector-specific regulations, e.g. health and hygiene issues.

While the franchisor will wish to distance itself from the franchisees' responsibilities in these areas they would be well advised at least to have a process for raising the awareness of these issues among their franchisees.

- **Director's duties, company law and accounting and reporting** are all topics where both the franchisor and the franchisee should be advised by their accountant or other advisers. Since the franchisor will almost certainly require sight of the franchisee's annual accounts well in advance of the lodging date they will be aware of whether or not the accounts have been prepared. However, there is no guarantee that this will result in the submission of the accounts to Companies House. The implication of a franchisee's failure in any of these areas is unlikely to have any direct adverse effect on the franchisor or the brand.

- **Employment law and health and safety issues** are both complex and continually changing. The franchisor is responsible for ensuring that it is kept up to date on these issues and then complies with them. While they may wish to raise their franchisees' awareness of their obligations in these areas and may even produce, in the operations manual, suggested procedures to assist compliance, they should make it clear that they are not offering legal advice and that the franchisee is responsible for keeping themselves up to date with the requirements of these laws. There are many companies that provide a service to small businesses in these areas and the franchisee could be directed towards one of these.

- **Tax, NI and VAT** advice is readily available from HM Revenue and Customs, both through enquiry offices and their comprehensive website. Both franchisor and franchisee can avail themselves of these facilities as well as seeking advice from the accountants.

- **Where franchisees or the franchisor keep personal information** on, for example, staff or customers, they must ensure that they comply with the Data Protection Act. They should look for advice on this from their own legal advisers and the relevant government website. Franchisors must be particularly careful to ensure that the processes that they put in place for franchisees to maintain these records comply with the provisions of the Data Protection Act.

- **Franchisees and franchisors that provide services or products to customers** will be subject both to contract law and in certain circumstances to the Sale of Goods Act or similar legislation. They may also be subject to Trading Standards regulations. These are, once again, areas where the same rulings are likely to apply to both franchisee and franchisor and in developing their own compliance with the regulations the franchisor may be able to incorporate compliance within its own systems without any implication that they are giving legal advice.

- **The growth of the internet and e-mail communications** has resulted increasingly in new regulation and legislation. This is likely to continue as new opportunities for communications and e-commerce develop.

- **Under the franchise agreement** the franchisee will have been granted the right to use the franchisor's trademarks. It is important that both the franchisor and its franchisees are consistent in the use of the trademarks not only for sound marketing reasons but also because any inconsistency in the use of the trademark may weaken any action to defend it.

- **In franchises providing food and drink** there will be specific regulations relating to health and hygiene issues and processes will need to be developed by the franchisor to reduce the risk to franchisees of prosecution under these regulations. Other sectors may have their own sector-specific regulations including licensing requirements etc.

Both the franchisor and its franchisees must ensure that they comply with all the legislative and regulatory requirements relating to running their businesses.

ADDITIONAL SUBJECTS RELATING TO THE FRANCHISOR'S SPECIFIC RISKS

Not only must the franchisor comply with general business legislation but they must also be conscious of the additional responsibilities that accompany the relationship with their franchisees. While litigation between franchisee and franchisor is not common there are a number of specific areas where it is possible.

These might relate to:

1. the franchisor's rights and responsibilities under the franchise agreement;
2. issues relating to the relationship between the franchise agreement and the operations manual;
3. the recruitment process.

- **Provided that the franchise agreement** has been prepared by an expert in the field it ought to comply with any relevant legislation at the time of preparation. However, laws change and there may be implications in such changes for the content of the franchise agreement. Many of the specialist legal firms and the bfa provide regular updates for their clients or members on changes in the law and its implications for franchising. However, if the franchisor has neither an ongoing relationship with the legal adviser who drew up the agreement nor with the bfa they are unlikely to be aware of such changes and might therefore be offering a franchise agreement that is defective.

A discontented franchisee or a franchisee whose business fails may choose to seek redress from the franchisor on the basis that the franchisor has not fulfilled its obligations under the terms of the franchise agreement. It is important, therefore, for the franchisor to ensure that it is fully compliant with the Franchise Agreement in relation to its responsibilities to the franchisee.

Both the franchisor and its legal advisers should regularly review the franchise agreement. The franchisor should check that any responsibilities it imposed upon itself remain both relevant and achievable. In the early days of a franchise the franchisor may, with the best of intentions, have committed itself to levels of support that are unattainable once the franchise has an increased number of franchisees. Moreover, it may be judged that that level of support is not necessary. The franchise agreement should be altered to reflect this situation while remembering that existing agreements cannot be altered without the consent of the franchisee. The franchisor's legal adviser should ensure that the agreement remains compliant with the relevant legislation and sector good practice.

- **The operations manual and the franchise agreement** are intrinsically linked and it is important therefore that any alteration to one document is reflected in the other where necessary. By the same token where operating methods change consideration should be given to whether this might require any change to the franchise agreement. For example, if changes are made to the induction training process this may require a change to be made to a schedule in the agreement.

- **The recruitment process** is the area of the franchisor's activity that is most likely to be challenged by a discontented franchisee. It is fair to say that successful franchisees are less likely to be dissatisfied than franchisees whose businesses have not achieved the levels of profitability for which they had hoped. This may give rise to accusations of misrepresentation by the franchisor during the recruitment process. Franchisors must therefore ensure that their recruitment process is beyond reproach.

Chapter 11, 'How to Recruit Franchisees', outlined the importance of providing full, fair and frank information through a formalised disclosure process. This information should be neither misleading nor ambiguous. Where financial information is provided to the franchisee it should be made clear what the information is based on, whether it reflects the franchisor's own performance or that of its franchisees, and the franchisee must be warned that this can in no way guarantee that they will achieve similar results.

The franchisor must ensure that any information imparted to the franchisee during the marketing and recruitment process matches

reality. This includes information contained in:
– advertising;
– websites;
– other marketing materials, e.g. brochures.

However, while it is relatively simple to control what information is given in the above situations, it is more difficult to ensure that information imparted during meetings and discussions is similarly controlled. Adequate training and monitoring of recruitment staff should be directed, among other things, at ensuring their compliance with and understanding of what should and should not be said. A major franchisor once had to answer to litigation by a franchisee based upon the fact that an overenthusiastic recruiter had described a particular opportunity as 'a licence to print money' and it had proved not to be the case!

HOW TO AVOID THE RISKS

- Make sure that you, the franchisor, and the franchisees are aware of the issues involved. Then put processes in place to monitor all those areas to ensure compliance. Explain the importance of compliance to both the franchisees and the franchisor's staff so that everyone understands the potential results of non-compliance.

- Regularly review, with your legal advisers, all the franchise documentation including not only the franchise agreement but also template documentation that you provide to your franchisees for use in their business, such as order forms, invoices, letterheads etc.

- Make someone within the franchisor's organisation responsible for following up on all these issues and keep field support staff informed of processes to include on field visits.

Legal problems, whether arising from prosecution or litigation, are not common within the franchising community. By following some simple precautionary processes you can ensure that it remains that way!

SECTION 3
ADVANCED FRANCHISING

22
Becoming an international franchisor

The battlefield of international franchise development is littered with the corpses of executives, business owners and indeed entire corporations who embarked on such expansion because 'it seemed like a good idea at the time and anyway everybody else was doing it, so why not us?' The truth is, even if everybody else *was* doing it, they were probably doing it for the wrong reasons and in the wrong way.

Having said that, like many aspects of franchise development, there is no 'right' way which applies to everybody. There are many ways of taking a business international and there is an almost infinite matrix of options. The task – hopefully with the help of some experienced advisers – is to come up with the mix that is 'right' for your business. Put some time into preparing the battle plan and the opportunities for success are abundant. Go blindly into the fray and you will become another of the corpses.

TAKING THE DECISION TO GO INTERNATIONAL

- **Prior to making the decision to develop your business in international markets**, whether by franchising or by any of the other strategies available to you, you will need to consider seriously some fundamental issues. The most important matter to be appraised pragmatically is the motive for such a move. Successful international expansion requires far more than just a wish to have a presence in other markets. Honestly and objectively assess the reasons for going international and ensure that they are based on sound commercial sense, rather than an

209

ego trip or PR exercise. If your motive for going international is short-term profit, you will need to think again.

- **You should then confirm that your domestic business is sufficiently strong** and independently stable to be able to support an international arm. An international operation will require substantial resources, enormous commitment and much patience. It will inevitably divert much of your attention away from the domestic operation and the international initiative will not succeed if you are constantly running back to put out fires at home. Ask yourself why you want to go abroad if you still have untapped potential at home.

- **Having assured yourself of your motives and capabilities**, next identify the key development criteria and aspirations for the business. Review all international development options and decide whether franchising is indeed the most appropriate. There are certain markets where orthodox franchising is not legally possible, or where it is wiser to have a joint venture partner on the ground to control the way in which the business is operating. Start to identify those markets which best fit your needs, more of which below.

- **Ensure the timing is right for the business to enter the international arena**. There is a fine line between taking a mature, strong system and an underdeveloped, evolving young system abroad. It is reasonably easy to identify the drawbacks of taking an underdeveloped, immature business to foreign shores. What may not be so obvious are the potential weaknesses of international expansion for a business which is too big and too mature. Regimented systems, which were developed to support a substantial domestic business, will need adaptation to support a much more flexible international operation, and although international will inevitably be a very small part of the big domestic brother, it cannot simply be made to fit existing systems.

Once you have satisfied yourself that you have the right answers to the above, only then should you proceed to prepare your international franchise development plan.

PREPARING THE INTERNATIONAL DEVELOPMENT PLAN

Your plan should include selecting priority markets where you can fully and relatively easily capitalise the business potential. Many firms consider the international development option simply because they receive numerous enquiries from various parts of the world. While receiving such approaches can be very flattering, ad hoc responses and sporadic franchise development in different parts of the world is unwise. There is very little sense in stretching your resources thinly across the USA, Poland, Spain and Thailand in the first phase of your franchise development. Entry into each foreign market should be well thought through, researched and developed only as part of the well-defined master international development strategy plan.

The process starts by selecting a list of target markets where you wish to have a presence. Then conduct market research to obtain the fundamental information on numerous factors to determine priority markets. Such factors include the following:

- size of the market (GDP, industry sector, growth potential);

- legal restrictions related both to the actual business and to franchise practices;

- local suppliers and distribution logistics;

- real estate availability and planning structures;

- degree of competition and presence of copycat systems;

- ease of doing business;

- current technological status in the local market, together with possible restrictions/promotional programmes for the transfer of technical know-how;

- geographical proximity to home country (ease of travel, local support, training and communication);

- language considerations;

- degree of acceptance of foreign franchises (previous success and failure);

- likely availability of investors to meet the franchisee financial profile;

- general cultural issues.

Other requirements are to identify and assess carefully the relevance of all the international franchise development options for each of the priority markets and carefully select the most appropriate entry vehicle for that specific market. Master franchise development with sub-franchise rights may be appropriate for Company A in Market A but not necessarily for Company B in Market A or for Company A in other markets.

Consideration of all of the above will enable the preparation of a plan which will detail where you want to go, when you want to be there, and how you want to go there. Preparing the plan will also start to make clear what staff you will need to recruit, how much it is all going to cost for development and marketing, and what the risks and returns are likely to be. This can be the point at which all international aspirations are abandoned and, for many potential international franchisors, that is often no bad thing. If however everything looks acceptable you can then move on to developing the offer.

DEVELOPING THE FRANCHISE OFFER PACKAGE

Developing the franchise offer package, remembering that its contents are likely to vary from country to country, requires all of the above research to have been completed. Doing so will provide you with valuable information on which to base your business plan and enable you to identify the most appropriate franchise development option. It will also demonstrate your commitment to the local franchise network; enable you to offer a much more comprehensive and targeted support package; and strengthen your bargaining position *vis-à-vis* the franchise candidate.

The preparation of the franchise offer package involves detailing what you are offering the franchisee and what he or she is expected to do in return. It may also include detailing the subsequent relationship between the master franchisee and their franchisees if master franchising with sub-franchisees is the chosen option. Existing franchisors will be familiar with what such a package should include, but examples are:

- size and characteristics of the franchisee's location and territory;
- franchise terms and conditions;
- sub-franchisee approval procedure;
- fees, royalties and advertising levy;
- renewal terms and fees;
- franchisor's rights and obligations;
- master franchisee's rights and obligations;
- sub-franchisees rights and obligations;
- rights for various parties to sell their business;
- termination of the franchise agreement and post-termination provisions;
- marketing and promotional investment.

SETTING THE FEE STRUCTURES

One of the questions which we are most frequently asked is 'How much can we charge for upfront and ongoing fees?' As usual, there is no 'right' answer to this question as the international fee structure is probably the most variable element of the franchise offer. Broad answers range from 'However much you can get' to 'It depends how badly you want to go there, how much you want that franchisee, or how much that franchisee wants your brand and system.'

Establishing the fee structure which is right for a particular business in a particular market is one area where professional guidance is invaluable.

Some of the types of fees which can be charged are as follows:

Initial franchise/territorial exclusivity fee

This is a fee charged by the franchisor to grant the franchisee the exclusive rights to develop the franchisor's concept within the defined territory. There may also be the opportunity to charge another fee on renewal.

Before setting this fee reasonably accurate information should be obtained on factors such as the length of the exclusivity agreement and the proposed renewal terms (the longer the contract, the higher the fee); the size and potential of the market (the bigger the market, the higher the fee); the pre-agreed development schedule (the more aggressive the schedules, the lower the fee); global brand value (the better known the brand name, the more valuable the exclusivity of its development); and the depth of the franchisor's expertise in supporting an international franchise network (the more previous success can be demonstrated, the more can be charged this time).

Some potential international franchisors imagine this fee to be a gateway to a fortune by selling off parts of the globe for exorbitant amounts. Such ventures, certainly for the master and sub franchisees, are doomed before they start.

Unit franchise fee

This is the fee payable on every store or outlet subsequently opened in the territory, whether sub-franchised or owned by the master. The fee should cover such things as the cost of supporting the franchisee to develop and open for business at that unit; the cost of the franchisor transferring its know-how to that unit management team; and some amortisation of the franchisor's development costs of the project.

Royalty/management services fee

This is the fee charged by the franchisor for offering continuous support and for the use of its trade name and marks. While this fee should be set at a level which covers the franchisor's ongoing support cost and the use of its industrial and intellectual property rights, it should not significantly erode the franchisee's profits which after all will be partly reinvested in the business.

There are a variety of ways in which this fee can be calculated, usually a percentage of the franchisee's turnover. This may not be at the same level in each country. Due to varying sets of local operating factors, a royalty of 4 per cent of turnover may be feasible for the Korean franchisee but totally impractical for the South African franchisee, or vice versa.

Other fees may be charged for provision of training or other specific services, such as global reservation or booking systems, and there may also be the opportunity for commission or mark-up on supply of raw materials and/or finished products. All have their own advantages, drawbacks and relevance to a particular network and the chosen options need to be carefully considered.

Marketing fee

This is the fee paid by all franchisees within a country into the master's joint marketing fund, part of which in turn may then be allocated centrally to the franchisor for global branding opportunities.

In principle whatever the mix and level of fees chosen, the structure has to be fair to all parties in helping them achieve their objectives from the relationship. In practice, provided the franchisee meets the required profile and criteria, it is frequently better for the franchisor to accept a lower upfront fee, which enables the local business to invest more in becoming established, and then to take more in continuing fees as the local business grows and prospers.

The days of large upfront fees followed by little support are gone – hopefully, for ever.

23
Becoming a master franchisee

When you consider that the master franchise fee for a whole country for a service-based franchise is often less than the cost of setting up a single unit outlet for some food service or premises-based retail franchises, you can see why more people are thinking 'Why should I just become a franchisee when I could be a master?'

Of course, the skills required of a master are very different, but for someone who is of the mindset of a typical franchisee, i.e. not too entrepreneurial and looking to be part of a proven system with established support structures, master franchising can offer far greater potential than simply running a single franchised outlet.

ADVANTAGES

Becoming the local operation of an overseas franchisor is not just an opportunity for individuals who are looking to start their own business. Many existing businesses look for opportunities from around the world, particularly those companies who are experienced in a particular field, say food service retailing, who have the operational expertise but perhaps lack the creativity, time or money to develop their own new products or services from scratch.

New products for an existing client base or distribution network, or even an opportunity to convert existing stores to a new brand, can quickly transform a business which has perhaps grown tired. Potential conversion works to the advantage of both franchisor and developer as they can more quickly achieve brand awareness than they would by opening one store at a time. Having an established network available for conversion is also a good bargaining point for the prospective developer in reducing the upfront fee on the grounds that income flow, from ongoing fees, will grow more quickly.

An interesting trend around the world is for existing franchisors (or indeed master franchisees) to be looking for another franchise system to operate alongside their original network. This often happens if they are nearing capacity, when they basically have two choices – either become an international franchisor themselves, and take their own brand overseas, or start another franchise at home, hopefully gaining some efficiencies from existing support team structures.

Looking at it from the overseas franchisor's point of view, someone who already has experience of running a franchised network may be a very attractive prospect as a master franchisee as they will already have many of the required skills, and maybe even the staff. This means the operation should grow faster than it would by taking on someone with no franchising experience.

POINTS TO CONSIDER

So what should you look for when considering becoming a master franchisee? For the purposes of this exercise we will assume that you have not previously been, or worked for, a franchisor.

Our international franchise development team spends about as much time advising UK franchisors how to find partners overseas, and overseas franchisors how to find partners in the UK, as we do working with people acquiring master franchises for the UK, and for both the points to consider are a mirror image of each other. Both sides should be looking for positive mutual commitment to building a sound business over many years, and this will involve working together with a common-sense approach to financing, training and support.

Unless the franchisor can show evidence of a policy decision to embark on, and properly resource, an international development programme, supported by a detailed business plan, with input from people who know the game, then neither they, nor the potential master franchisee, should go any further.

Something to look for specifically is: what basic market research has been done by the franchisor on their product or service in the target country? If none, what makes them think a franchised network can succeed there? Obviously, even if the franchisor has done some research, you will need to verify it with some of your own when preparing your business plan, as well as considering the potential differences in key ratios such as property costs, wage rates or petrol prices. You also need to build in some franchising research – how does the franchising market for potential franchisees differ in your country from that in the franchisor's home country, and is the proposed fee structure and rate of franchisee roll-out realistic? What about the costs of franchisee recruitment, or local laws and cultural differences that may affect the operation?

Please note, comparing the population of the USA or Australia with the population of your country, and extrapolating figures from there, is *not* market research!

You will also want to know about the franchisor's track record. If they come from a country that requires pre-contract disclosure for domestic operations then ask for a copy of the relevant disclosure document.

Ask for contact details of their other master franchisees so you can ask them about their experiences – and if the franchisor doesn't have any others, or won't let you speak to them, consider that carefully in your decision-making process.

24
Meeting your international match

Having been involved with the search for master franchisees for many years, the first point we must make is that finding an overseas partner is *not* where the international franchising process starts! In the unlikely event that your business is considering international development because 'everyone else is doing it, and it seems like a good idea' then we urge you to do some serious research to ensure you know what you are getting into.

We will assume that if you are planning to franchise your system into other countries you have at least read the parts of this book dealing with how to structure your international franchise package, how to build your international support infrastructure, how to decide which countries are your prime targets, and how to build the profile of the individual or organisation that would make an ideal partner in each market.

If we have the above, we can now get on to how we generate and process enquiries from suitably qualified candidates.

For a franchisor whose network is well established, perhaps even nearing capacity in its home market, the lure of international franchising can often be irresistible. The dream is often made more attractive when individuals or businesses from foreign countries approach that franchisor with the question: 'Can I do what you do in my country?'

Such approaches are fine if they become the trigger for beginning to think about an international franchise development strategy. However, if they become the trigger for starting that development, without properly researching and planning it, then the dream will turn into a nightmare.

THE PROCESS

Why should someone who approaches you out of the blue be the right person to operate your system in their country? Indeed, who says their country is right for your system?

As one experienced international franchise development director says, 'If you received an e-mail from a girl in China you knew absolutely nothing about, saying she was looking for a husband, would you jump on the next plane and go over there to meet her family and marry her?'

Probably not, and nor should sensible business people react in more or less the same way with a business system that has taken them years to develop and become profitable.

So how *do* you meet your ideal match?

Many years' practical experience of helping businesses move into the UK and Europe, typically from the USA and Australia, and also of helping them move between various EU and Middle East countries. Our experience leads us to believe that it will be a much easier, and much more successful, process if you engage with a network of professionals, such as that operated by the International Franchising Centre who know their local markets, than it will be if you try to do it all yourself.

Material review and adaptation

Businesses looking for a master franchisee in the UK and Ireland (and often then onwards into the rest of Europe) are frequently referred to us by their professional advisers in their home country, or we are contacted by their government department which helps businesses from their country to export. In either case we ask for details of the franchise offer package, the development plan, and some information about what research they have carried out into the market for their product or service in the target market. All that information is reviewed by a specialist consultant and feedback is provided as to whether any of the documentation needs to be improved or adapted in order to fit better with the requirements of the destination market.

Should the franchisor need any help with 'closing the gaps' then the consultant will advise how that can best be achieved.

Once the franchisor and the local market consultant are confident that a marketable package has been produced then a marketing plan and budget to promote the opportunity are devised and managed by the consultant on the franchisor's behalf. All enquiries are directed through the consultant's office, not least because candidates initially prefer to be dealing with people in their own country, and an agreed screening process commences.

Promoting the opportunity

So where will the marketing be placed? The answer to that, of course, varies from franchisor to franchisor and depends very much on the profile of the candidate being sought. Sometimes the target could simply be any individual with enough money and business experience; sometimes it will need to be an existing corporation with a synergistic operation – particularly for an add-on opportunity; sometimes it will be an existing franchisor, or master franchisee, who is looking to add another system to its stable. Sometimes it could be any or all of these.

The inexperienced will say the answer to where to promote is obvious. Place plenty of advertising in traditional franchising media and websites, and attend the relevant franchise exhibitions. While these avenues may indeed be part of the marketing mix for a particular system, experience suggests they should not be the sole, nor are they likely even to be the best, sources of enquiries from master franchisees or developers – and this is where local knowledge of the market comes into play.

Many potential master franchisees do not *know* they are potential master franchisees! Existing franchisors may not realise they could take on another system. Experienced business people, or existing corporations, may not realise they could grow their businesses by developing someone else's successful concept. All these potentially exciting candidates will not be reading the franchising press, nor will they be attending franchise shows, so they will not see the opportunities promoted there. They need to be reached some other way.

One way to do this is for the local market consultant to provide generic articles for the general business and investor press, and make presentations to investor groups and individuals who are outside the franchising community, extolling the virtues of becoming a master franchisee. Generic advertising in the national business press – sometimes supported by specific advertising for a specific client – is also an option.

The outcome of these activities is that a database is built of known investors, together with details of their business experience, the sectors in which they are interested, and the amount of money they have available. Members of this database therefore become prime targets for appropriate incoming systems and can be directly approached when a suitable opportunity becomes available. Because they already know the consultant, they tend to listen to the details of an offer because they are not just being marketed to 'out of the blue', and will only be approached with something likely to be of interest.

A recent development of the database system has been to invite pre-qualified potential investors to 'Master Franchising in the 21st Century' events, which happen twice a year in London and Dublin and are being launched in many other markets.

With the support of various consultants, law firms and banks, the sessions start with some general educational sessions about master franchising. These are followed by presentations of up to six non-competing systems who are actively seeking master franchisees or developers in the local market. These presentations are ideally done by a senior executive from each of the systems, not only because they can answer all the questions but also because they can demonstrate true passion for their opportunity. Meeting rooms are made available for post-seminar meetings should individuals want to know more from a particular franchisor at that time.

Sometimes, an executive recruitment service can help to team up serious investors ('the money') with an ambitious franchise develop-ment manager ('the man') in order to create the 'dream team' to develop the new master franchise operation. After all, a good franchisor will want to be convinced that the chosen partner has as many of the necessary resources for success as possible.

Recruitment

Whatever the source of an enquiry, it is more likely to move through the recruitment process if it is professionally followed up and there is a clear process of stages through which it must pass. This can start with simple telephone screening to decide whether there is a potential match, based on the profiling criteria established before the recruitment project starts, through despatching marketing materials, following up with further telephone or personal meetings, establishing that appropriate finance and experience exists, all leading up to the all-important Discovery Day at the franchisor's office in their home country.

By the time the candidate gets to this stage they will need to be pretty well sold on the opportunity because it is obviously a serious commitment to make such a trip. Similarly the franchisor will need to be pretty well sold on the candidate to devote the required amount of time and personal resource to the visit. It would be difficult to achieve such commitment without the involvement of a mutually trusted third party.

After the Discovery Day, when the candidate returns to their home country, the local consultant can help to keep the impetus going by obtaining feedback from, and providing it to, both parties as to how things went and what outstanding issues need to be resolved. Assistance with development of the roll-out plan and obtaining working capital finance from local banks is an added benefit at this stage, as is access to qualified legal support to deal with negotiation of the agreement.

Of course, a franchisor can do all, or most of, the above themselves if they have enough experienced staff and plenty of resources, but this is rarely the case and the added complication of time differences makes it worse. Having a third party, who understands franchising, to nurse both parties through the process can be invaluable.

Post-sale support

One final advantage to be considered when using a local market consultant is the availability of ongoing support for the master, particularly at times when it is impractical for the franchisor to make as many country visits, or even provide as much telephone support, as they would like. Entities such as the Franchise Training Centre and the Franchise Support Centre are able to provide such services, including marketing the franchise and recruiting unit franchisees. For the latter they would likely be directly engaged by the master franchisee, but they can also act as an outsourced monitoring and support service for the franchisor.

Until such time as the international franchising operation can afford its own in-house team of experienced operators it may make good sense to outsource the whole lead generation, enquiry processing and subsequent support services to others. This can often be done on a share-of-fees basis which reduces the risk and financial commitment for the franchisor, but provides better local service for the master and their franchisees.

25
Negotiating the international agreement

The biggest difference between domestic and international franchise agreements is that the latter will always be negotiated, whereas the former are most often presented as 'take it or leave it'.

MASTER FRANCHISE AGREEMENTS
The master franchisee basically becomes the franchisor in its country, and has all the dealings with its domestic franchisees that the franchisor has with those in its own country. Therefore the gist of the master franchise agreement is to confirm the commercial arrangements which have been made between the parties and to make clear their respective responsibilities. In a nutshell, it is the responsibility of the master franchisee to introduce and grow the franchisor's business effectively in the territory, maintaining all the required standards; and it is the franchisor's job to train them how to do it and subsequently support them in doing so.

Franchisors must realise that there is no point setting unrealistic upfront and ongoing fees that will be unmanageable for the master if they are to build a successful network. In many cases if the proposed fees were to be implemented in the franchisor's domestic business, purely on paper and for illustrative purposes only, it would immediately become clear that they were unrealistic.

Master franchisees must realise the importance of having a Network Development Plan prepared by experienced franchise consultants from their own country in order to embark on a credible and properly costed project. Not to do so will cause them to overestimate the speed at which they can get pilot operations under way and subsequently recruit franchisees, and to underestimate the cost of recruiting those franchisees and putting in place the required support infrastructure for them.

Both parties must realise that all the legal, marketing and operational documentation will need at least some adaptation for the new market, and quite how much adaptation may not become apparent until the business gets under way.

Note that the legal situation regarding franchising in various countries around the world changes quite quickly and there is no point in this, or any other, book listing any specific countries or their current regulations. It is essential to engage the services of a law firm with thorough experience of international franchising, such as Eversheds in the UK or DLA Piper Rudnick in the USA, when finalising the detail of any agreement for any international territory.

So, what are the matters to be negotiated? They will include:

Rights granted

This details the rights granted to the master franchisee to use the name, system, trademarks, software and other relevant intellectual property owned by the franchisor, and in what territory they can be used. Unlike unit franchise agreements, it is highly likely that these rights will be exclusively granted in the territory, provided that the franchisee maintains the agreed opening schedule.

Should they not do so, they may lose the right to exclusivity, unless they pay whatever fees they would have paid had they maintained the schedule. However, the practicalities – or more likely the impracticalities – of such an arrangement need to be carefully considered and discussed, not least because if the franchisee has not maintained the opening schedule then they probably do not have the money to pay the fees.

Term of agreement

Defines when the agreement starts and how long it lasts. It is only common sense that a master franchise agreement should be for at least

20 years which, if nothing else, should focus the mind of both parties on finding the right partner!

It's going to take at least three years to get the master properly established in their country – they have to be trained how to operate outlets, they have to open pilot outlets and make them successful, then they have to be trained how to franchise, then they have to launch the franchise and start recruiting franchisees. Franchisee recruitment is a slow process and it may be five years or more from launching the franchise to signing the final franchisee to complete the network. (In practice this never happens, but bear with us for the sake of illustration.) We are now eight years into the relationship and the master has just signed a franchisee on, perhaps, a ten-year agreement. That means 18 years from the start until the last franchisee finishes – but remember there are almost certain to be renewals so the sub-franchise agreements could go on for much longer. So maybe even 30 years for the master agreement, with a right of renewal, is more sensible. The franchisee can always sell the business (subject to the franchisor's approval) if they have had enough, and the franchisor will be able to take appropriate action if the franchisee is failing to meet the required standards or targets.

Opening and performance schedule

This is a matter of great importance to the franchisor because if a realistic opening schedule cannot be agreed then there may be little point in entering the market – unless he can get an exorbitant upfront fee, but hopefully we've established by now that such considerations are not good franchising practice.

Agreeing what is realistic is never easy – particularly when a new concept is entering a new market, because there is very little evidence on which to base projections. Both parties should do their own independent research on both the market for the product or service and the market for franchising, then combine their findings to prepare a mutually agreed business development plan with which they can both be happy. That plan can then be regularly reviewed in the light of experience and discussions can be had when a shortfall looks likely.

If the franchisee can explain that they cannot meet the schedule because some of the assumptions in the plan have turned out to be inaccurate then a modified schedule can be agreed; if it is clear that the franchisee will not, rather than cannot, meet the schedule – perhaps because they are not investing enough in marketing – then the franchisor can either show them how to do it, help them to do it, or if necessary start to talk about loss of exclusivity or even termination.

The point is, these matters have to be discussed. Actions cannot simply be taken based on black-and-white facts.

Fees

The types of fees have been listed in Chapter 9 'International franchising'. Their levels are what need to be negotiated.

- **Country and exclusivity fees** There are as many ways of coming up with an upfront fee as there are international franchisors, but suffice to say an amount has to be agreed which covers the franchisor's costs of finding and training the franchisee, reflects the value of the opportunity to the franchisee in the market, but leaves the franchisee with enough funds to develop it properly.

  We have seen formulae based on so many cents per head of population; the total value of all the upfront fees unit franchisees will pay when they join the system; and multiples of what was paid by someone in a country with a smaller population. None of these makes any sense if the aim is to give the franchisee a fair crack of the whip. What does make sense is something that can be shown to be affordable if the franchisee works hard to develop the business in line with the agreed business plan – and that will vary with every franchisor, and every potential master franchisee, in every market.

- **Ongoing fees** Once again these have to be at a level which will make it worthwhile for the franchisor to be in that market, and cover their costs in providing the necessary support, but they also have to allow the master franchisee sufficient funds to recruit and support their own sub-franchisees. The mutually agreed business plan will again demonstrate whether this is likely to happen. If it is not, then there should be no deal.

- **Transfer of funds, exchange rates and taxes** This is a complicated area which needs to be considered by both parties and their financial advisers, as timing of funds will have cash flow implications, as will fluctuating exchange rates, efficiency of the respective banking systems, and possible future local legislation. A book like this cannot go into all the detail of all the possible hurdles in all the likely countries so professional advice must be taken at the time the agreement is being prepared.

Selling the business

Franchisees typically have the right to sell their business as a going concern, but only to a buyer approved by the franchisor, using the same criteria as they would for a new master franchisee. These criteria will not just consider whether the incoming franchisee has the right skills and attitudes, but also whether they can afford to buy at the price agreed, depending on how the deal is being financed. The franchisor will usually have the right to pre-empt the purchase by acquiring the business themselves (either to operate as a company-owned unit or to sell on) on the same terms as those agreed with a third party.

Termination and post-termination

The franchisor will need to be able to terminate the agreement in the event of the master franchisee failing to perform their duties, including those relating to maintaining the quality of products or services provided through the sub-franchised network. It is necessary therefore for those duties, and their associated standards, to be clearly defined in the operations manual.

One of the biggest issues to consider post-termination is what happens to the sub-franchisees? The franchisor may or may not want to take on some or all of them, but how will they decide? For the master franchise agreement to have been terminated, it is possible that the unit franchisees will have been poorly serviced and will therefore be demotivated at best, or decidedly non-compliant at worst.

Not surprisingly, neither party is likely to want to think about termination before they have even signed what might be a 30-year agreement but it is a matter which must be considered.

International franchise agreements are extremely complex and can best be devised by working with an experienced consultant who can then brief an equally experienced lawyer, and can then negotiate on your behalf with the other party. Far too many franchisors and master franchisees rush into signing agreements without considering, or even realising, what can go wrong in practice. A two-handed team of consultant and lawyer is the best asset you can have, whichever side of the deal you are on.

26
Buying or selling a franchised network

Buying or selling an established franchised network is similar in many ways to the sale or purchase of a non-franchised business, but there are some very specific areas, unique to franchising, where care needs to be taken. For this reason it is advisable for both parties to involve experienced franchise consultants as soon as they embark on either the buying or selling process. In due course expert legal and accounting advice, again from within the franchising community, will also be required, but practical franchising advice comes first.

The purchaser needs to ensure that they are making a wise investment, they are paying a sensible price for the business, and they understand what they are getting into – particularly if they have no previous experience of how franchising works.

The seller will often just want to ensure that they optimise the consideration they receive for the business, but if they are the person who created the business in the first place they may also be concerned about how their franchisees will be treated in the future. Franchising is an emotional business and the creator of a network may want to ensure that it 'goes to a good home'.

ITEMS FOR CONSIDERATION
Intellectual property rights – who owns the rights for the trademark(s), brand name, systems and processes which are licensed to franchisees? If you are buying or selling a franchising subsidiary of another company, or the country master licence for an overseas franchisor, then the vendor will normally only have the right to use the IPR in the

assigned territory for the term of the master franchise agreement – ownership may reside with the parent company or the overseas franchisor.

Franchisee agreements – are all franchisees operating to the same version of the franchise agreement? If not, what are the differences – fee structure? Term? Renewal rights? Obligations of both parties? When are the renewal dates for the agreements?

Systems – are the franchise systems well documented? Is there an up-to-date operations manual? Is it used by franchisees? Is there a structured training programme? What happens about field support? Is there a franchisee development programme, with benchmarks?

Litigation – is there any ongoing/pending litigation between franchisor and franchisee? If so, what is the nature of the issues, and at what stage is each case? What are the likely outcomes and costs – and would a new owner be likely to be able to encourage some form of alternative dispute resolution?

Network performance – how are individual franchisees performing against the system benchmarks? How many poor performers are there in the network? What are the issues associated with these franchisees? How many franchisees are actively looking to sell their franchises? Why? Do current franchisees meet the current franchisee profile? Is there 'churning' in the system – are most new franchise sales merely replacing franchisees who close/sell their businesses or is there potential to open more 'greenfield' sites?

Franchisee relations – how good is the general relationship between franchisor and franchisees? Is there a franchisee council? What do the franchisees perceive to be the major issues facing the network? How happy are they with their lot?

Company-owned outlets – are there any, and if so, how are they performing? Are they to be included in the business sale, or sold off as going-concern franchises?

Growth potential – is the network complete? What is the scope for the sale of additional franchises (in addition to resales)? Are franchisees achieving good local market penetration – or are the territory sizes too large? Can sales be improved through more national account development, or by expanding the product/service lines? Has the company been working to a strategic plan and how close is it to achievement?

Financial performance – does revenue from management service fees more than cover the franchisor's fixed overheads? Does the franchisor need to sell franchises in order to be profitable – if so, how many? Sales track record? Has there been a consistent performance over the past three to five years, or have revenue/profits been up and down? Is there an upward trend in both revenue and profits? How controllable are costs? Could a purchaser leverage their own management and administration capability, and so strip out overheads?

Management team – when the current owners sell the business, is there sufficient knowledge/expertise in the remaining management team for the business to continue to operate effectively? Does there need to be a tapered exit strategy to effect a knowledge transfer? What is the overall quality of the management team?

Property leases – some franchised businesses (especially those in the quick service restaurant sector) will take the head lease on the premises used by the franchisee – firstly to secure the site for the brand, and secondly because the covenant strength of the franchisee may be inadequate to secure the lease from the landlord. If a site is performing well, these leases will be viewed as a major asset of the businesses – if a site is not trading well, then the site is a potential liability. Are there major restrictions associated with the lease for headquarters premises? Expert legal advice should be taken when looking at the issues surrounding lease transfer.

Business valuation – all of the above will have some bearing on the price a buyer is willing to pay for the business; in addition, the valuation formula used will be dependent to some extent on the nature of the business – most sales will be asset-based rather than share-based, on the grounds that the purchaser will not wish to acquire any of the known (or potential) liabilities of the vendor company. If asset-based, the process for determining the value of the tangible assets is normally fairly straightforward; the element which can be more challenging is goodwill. The price a purchaser is willing to pay for goodwill is normally linked to EBITDA based on management services fee income (rather than on franchise sales income), and would typically be based on a multiple of five to ten. Most vendors believe that their businesses have huge development potential, and that this should be recognised in the sale price – however, by contrast, most purchasers are unwilling to pay for potential, taking the view that they are not going to pay someone else for the work they will have to do. If there is a proven and steady trend of profit growth, or if both parties are prepared to look at an 'earn-out' arrangement, then the price agreed for goodwill could be higher.

PREPARING THE BUSINESS FOR SALE

The seller will need to take account of all of the above points when preparing or 'grooming' the business for sale. We will consider their implications in more detail shortly, but first, it's vital that the vendor is clear about why they wish to sell the business – this may seem to be an obvious point, but dependent on the vendor's objectives, there could be very different sales strategies (and associated grooming activities). By way of illustration, consider the following three scenarios:

- The vendor's spouse has a serious illness, and they wish to dispose of the business to spend more time together. Clearly, speed will be important, and consequently the vendor may be prepared to accept a lower offer for the business, subject to ready availability of purchaser funds, and the purchaser's ability to complete quickly.

- The vendor wishes to release funds from the business to invest elsewhere, but is in no desperate hurry; in addition she believes that the business is about to enter a significant growth phase. To maximise their return, it is very likely that a purchaser would look for an earn-out arrangement over say two years – an initial consideration would be paid, with either a phased or back-ended payment which would be paid against pre-agreed performance criteria.

- The business has had a variable trading performance in recent years; the vendor wishes to retire in three years' time, and would like to release the equity in his business at that time. To maximise the potential value of the business, he should produce a business plan which gives a growing profit profile over the next three years – and if there is the possibility of selling to an investment group, then succession management planning will be important.

THE FRANCHISED NETWORK HEALTHCHECK

If there is time to groom the business, it is a good idea to commission a franchised network healthcheck, including a franchisee satisfaction survey (see Chapter 20), which will establish where the business currently stands against good practice. The subsequent report will make appropriate recommendations for closing any gaps. These may include:

- Ensure that all trademarks/domain names are registered. If there is potential for international expansion, consider trademark registration for the likely target countries.

- If there are different franchise agreements in use by the network, take legal and practical advice to identify ways in which all franchisees can be moved to a single version. Normally, this will mean that those working to older versions, will have to perceive a benefit to change.

- Ensure that the documented 'know-how' of the business reflects current best practice – this will include the operations manual, training programmes and manuals. Consider making the operations manual available 'online'.

- Does the image of the business need overhauling – logos, website and literature? If yes, get professional input and ensure image consistency in all areas which project the brand.

- If there is ongoing litigation with one or more franchisees, look for ways to resolve the situation – even if this means taking a short-term hit. Ongoing legal issues will be perceived in a very negative light by potential purchasers.

- Ensure that all franchisees have development plans – to make the good better, and to identify appropriate strategies for those which are struggling. This could mean an exit strategy for those franchisees where the core attributes or attitudes are no longer in line with the preferred franchisee profile.

- Ensure that there are excellent vehicles in place for franchisor–franchisee communication, and also for peer-to-peer communication between franchisees. These could include intranet, franchisee meetings, annual convention, franchisee council, regular in-house publication etc.

- If the business plan calls for the recruitment of additional franchisees, ensure that the recruitment methodology used is likely to produce the desired results – if not, change it. Consider changing media used for lead generation, and recruitment of additional/replacement franchise sales staff; consider also outsourcing of franchisee recruitment, use of referral networks etc.

- If the current owner's exit from the business would leave a critical knowledge or capability gap in the management team, take steps to close the potential gap either through knowledge/skills transfer to existing members of staff, or through the recruitment of additional staff.

- If there are property leases due for renewal, try to avoid entering into long-term arrangements that remove flexibility for a new owner.

- Ensure that all business documentation is in good order, and complete – this will include accounting records, franchisee files, supplier agreements etc. Make due diligence easy for the prospective purchaser.

- Get any skeletons out into the open – if a seller tries to hide bad news, and it is subsequently discovered during the due diligence process, not only will it normally result in a downgrading of the business valuation, but is also very likely to cause a lack of trust on the part of the purchaser towards the vendor, and any statements made about the business. It has the potential to drive away some purchasers – so the golden rule is to disclose everything, and try to address potentially difficult issues during the grooming process.

Depending on its findings, the network healthcheck report, or evidence of its implementation, can be used as a sales tool to be included in the buyer's information pack. Should such a report not exist there is the option for the purchaser to commission one themselves with the vendor's approval.

TYPES OF BUYER

There are various categories of potential buyer, each of whom will have different motivations for their purchase.

- A **'financial'** buyer will focus on the numbers, and will be looking very closely at potential return on investment, payback periods, possible future exit options etc. For this type of buyer, integrity in the financial information will be very important.

- A **'strategic'** buyer by contrast will be looking for potential in the business model/system. Is it complementary to their existing business? Does it provide potential to leverage existing assets – support infrastructure, customer base etc.? Does it spread risk? This type of buyer may well be prepared to pay more for perceived potential, especially where they see a strategic fit with an existing business.

  Currently, there are several multi-brand franchise groups developing in the UK, and should the business in question complement those already in the 'stable', then it may be possible to negotiate a premium over and above the standard valuation – however, this will be down to buyer and seller to negotiate.

- An **'emotional'** buyer – may possibly be one or more of the existing franchisees or members of the existing management team. This type of buyer will often pay well over the odds if they can raise the money or find a backer. However, they also know the business and its potential problems intimately. With the right advice, they can drive the price down or even instigate unrest in the network in order to do so – so beware.

THE SALES PROCESS

Having made the decision to sell their business, the vendor has several options in terms of securing a purchaser:

- If the vendor wishes to 'groom' the business to try to optimise the sale price, then they can either undertake the process themselves, or use an experienced third party, such as the Franchise Sales Centre, to assist.

  The latter route is often the best one, because an experienced third party can be totally objective whereas the vendor, by definition, cannot. In addition, most vendors do not make a habit of building and selling businesses, whereas an appropriate consultant will bring experience of a good number of business sales to the table. The consultant's fees should be more than covered through added sales value – and they will also be able to advise on which aspects of grooming are likely to add value to the business.

- Once 'groomed', the vendor again has the option of either a DIY approach, or using an experienced broker.

Whichever route is chosen, a certain amount of documentation will be required:

(a) non-disclosure agreement;

(b) business prospectus/information memorandum;

(c) audited accounts for the last three years' trading;

(d) sales/marketing pack for both end-user service, and franchisee recruitment;

(e) full system disclosure document;

(f) memorandum of understanding/intent to proceed document;

(g) sale and purchase agreement (normally prepared by a solicitor).

Use of a third party will have benefits, since a competent broker should have access to a number of potential buyers, and will be able to market the opportunity through their established channels without getting too emotionally involved in the outcome.

Appendix A
A typical franchise development work programme

(See Chapter 3)

STEP	TASK	WHO	DATE	END PRODUCT

1. SHOULD YOU FRANCHISE?	ESTABLISH VIABILITY OF FRANCHISING THE BUSINESS
	Visioning process
	Establish base model for business
	Establish financial consequences of franchising
	Produce network development plan and comparison
	   with criteria for successful franchise
				Stated vision for franchise business
				Initial draft model of franchise
				Detailed five-year franchisor and
				   franchisee P&L and cash flow forecasts
				Establish funding requirement
				Case for and against franchising

2. THE FRANCHISE PROJECT PLAN	MAKE THE FRANCHISE DECISION
	
	DEVELOP WORK PROGRAMME
	Establish project team
	Who is in team, allocate tasks/roles, time-scales
	Check trademark status
	   Name/marks protected?
	   Apply for registration
	Corporate structure of franchisor business
	   Form legal entity, constitution, framework
	Communications programmes
	   Develop and implement ongoing internal programme
	   Develop and implement ongoing external programme
				If no, project ends here
				
				Written project work programme
				Defined personnel and roles
				Protected name and marks
				Vehicle for franchisor business
				Written internal communications plan
				Written external communications plan

3. THE FRANCHISE BUSINESS PLAN	DEVELOP FRANCHISE BUSINESS PLAN
	Write business plan narrative
	   (include network development plan and franchise
	   marketing plan)
	Incorporate financial projections from Step 1
				Detailed business plan tailored to
				   audience e.g. bank, investors, internal
				   working document etc.

STEP	TASK	WHO	DATE	END PRODUCT
4. THE FRANCHISE OPERATING SYSTEM	DEVELOP DETAILED FRANCHISE BUSINESS MODEL Territories – size, location analysis, mapping, capacity Business set-up procedures Establish IT policy and systems Initial and ongoing training programmes Support and communication systems Reporting/accounting systems – group accounting Marketing, admin, HR etc. Stock ordering and control Invoicing systems and credit control Establish property/leases policy, etc. Develop final franchise package			Detailed franchise operating system in note form Stated franchise offering – franchise fees, the package and benefits
5. THE FRANCHISEE OPERATIONS MANUAL	WRITE FRANCHISEE OPERATIONS MANUAL Produce Step 4 in manual form			Manual(s), training workbooks etc. documenting franchisee operating system
6. THE FRANCHISOR OPERATIONS MANUAL	WRITE FRANCHISOR OPERATIONS MANUAL Develop template/systems for running franchisor business Produce in manual form			Manual covering franchise marketing and recruitment, training, support, contact programme, dispute procedures, managing marketing fund, job descriptions etc.
7. THE FRANCHISEE BUSINESS PLAN TEMPLATE	DEVELOP STANDARD FRANCHISEE BUSINESS PLAN TEMPLATE			Business plan template for franchisees with narrative, P&L and cash flow guidelines
8. THE FRANCHISE AGREEMENT	PRODUCE FRANCHISE AGREEMENT Develop briefing document for lawyer Lawyer to produce final agreement			Brief containing basic requirements Final franchise agreement

STEP	TASK	WHO	DATE	END PRODUCT
9. FRANCHISE MARKETING AND RECRUIT-MENT	PRODUCE FRANCHISE MARKETING AND RECRUITMENT PLAN Develop franchisee profile Develop franchise marketing and media plan Develop recruitment and selection process Produce franchise prospectus and application form Produce disclosure document Develop franchise website/web page Contact franchise banks Investigate benefits of joining the BFA Appoint franchise PR consultant			Documented franchisee profile Documented franchise marketing plan Documented recruitment and selection process Franchise prospectus and application form Recruitment disclosure document Website/franchise web page Approval from major franchise banks BFA membership PR machine in place
10. FRANCHISOR STAFF TRAINING	ATTEND FRANCHISE TRAINING CENTRE How to find franchisees How to recruit franchisees How to monitor franchisee performance How to motivate franchisees Franchise awareness training for non-franchise staff			Trained franchisor staff Exposure to other franchisors and learning from their experiences and collective knowledge
11. BUSINESS LAUNCH AND ONGOING SUPPORT	SUCCESSFUL/HIGH PROFILE LAUNCH OF FRANCHISE Maximise PR and franchise marketing opportunities SUCCESSFUL INITIAL TRADING PERIOD Implement franchisee and franchisor operating systems Recruit first good, high-quality franchisees Ensure successful launch/initial trading period for new franchisees Attend support meetings − BFA regionals, Third Wednesday Avoid expensive mistakes!			Business started successfully Generate enquiries from good prospective franchisees Recruit good-quality franchisees Happy, motivated, successful franchisees Meet objectives of business plan!
12. FRANCHISEE BUSINESS PLANS	GUIDE NEW FRANCHISEES THROUGH BUSINESS PLANNING PROCESS Ensure new franchisees have realistic, achievable plan Ensure new franchisees are able to secure funding Avoid making false/unsubstantiated claims			Franchisees have robust business plan and funding to carry it out and be successful Avoid future litigation

Appendix B
Franchised network development plan
Example contents

(See Chapter 3)

1. Introduction

2. Management summary

3. Appraising a franchise

4. Client company v. franchising fundamentals

5. Franchising in the UK

6. Franchising in client company business sector

7. The franchise development process

8. Conclusion

9. The financial model

   - Introduction

   - Data and assumptions

   - Franchisor development and costs

   - Franchisor ongoing cost assumptions

   - Bank lending

10. The role of a client company franchisee

Appendix C
Franchised Network Development Plan
Financial factfind questionnaire
Data collection and assumptions

(See Chapter 3)

For best results, collated data should be input to Howarth FranchisedNetworkBuilder software

FRANCHISEE – SET-UP AND PRE-TRADING COSTS

	Amount	To whom payable?	When payable?	VAT?	Comments
Franchise joining fee					
Training package					
Lease premium					
Legal fees **Franchise agreement** *Lease* *Licences* *Other*					
Accountants **Business plan** *Company set-up*					
Premises plans/ approvals					
Premises improvement					
Turnkey					

FRANCHISEE – SET-UP AND PRE-TRADING COSTS (continued)

Management fee								
Pre-opening rent and rates, insurance, utilities								
Operations equipment [list]								
Fixtures, fittings and fitout [list]								
Office equipment and IT package [list]								
Marketing/stationery pack [list]								
Marketing launch activity								
Opening stock – goods for re-sale [list]								
Opening stock – consumables [list]								

FRANCHISEE – SET-UP AND PRE-TRADING COSTS (continued)

Vehicle deposits and pre-trading running costs				
Staff recruitment				
Staff training				
Pre-trading wages				
Pre-trading owner's drawings				
Other pre-trading costs				
Contingency				

Franchisee directors and relevant staff will need full business training as per the training schedule regardless of previous experience

Franchise will trade from owned/leased retail/commercial/home premises

New or existing vehicle(s)?

Total set-up costs of . . . . of which . . . . will need to be borrowed over . . . . years @ . . . . per annum

Franchise fee, premises improvement, F&F, equipment package written off over . . . . years

Training fee, marketing launch, IT costs written off in first year

FRANCHISEE – SALES

MONTH	1	2	3	4	5	6	7	8	9	10	11	12	TOTAL
MONTH	13	14	15	16	17	18	19	20	21	22	23	24	TOTAL

YEAR THREE TOTAL

YEAR FOUR TOTAL

YEAR FIVE TOTAL

Any special product types/groups?

Seasonality?

Sensitivities?

Terms of business – credit periods?

FRANCHISEE – ONGOING COSTS

	Amount	Payable to franchisor?	When payable	VAT?	Comments
COST OF SALES					(Split by group?)
OVERHEADS					
Staff wages					
Owner's salary					
Staff training					
Staff recruitment					
HR support e.g. Peninsula)					
Other staff costs					
Insurance					
Utilities – heat, light, water					
Communication – post, phone, e-mail inc. mobiles					

FRANCHISEE – ONGOING COSTS (continued)

Vehicle running costs			
Print and stationery			
Local marketing			
Premises – rent, rates, insurance			
Repairs and renewals			
Refits			
Equipment purchases			
Franchisor meetings and conference			
Miscellaneous – client specific items			
Contingency			
FINANCE and ADMIN COSTS			
Book-keeping, invoicing, payroll and credit control			

FRANCHISEE – ONGOING COSTS (continued)

Accountancy inc. year end				
Legal and licensing costs				
Bank charges				
Overdraft interest				
Bad debts				
Loan repayments				
Vehicle and equipment				
Leasing costs				
Depreciation				
MANAGEMENT SERVICES FEES			Percentage or fixed	
MARKETING CONTRIBUTION			Percentage or fixed	

FRANCHISOR – SET-UP COSTS (PRE-LAUNCH)

PROJECT START DATE?: . . . .

	Amount	When payable	VAT?	Comments
Development plan and financial projections				
Master franchise fee				
Market research – territory and location analysis				
Trademarks registration				
Accounting – creation of new company				
Accounting – creation of reporting systems				
Corporate identity design and development				
Pilot operation costs (net)				Account as for franchisee
Franchisor premises acquisition and occupancy costs				
Office fixtures, fittings and equipment inc. IT				

FRANCHISOR – SET-UP COSTS (PRE-LAUNCH) (continued)

Website development			
Staff recruitment			
Staff training			
Staff salaries			
Preparation of franchise manual			
Preparation of franchise agreement			
Other legal advice – property employment			
Preparation of franchise marketing materials			
Preparation of recruitment process			
Preparation of franchisor office manual			
Launch marketing and promotion activity			
Consultancy support			

OUTLET OPENING SCHEDULE

Assumed capacity is locations/territories. . . . .

First/franchisee starts trading in Month 1 which is estimated to be . . . .

	Franchisees open	Cumulative
Year One		
Year Two		
Year Three		
Year Four		
Year Five		

MONTH	1	2	3	4	5	6	7	8	9	10	11	12	TOTAL
MONTH	13	14	15	16	17	18	19	20	21	22	23	24	TOTAL
MONTH	25	26	27	28	29	30	31	32	33	34	35	36	TOTAL
MONTH	37	38	39	40	41	42	43	44	45	46	47	48	TOTAL
MONTH	49	50	51	52	53	54	55	56	57	58	59	60	TOTAL

FRANCHISOR – INCOME

	Gross amount	Direct costs	Net receipt	When receivable	VAT?	Comments
Joining fee per franchisee						
Initial training fee per franchisee						
Turnkey fee per franchisee						
Premises approval and plans per franchisee						
Operations equipment package per franchisee						
Office and IT equipment package per franchisee						
Fixtures, fittings and fit-out fee per franchisee						
Marketing materials and stationery per franchisee						
Opening stock for resale per franchisee						
Opening stock consumables per franchisee						
Handover services fee per franchisee						
Franchisees continuing purchases of goods						
Franchisees containing purchases of services						

FRANCHISOR – INCOME (continued)

Franchisees insurance							
Franchisees rent							
Management services fees @ % of all franchisees sales							
Management services fees @ % per month per franchisee							
Franchisees marketing contribution @ % sales per franchisee							
Franchisees marketing contribution @ % per month per franchisee							
Other income from franchisees							
Contributions from approved suppliers							
Contribution from own outlets							

FRANCHISOR – ONGOING COSTS

	Amount	When payable	VAT?	Comment
Master franchise fees				
Staff salaries				
Staff training				
Staff recruitment				
HR support (e.g. Peninsular)				
other staff costs				
Utilities – heat, light, water				
Communication – post, phone, e-mail inc mobiles				
Vehicle running costs				
Other travel and accommodation				
Print and stationery				
Franchise advertising and exhibitions				
Product/service advertising				
PR – franchise product/service				
Market research				
New product development				
Franchise association subscriptions				
Premises – rent, rates, insurance				

FRANCHISOR – ONGOING COSTS (continued)

Repairs and renewals							
Equipment purchases							
Franchisee communications meetings, conferences, newsletters, website							
Contingency							
FINANCE/ADMIN							
Book-keeping, invoicing, payroll, credit control, internal audit							
Accountancy inc. year end							
Legal costs							
Consultancy support							
Bank charges							
Overdraft interest							
Bad debts							
Loan repayments							
Vehicle and equipment leasing costs							
Depreciation							

Appendix D
Franchise agreement
Example contents

(See Chapter 8)

1. Parties
2. Interpretation
3. Rights granted
4. Term and rights of renewal
5. Franchisor's initial obligations
6. Franchisor's continuing obligations
7. Franchisee's obligations
8. Training
9. Fees and payments
10. Accounting records
11. Advertising
12. Insurance
13. Trademark
14. Sale of business
15. Non-competition and confidentiality
16. Death or incapacity of guarantor
17. Termination
18. Consequences of termination
19. Post-termination restrictions
20. Buy back
21. Guarantor's obligations
22. Representations
23. Indemnity
24. Improvements
25. Operations manual

26. Data protection
27. Agency
28. Force majeure
29. Trading Schemes Act 1996
30. Waiver
31. Continuing provisions
32. Severability
33. Modification
34. Set off
35. Notices
36. Rights of third parties
37. No warranties
38. Assignment
39. Alternative dispute resolution
40. Jurisdiction
41. Schedules
42. Territory or location maps

Appendix E
The Diploma in Franchise Management Programme

(See Chapter 6)

The Diploma in Franchise Management is awarded to candidates who have attended a minimum of eight core workshops and successfully completed a dissertation on some aspect of franchise management either particularly relevant to their business or of general interest.

CORE WORKSHOPS

The eight core workshops that must be attended within a period of two years are:

- How to find franchisees
- How to recruit franchisees
- How to monitor franchisees' performance
- How to get the best from field visits
- How to motivate franchisees
- How to manage franchise resales
- How to avoid litigation against franchisors and franchisees
- How to understand franchisees' financial performance

Where a candidate believes they can already demonstrate competence in any of these areas they can apply for Recognition of Prior Learning or Recognition of Current Competence in that area and may then not need to attend the relevant workshop. Application for such recognition must be accompanied by a paper prepared by the candidate which demonstrates that they have not only an understanding of how their own franchise system operates but also a more general understanding of the options available within franchising for the structure of such systems.

THE DISSERTATION

Following or during attendance at the workshop modules the candidate must write a dissertation of not less than 5,000 words on a franchise-related subject. The subject must be agreed with the Franchise Training Centre. The dissertation should address the chosen subject under two headings: the theory of this aspect of franchise management and its practical application within one or more franchises. Wherever possible it should include elements of original research that will contribute to the general fund of franchising knowledge. Where applicable the dissertation should be endorsed by a senior manager within the applicant's franchise operation.

The Diploma recognises that the candidate has committed to a process of formal training and development and has acquired skills relevant to the franchise sector.

The Diploma is awarded in the UK by The Franchise Training Centre.

Appendix F
The Franchise Training Centre Workshops

(See Chapter 6)

INTRODUCTORY MODULES

How to find potential franchisees

Generating enquiries from motivated and suitably qualified potential franchisees is critical to the recruitment process. This workshop addresses the issues of how to do it.

Objectives

By the end of the session delegates will have:

- considered all elements of the Franchise Marketing Plan;
- reviewed the methods and media for franchisee marketing;
- discussed creative marketing techniques;
- built a franchisee profile for their business;
- completed a personal action plan to improve their franchise marketing.

Course outline

- An introduction to the current recruitment environment
- The Franchise Marketing Plan – how many, where and when?
- The franchisee profile – knowledge, skills, attitude, resources
- The approach – define and design to hit the target
- The media – advertising, the internet, exhibitions, PR, and others
- The legal and ethical aspects – misrepresentation, misleading or ambiguous statements

How to recruit franchisees

Your marketing activities have found interested applicants – now, through your recruitment process, you need to ensure that the best candidates choose your franchise.

Objectives
By the end of the session the delegates will:

- have reviewed the detail of their franchisee recruitment process;
- understand the multi-skilled approach – recruiting, interviewing, selling;
- understand the motivations of prospective franchisees;
- have completed a personal action plan to improve their franchise recruiting.

Course outline
- The fundamentals of the recruitment process
- The legal aspects – disclosure, confidentiality, misrepresentation
- The prospectus – what to say, how much to say, how to say it
- Developing the detail of the recruitment process – screening enquiries, meetings and interviews, follow-up
- The financial aspects – deposits, projections, business plans, raising finance

How to monitor franchisees' performance

In granting a franchise you are giving your franchisees access to your most important assets: your brand, your systems and your customers. How can you ensure they will treat them all with respect?

Objectives
By the end of the session delegates will have:

- reviewed the roles of franchisor and franchisee in maintaining standards;
- discussed where standards are set down or agreed;
- considered ways of monitoring performance;

- completed a case study exercise to evaluate monitoring techniques;
- prepared a personal action plan to improve their own performance.

Course outline
- The franchisor–franchisee relationship
- What needs monitoring
- Setting the standards – the franchise agreement, the operations manual, the franchisee business plan
- Audit processes
- Case study practical exercise

How to motivate franchisees

The success of your franchise rests on the commitment and hard work of your franchisees but what happens when either or both of these are missing?

Objectives
By the end of the session delegates will:

- have discussed what motivates franchisees at different stages of their development;
- have reviewed the methods for communication with franchisees;
- be aware of the skills required to motivate individual franchisees;
- have prepared a personal action plan to improve your communication with franchisees.

Course outline
- The franchisee life cycle
- Theories of motivation
- Leadership styles in motivational situations
- Recognising and rewarding achievement
- Communication media – written, verbal, individual, group

INTERMEDIATE MODULES

How to get the best from field visits

By careful planning and organisation you can ensure that field visits benefit both franchisees and franchisors.

Objectives

By the end of the session delegates will have:

- considered the function of the field visit;
- reviewed their role as a member of the franchise support team;
- considered the various elements of franchisee support;
- discussed the structure of the visit;
- developed a strategy for enhancing their support to their franchisees;
- completed a personal action plan to implement that strategy.

Course outline

- What do franchisees/franchisors want from field visits?
- The key elements of the support staff role
- The structure of the field visit
- Preparing for and following up field visits

An introduction to coaching

As in sports activities, using coaching to enhance the franchisee's business performance is all a matter of getting them to 'raise their game'.

Objectives

By the end of the session the delegates will:

- understand the role of coaching in motivating franchisees;
- understand the basic principles of the coaching process;
- have considered how to support franchisees in setting and achieving new goals;
- have practised basic coaching techniques.

Course outline
- What is coaching?
- When is coaching appropriate?
- How can coaching help to improve franchisee performance?
- The relationship between coach and coachee
- Basic coaching skills ʿ
- Interactive coaching practice

How to manage franchise resales

As franchise networks mature, resales activities can increase to a level where recruitment for resales outstrips recruitment for new units – but the two processes can be very different.

Objectives
By the end of the session delegates will have:

- considered the need for re-sales both voluntary and 'encouraged';
- discussed options for the structure of the resale process;
- reconsidered their franchisee profile for purchasers of resale territories;
- reconsidered their marketing activity to attract such purchasers;
- considered the process of business valuation and the role and responsibility of the franchisor in such a valuation.

Course outline
- The role of resales in a maturing network
- The role of the franchisor in preparing for resales, the processes and documentation
- The franchisee profile of the purchasing franchisee
- Marketing the resale opportunity
- The rights and responsibilities of the franchisor in approving the resale
- Business valuation – is there a simple formula?

How to understand franchisees' financial performance

Almost every franchisor will have the right to see their franchisees' annual accounts. This two-day workshop will ensure that relevant support staff understand and feel confident in discussing these accounts with their franchisees.

Objectives
By the end of the workshops the delegates will:

- have understood and practised basic accounting principles;
- be better able to read and understand profit and loss accounts and balance sheet statements;
- have considered the factors which affect profitability;
- have prepared a profit and loss and cash flow forecast for a new case study franchised outlet;
- have analysed the case study business's first trading results.

Course outline
- The need for businesses to keep accurate accounts
- What makes the balance sheet balance and how the profit and loss account calculates profits
- The principles of accounting
- Analysing annual accounts
- The role of the cash flow statement
- How profit is made and retained
- Case study franchised business forecasts and results

SPECIALIST MODULES

How to avoid litigation for you and your franchisees

Whether from complicated legal issues or simply overpowering red tape both franchisors and franchisees find themselves increasingly exposed to possible litigation. Simple processes and procedures can dramatically reduce your own and their exposure.

Objectives

By the end of the session delegates will have:

- become aware of the legal issues that can affect their business;
- identified the specific functions of their business that they relate to;
- discussed model procedures for minimising risk;
- discussed implementing these procedures;
- prepared an action plan for implementing them.

Course outline

An overview of laws/legal issues affecting franchisors

Model operational procedures for minimising risk:

- Marketing
- Training
- Recruitment
- Support

Note: This seminar does not contain legal advice – it suggests practical operational steps that can be put in place to reduce your exposure to potential legal action. We strongly recommend that you seek legal advice from a suitably experienced lawyer where required.

How to prepare to franchise internationally

Growth potential at home limited? Is your product or service relevant for other market places?

Objectives

By the end of the session the delegates will have:

- considered the role of international franchising in business development;
- considered the validity of their existing offer in international markets;
- considered the various structures available;
- discussed the role of market research;

- identified the external assistance required to develop the franchise.

Course outline
- Why franchise internationally? What can it achieve?
- Is the existing structure valid for international markets?
- What structure will the franchise relationship take?
- How different is the culture and business practice in the target market?
- Franchise legislation in target territories
- Funding and income streams

How to get the best from franchise exhibitions

Did you know that research shows that only 15 per cent of companies that use exhibitions achieve a return on their investment? So what do those 15 per cent do differently?

Objectives
By the end of the workshop the delegates will be able to:

- set realistic goals to achieve whilst at the exhibition;
- attract people onto your stand elegantly and effectively;
- influence and persuade prospects whilst they are on your stand;
- deal with difficult situations on the stand.

Course outline
- How to plan to achieve your objectives for the exhibition
- How to attract the right people onto your stand
- How to promote to them elegantly while on the stand
- How to deal with difficult situations on the stand
- Professional exhibition behaviour

The techniques and principles discussed in this workshop apply equally to any exhibition, whether recruiting franchisees or selling your products or services.

Appendix G
Further reading

Mendelsohn, Martin (2005) *The Guide To Franchising*. Thomson Learning.
Pratt, John H., *The Franchisor's Handbook* (available only from *Franchise World* magazine, details below).
Franchise World Directory, 2007 (available from *Franchise World* magazine, details below).

All of the above are available from *www.franchiseworld.co.uk*

Appendix H
National Franchise Association and other useful websites

NATIONAL FRANCHISE ASSOCIATION WEBSITES

ARGENTINA	www.aafranchising.com
AUSTRALIA	www.franchise.org.au
AUSTRIA	www.franchise.at
BANGLADESH	www.kingshuk-bd.com
BELGIUM	www.fbf-bff.be
BRAZIL	www.abf.com.br
CANADA	www.cfa.ca
CHINA	www.ccfa.org.cn
CZECH REPUBLIC	www.czech-franchise.cz
DENMARK	www.dk-franchise.dk
EGYPT	www.mife.com.eg
EUROPEAN Franchise Federation	www.eff-franchise.com
FINLAND	www.franchising.fi
FRANCE	www.franchise-fff.com
GEORGIA	www.franchise-geo.org.ge
GERMANY	www.dfv-franchise.de
GREECE	www.franchising.gr
HONG KONG	www.franchise.org.hk
HUNGARY	www.franchise.hu
INDIA	www.fai.co.in
IRELAND	www.irishfranchiseassociation.com
ITALY	www.assofranchising.it
JAPAN	www.jfa-fc.or.jp
MALAYSIA	www.mfa.org.my
MEXICO	www.feherandfeher.com
KAZAKHSTAN	www.franchising.kz
LATVIA	www.franch.lv

MALAYSIA	www.mfa.org.my
NETHERLANDS	www.nfv.nl
NEW ZEALAND	www.franchise.org.nz
PHILIPPINES	www.philippinefranchiseassociation.com
PORTUGAL	www.apfranchise.org
ROMANIA	www.francizor.ro
SINGAPORE	www.flasingapore.org
SLOVENIA	www.franchise-slovenia.net
SOUTH AFRICA	www.fasa.co.za
SOUTH KOREA	www.ika.or.kr
SPAIN	www.franquiciadores.com
SWEDEN	www.franchiseforeningen.se
SWITZERLAND	www.franchiseverband.ch
TAIWAN	www.tcfa.org.tw
UNITED KINGDOM	www.thebfa.org
USA	www.franchise.org
VENEZUELA	www.franquiciasonline.co

OTHER USEFUL WEBSITES

HOWARTH FRANCHISING	www.howarthfranchising.com
THE FRANCHISE DEVELOPMENT CENTRE	www.thefranchisedevelopmentcentre.co.uk
THE FRANCHISE TRAINING CENTRE	www.thefranchisetrainingcentre.com
THE FRANCHISE SUPPORT CENTRE	www.thefranchisesupportcentre.co.uk
THE FRANCHISE SALES CENTRE	www.thefranchisesalescentre.com
THE FRANCHISE CAREERS CENTRE	www.thefranchisecareerscentre.com
THE INTERNATIONAL FRANCHISING CENTRE	www.theinternationalfranchisingcentre.com

Index

action plan, 20, 68, 174, 175, 177
area developer, 54–5, 58–9

BFA/British Franchise Association, 20, 76, 92, 100, 105, 203
branch network, 4, 9
brand, 7, 25, 28, 53, 55, 59, 66–8, 76, 78–80, 114, 120, 122, 138–41, 143, 199–201, 213–14, 216–17, 231, 235
business format franchising, 5, 9–14, 138
business management, 110, 129–30, 133–4
business plan, franchisee, 15–18, 91, 108–17, 144–9, 187, 189
business plan, franchisor, 18–21, 110, 216–18, 228–9, 235–6

coach, 37, 161, 167, 169, 267
comfort zone, 155–7
communications, franchisee, 24, 40, 45, 123, 151, 162, 167, 170, 171, 177, 236, 266
compliancy, 28, 49, 123, 141, 142, 149, 167, 170, 200–5, 230
conference, 27, 36, 163
customer satisfaction surveys, 153, 197

data protection, 124, 200–2, 260
deposit, 93
diploma, 4, 34, 37, 262–3
disclosure, 92
discovery day, 86, 90, 223

enquiry, initial, 68, 82, 83, 103
Ethics, Code of, 92
European Franchise Federation, 92
exhibitions, 72, 74–5, 98–107, 221
exit planning franchisor, 231–9
exit planning, franchisee, 50, 123, 178–92

fees, initial/upfront, 15–18, 49
fees, international, 54–6, 213, 215, 225–6, 228
fees, marketing, 17, 56, 215
fees, ongoing, 15–18, 19, 49, 54, 56
field visits, 27, 36, 152, 165–77, 267
finding franchisees, 63–82
franchise agreement, 38, 41–2, 46–52, 94, 127, 138, 144, 148, 150, 184–5, 189, 203–4, 232
franchise agreement, international, 225–30
Franchise Careers Centre, 34, 37
franchise consultant, 11, 17, 34, 42, 44, 42, 47, 51, 119, 122, 194, 220–4, 225, 230, 231, 238
franchise marketing, 63–82, 190, 264
franchise operations manual, 31, 38–45, 118–27, 144, 151
franchise resales, 123, 178–92, 268
Franchise Support Centre, 34, 35, 124, 193, 224
franchise surveys, 4, 153, 154, 193–8, 235
Franchise Training Centre, 4, 34, 37, 224, 263, 264–71
franchisee, master, 54, 57–8
franchisee, monitoring, 35, 108, 116
franchisee profile, 12, 70–2, 85, 90, 99, 128
franchisee, recruitment, 20, 24, 25–6, 34–5, 65, 69, 83–97
franchisee, training, 35, 38, 40, 123, 128–37
franchisees, potential, 3, 5, 25, 104
franchisees, finding, 63–82, 190, 264
franchising culture, 13, 22–8
franchising, international, 53–9, 209–15, 216–18, 219–24, 225–30
franchising, principles, 6–8, 9–14
franchisor/franchisee relationship, 4, 6, 13, 22–8, 36, 165, 266

franchisor, support team, 4, 13, 26–8, 33–7, 44, 150, 151–2, 163, 164, 166–77, 267, 269
funding, 20, 108, 115

going concern, 50, 184, 229, 232
goodwill, 180, 182, 184, 190, 234

healthcheck, 193–4, 235, 237

intellectual property, 10, 48, 51, 214, 226, 231
International Franchise Association, xi
international franchising, 53–9, 209–15, 216–18, 219–24, 225–30
internet, 42, 72, 75–6, 80, 87, 136, 195, 200, 202, 264

lawyer, 11, 46, 47, 50–2, 69, 91–2, 111, 150, 201, 203–5, 230
lease, 11, 49, 50, 182, 184, 233, 236
life cycle, franchisee, 27, 157–8, 266
life–style, 12, 25, 64, 71, 80, 156, 159
litigation, avoiding, 91–2, 94, 111, 199–205, 269

management services fees, 15–18, 19, 49, 139
Management team, Franchisor, 33–7
marketing and sales, 129, 131–2
marketing, fees, 17, 49
marketing, local, 17, 66, 112, 114
marketing, messages, 67, 77, 80, 102
marketing plan, 77–82
Martin Mendelsohn, ix, 92
master franchisee, 47, 54–9, 212–13, 216–18, 219–22, 224, 225–30
media, 72–4
monitoring performance, franchisee, 35, 108, 116, 138–54
monitoring performance, franchisor, 193–8
motivating franchisees, 27, 36, 155–64
mystery shopper, 152, 154, 177

Natwest/BFA surveys, xi, 72, 155, 178, 195
network development plan, domestic, 12, 15–21
network development plan, international, 211
network healthcheck, 193–4, 235, 237

operations manual, 31, 38–45, 118–27, 144

pilot operations, 29–32, 125
PR, 74, 100, 105
premises, 8, 11, 15, 16, 48, 9, 51, 118–19, 154, 172, 173, 184, 216, 233
press, the, 72–4
pre–trading set–up, 96–7, 118, 122
profitability, franchisee, 12, 1, 79, 109, 111, 115, 116, 141, 143, 146, 147, 156, 159, 170, 171–4, 179, 190, 204, 269
profitability, franchisor, 10, 11, 12, 16, 17, 20, 55, 57, 91, 110, 210, 233, 235
prospectus, 86, 88, 90, 186, 187, 189, 238, 243, 265
protection, 44, 86, 126–7, 138, 142–4
proven format, 10

recruitment process, 84, 86–96, 107, 109
recruitment, support staff, 34, 36
recruitment, franchisees, 83–97
report(ing), 9, 54, 58, 116, 134, 145, 14, 152, 172–3, 194, 200

salary, franchisee, 15, 64, 145, 147–8
satisfaction surveys, customer, 197
satisfaction surveys, franchisee, 195
satisfaction surveys, staff, 196
support, 4, 13, 17, 18, 19–20, 23, 25–8, 33–7, 41, 43, 44, 49, 55, 57–9, 66–7, 112–14, 121, 138, 155, 165, 193, 204, 212, 214, 217, 224, 228, 232

territory, 16, 19, 25, 48, 54, 65, 78, 85, 93, 109, 155, 58, 179, 10, 11, 213, 214, 225, 226, 233
trade marks, 10, 48
training, franchisee, 35, 38, 40, 123, 128–37
training, franchisor, 36–7, 262–71
TUPE, 182, 185

valuation, 123, 181, 182, 183–5, 189, 233, 236, 237, 268

World Franchise Council, xi